The Final Kingdom

Where all kingdoms bow to the Ancient of Days

Ron Cantrell

*This book is dedicated
first of all, to the God of Israel,
whose Word is my constant delight
and to
Carol, my wonderful wife of twenty-seven years,
and my three children,
Heather, Michael, and Raquel,
who are my inspiration for everything.*

*It is also dedicated to Carol Carlson and Deborah Tyler
who convinced me to put these thoughts down
on paper.*

*We greatly miss Deborah Tyler.
Deborah died in the service of her King
on November 15, 1999, in Jerusalem, Israel.*

aramaic logo of   Yahweh, God's name

Cover Art
Ted Larson has been creating digital Christian art for about five years.
Computer illustration was an exciting way to branch out from his
traditional media work. He is currently designing a large series of digital
paintings that illustrate dramatic scenes from Genesis to Revelation. Ted
resides in Seattle, Washington. He can be reached by e-mail:
theoson@earthlink.net.

Aramaic Logo
The logo at the top of this page, and found on every other chapter title
page, is comprised of two letters of the Aramaic alphabet, "yod" and
"heh." These are the first two letters of the four letters that make up the
name of God יְהֹוָה "Yaweh." This logo was adopted by the early Eastern
church, with the addition of the three dots above, signifying the Trinity,
and one dot below, proclaiming the unity of the Godhead.
For those interested in more information about Aramaic, the web site:
www.aramaic.org (sponsored by the Aramaic Bible Society) has
information on Aramaic as a language as well as current and historical
articles.

Table of Contents

Mesopotamia and the Fertile Crescent

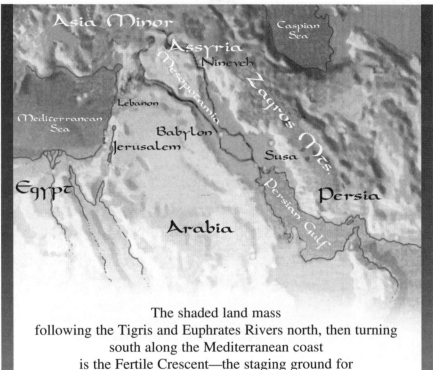

The shaded land mass
following the Tigris and Euphrates Rivers north, then turning
south along the Mediterranean coast
is the Fertile Crescent—the staging ground for
the drama of the book of Daniel.

Our captive travelers were led from Jerusalem along this route
for several months, staying close to the river's life-giving water,
to arrive at the city of Babylon.
Here they dwelt for seventy years awaiting God's deliverance.
They longed for a word from Heaven that
their time of exile was over.

No longer did the Temple musicians of Zion sing their
joyous songs or play upon their devoted Temple instruments.
The mocking crowds of Babylon,
who longed only to hear "something new",
were astounded to find that these harp players had bitten the
ends of their fingers off in mourning (Psalm 137:1-7).

By the rivers of Babylon . . .

Reliving the Days of Haggai

Standing like parentheses in the midst of Jewish history, are the exile and return of the Jewish people from Babylon. The well-known opening of that phase of the Jewish story is the Babylonian captivity which happened in three phases, the first in 605 B.C., the second in 597 B.C., and the third in 586 B.C. The exile happened in stages and, their return happened in stages as well. Just as intriguing is the little-known closing parenthesis—the final return from Iraq of those captives to modern Israel. This happened in the last century between the years 1947 and 1952, during the dramatic Israeli rescue known as "Operation Ezra and Nehemiah."

The close of this 2,550 year captivity and the birth of the new State of Israel is no coincidence. Indeed it is part of a much larger picture—the regathering of the Jewish people to their homeland. In this phase, we are reliving the book of Haggai when the prophet exhorted the people to lay the foundation stone of the Temple.

> *From this day on, from this twenty-fourth day of the ninth month, give careful thought to the day when the foundation of the LORD's temple was laid. Give careful thought: Is there yet any seed left in the barn? Until now, the vine and the fig tree, the pomegranate and the olive tree have not borne fruit.*
>
> *'From this day on I will bless you.'*
>
> Haggai 2:18,19

Each turn of prophecy is different though. Haggai's generation suffered lack for not laying the foundation stone of the Temple. In this rerun of "return and rebuild," the abundant blessing of the modern land of Israel cannot be disputed. It is obvious that the reemergence of the Temple in our day has been reserved by God for the right moment, and yet the cycles bring us ever closer to the end of time.

Israel has not laid the Temple foundation yet, but there is an important parallel: The proclamation of statehood. Contrary to popular belief, without fail there has always been a Jewish population in Israel, but the proclamation of statehood was the start button on God's stopwatch. From that moment the State of Israel blossomed and filled the earth with goods: flowers, fruit, technology in irrigation of arid lands, the use of brackish water for agriculture, and on and on. Yearly, the technological innovations from the intelligence pool being created here in Israel astound the world. Top intellectuals from every field have populated Israel from over one hundred and twenty different countries, bringing with them know-how on almost every subject.

A down-home illustration comes to mind. When my children were smaller, computer games were coming out with alarming frequency. Who could keep up with all the tricks and shortcuts to staying a winner? Standing, unnoticed, behind my son and several of his friends one day as they jumped through hoops of fire and traveled hidden underground caverns in stone castles, I got a lesson. Each one had a tiny bit of information to share with the others about how the game worked. This was, and still is, the secret of staying a winner of digital games. What child has time to read the manual? Plus, there are hidden tricks not written in those manuals that kids discover by accident and share with their friends.

Likewise, Israel's population represents the best brains of the world all sharing their wisdom and innovations with each other. The evil that the world planned against the Jewish people to suppress them and either hold them captive, or expel them as the "dregs" of society, has only turned out for good for this tiny nation.

Isaiah declares to the Jewish nation:

Although you have been forsaken and hated, with no one traveling through, I will make you the everlasting pride and the joy of all generations. You will drink the milk of nations and be nursed at royal breasts.

Isaiah 60:15-16

This finds its flip-side later in Isaiah when God says to the Gentiles who have loved Israel:

Rejoice with Jerusalem and be glad for her, all you who love her; rejoice greatly with her, all you who mourn over her. For you will be satisfied at her comforting breasts; you will drink deeply and delight in her overflowing abundance.

66:10,11

These nurturing prophecies stand as true as God's promise to Abraham that those that bless "Abraham" and his descendants would in turn receive blessing (Gen. 12:3).

Here in this book, the "parentheses" are examined and the place we now stand in prophecy becomes more clear. I believe firmly that there is a "practical prophecy," whereby we do not just stand back and watch, or simply read about unfolding events, but rather, we would catch the vision and participate in the opportunities God affords us.

Ron Cantrell
Jerusalem, Israel
August, 2000

Seek the peace
and prosperity of the city
to which I have carried you
into exile.
*Pray to the L*ORD *for it,*
because if it prospers,
you too will prosper.

He has sent this message to us
in Babylon: It will be
a long time. Therefore build houses
and settle down; plant gardens
and eat what they produce.

Jeremiah 29:7, 28

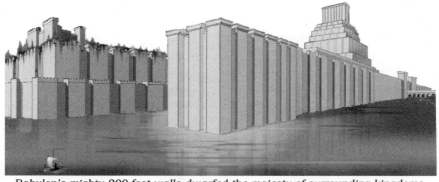

Babylon's mighty 200-foot walls dwarfed the majesty of surrounding kingdoms.

 # First Things First

Short curled beards, domed felt caps, knee-length leather tunics, and high laced shoes stretched as far as the eye could see. A sea of brass-embossed leather shields would have encircled the whole of Mesopotamia, if stretched end to end.

Finally, to fulfill a promise given two hundred years earlier, heaven stooped down to touch the earth in judgment. The dam of tolerance burst and thousands upon thousands of Chaldean and Median soldiers, led by Nebuchadnezzar's father, Nabopolassar, King of Babylon, marched north to Nineveh. In the sweltering summer heat of the month of Av they followed the Fertile Crescent valley between the Tigris and Euphrates Rivers. Staying close to the water was the only relief from the heat.

Tolerance for their cruel northern neighbor, Sin-shar-ishkun, King of Assyria, had come to an end. Thirst for justice melded the two peoples into an iron fist of retribution. Like a hord of locusts, they targeted the wicked capital city of Nineveh. No longer would they stand the ever-increasing humiliation of being a small abused vassal of the powerful northern empire. Their chances of victory matured when Assyria's might was weakened as Sin-shar-ishkun's twin sons pulled and tore at their own kingdom in hatred for each other.

In the long operation, blood flowed, men died, and women were widowed. Entire villages in the path of the warriors scattered to save their lives. The final blow fell on Nineveh in the fall of 612 B.C. Sin-shar-ishkun's palace was burned to the ground and Babylon began to rule.

At last, the promise made to Israel's prophet Jonah, two hundred years earlier, had come to pass. Nineveh ceased to be, never to rise again. At the end of the battles, King Nabopolassar and his handsome young son, Nebuchadnezzar, turned south to return home to Babylon. Upon arriving, they would enter one of the most vigorous building campaigns in history, resulting in Babylon becoming the capital city of the rising world power. The mighty jewel among empires—fine gold in the eyes of Heaven.

The Final Kingdom

Daniel, his friends, and most of the population of Judah and Benjamin, were taken captive in 605 B.C., and marched off to Babylon. The prophet Ezekiel was exiled in 597 B.C.

Babel in the Aramaic language means "Gate of God." In ancient times the gates of a city were places where the elders and judges of the city sat and oversaw the comings and goings of all. Interestingly, Daniel's name in Hebrew (Dan-i-el) means "judge of God." The names of the characters and the place are really a hint at what we have waiting in store for us in the pages of the book of Daniel. It is a masterful twist of literary irony to have God's judge sitting in the gate of God. And from the gate of God proceeded situations and circumstances, directly through Daniel and his compatriots, that minimized the culture and gods of Babylon and maximized the one true God of all the Universe.

The Secret of the Citrus Grove

An ancient Mesopotamian word meaning "paradise" is a key to understanding Daniel. In modern Persian, the word means "garden." The four letters P-R-D-S which make up the word, *pardes*, have found their way into modern Hebrew and specifically mean "a citrus grove."

According to the *Encyclopedia of Jewish Life and Thought*, the word PaRDeS is also an acronym standing for a method of exegesis the Jewish world uses to understand Scripture. Semitic languages use only consonants. So, vowels are added here for aid in pronunciation. PaRDeS, is four Jewish methods of understanding Scripture and are really the secret to the citrus grove—the book of Daniel.

An unusual variety of citrus lies within this grove. The most common are there, but deeper in the grove grow the most rare.

Each of the capital letters of the word PaRDeS stands for a Hebrew word. The "P" stands for the Hebrew word, *pashat* which means, "simple." In other words, what it says is *literally* what it means, in context of the time period in which it was written and of the people to whom it was written.

The letter "R" stands for the Hebrew word *remez* which means "hinting." In explanation, one Scripture sheds light on another Scripture, giving them both a fuller meaning.

The letter "D" stands for the Hebrew word *derash*, which means "to search." You might recognize the word *midrash* which comes from the word *derash*. The Midrash is rabbinic literature, a section of the Talmud, the voluminous work in which the Jewish Rabbis explain how to act out the holiness of the first five books of Moses (Genesis through Deuteronomy). The *Midrash* consists of homiletical stories that actually shed light on the Bible's deeper truths. Derash is not Scripture; it is a creative interpretation of Scripture. Derash are parables, or stories that open up a section of Scripture in a more meaningful way.

Finally, the letter "S" in the Hebrew word PaRDeS stands for *sod* meaning "secret." Books like Michael Drosnin's New York Times bestseller, *The Bible Code* attempt to explain the seemingly hidden messages in the Hebrew Scriptures. Caution is advised in this field as it can range from the interesting to the absurd. Some of the more readily accepted instances of hidden meanings explain, for instance, how we arrive at the knowledge that the number seven is an important number in the pages of the Bible. This concept is not spelled out plainly, but the number recurs so many times that it demands that you take notice. The idea of a mysterious meaning is also portrayed for us when the book of Revelation reveals that the number of the name of the antichrist is 666 (Rev. 13:17,18).

The PaRDeS methods of Scripture interpretation suggest that we remember first things first. *Pashat* should take precedence. Only after understanding the simplicity of a passage of Scripture, is an up-to-date application permitted.

The Aaronic Benediction and the "Hinting" Method

The story of Jesus bidding goodbye to His disciples on the Mount of Olives is a good example of *remez*—the hinting method.

> *When he had led them out to the vicinity of Bethany, he lifted up his hands and blessed them. While he was blessing them, he left them and was taken up into heaven. Then they worshiped him and returned to Jerusalem with great joy.*

> Luke 24:50

When Gentiles read this section of Scripture, they may simply see an intimate farewell between Jesus and His disciples. But with a Jewish background of this Scripture, a different mental picture may present itself. Anyone in a priestly office or in an itinerant teacher's position, when lifting the hands to bless any group of people, calls to mind the book of Numbers 6:22-27. This is the Aaronic benediction given to Aaron, the brother of Moses, with which to bless God's chosen people in the wilderness of Sinai.

This benediction has found its way into Christian liturgy. It has also successfully transcended denominational barriers. Many formal Christian churches end their services with this benediction. The underlying power in the Aaronic benediction has undoubtedly been the reason for its widespread adoption.

In Judaism, the benediction also calls for inherent physical ceremony performed by the one reciting the blessing. The Temple priest, rabbi, or itinerant teacher pronouncing the Aaronic benediction over the people will make a sign with his uplifted hands. The formation of his hands will be as close as human hands can come to the Hebrew letter *shin* which looks much like a "W" in English. This Hebrew letter stands for God's name "*El Shaddai.*" This name, which God revealed to Abraham, is translated into English as "God Almighty."

The Hebrew letter ש (*shin*) adorns the door of every observant Jewish home around the world. It is the decoration on a small ornament called a *mezuzah* which is affixed to the doorpost. The mezuzah has the letter *shin* beautifully done in calligraphy ornamenting the front. There is a niche in the back where an important section of Scripture which was written by a scribe on a tiny scroll is placed. The scroll is rolled tightly and placed in the mezuzah as a reminder of God's word and to invoke a blessing on their home.

The priest, having made the symbol of the *shin* with his hands, repeats the Aaronic benediction over his congregation.

> *The LORD said to Moses, "Tell Aaron and his sons, 'This is how you are to bless the Israelites. Say to them: "The LORD bless you and keep you; the LORD make his face shine upon you and be gracious to you; the LORD lift up his countenance upon you and give you his peace."*

Numbers 6:22-26 (NKJV)

The benediction itself demonstrates that God delights to bless His people. It is the verse following the benediction that explains its unusual power.

So they [meaning the priest pronouncing the blessing] *will put my name on the Israelites, and I will bless them.*

v. 27

The word "put" in the verse is *sim* in Hebrew, and it means "to make a mark on." We see God inscribing His name upon His people through the priestly blessing of the Aaronic benediction. The power of this blessing comes from the awe inspired by His name.

With this understanding we can reconsider Luke's description of that day on the Mount of Olives. *"He lifted up His hands"* now calls forth a different image to both Jewish and Gentile reader.

A fuller understanding of the blessing brings even more reason to be encouraged. The *Encyclopedia Judaica* has a praiseworthy section on the Aaronic Benediction under the heading "Priestly Blessing," or the *Birkhat Cohanim,* as it is called in Hebrew. It says:

> PRIESTLY BLESSING (Heb. כהנים ברכת - Birkhat Cohanim), the formula in Numbers 6:24-26 ordained by God and transmitted to the priests by Moses for the blessing of Israel. Verse 27, *"They shall invoke My name on behalf of the Israelites and I will bless them,"* makes explicit the intent of the ordained formula: to invoke the power of the Lord, who alone dispenses blessing. The threefold arrangement of the benediction may reflect an older incantation form; the three verses probably represent synonymous rather than climactic parallelism.
>
> The blessing has been customarily translated:
>
> *"The Lord bless you and keep you; the Lord make his face to shine upon you and be gracious to you; the Lord lift up His countenance upon you and grant you peace."*
>
> The literalness of this translation obscures the force of the Hebrew and fails to convey the court imagery of the biblical idiom. In biblical idiom the king shows favor (the verb *hanan*) to his subjects by giving them audience, access to *"the light of his face,"* whereas his disfavor is expressed by "hiding" his face from them.
>
> The third verse of the benediction presents a problem, for the king never "lifts up his face upon" his

15

subjects as a token of favor: "to lift one's own face" means "to look up" (II Kings 9:32), and it is rather the recipient of favor whose "face is lifted up" (who is *nesu panim* by the one who shows favor, see II Kings 3:14; Job 42:8-9). In the blessing, however, the idea seems to be that of raising the features in a smile, the opposite of dropping them in a frown (cf. *lo appil panai ba-khem;* lit. *"I will not drop my face against you,"* [Jer. 3:12; cf. Gen. 4:5-6; Job 29:24]). Finally, favor is a good deal more than the mere absence of hostility; consequently not just "peace" but friendship is what *shalom* means here, as in Judges 4:17 and in *beriti shalom* (Num. 25:12), and *berit shelomi* (Isa. 54:10), both of which mean *"my covenant/promise of friendship."*

Therefore, during the blessing, we are transported to the court of "the King." As the encyclopedia points out, it is not that someone has approached the king and physically taken his face and lifted it up so he can look at his subjects. This misses the reality of the court of an ancient king. No king has ever had to have his face "lifted" in order to view his subjects, because the king's throne is situated *above* his subjects.

As we can see, this is not what the Hebrew means. The royal imagery becomes even stronger and more endearing as we place the blessing in the context of the customs of Israel's surrounding nations. We can appreciate our heavenly King in a new and different way when we understand the differences of His kingdom and the kingdoms of surrounding nations.

For instance, when coming into his presence, the Pharaoh of Egypt's subjects were forbidden to look in his face unless directly requested to do so. Pharoah's subjects looked off to the side as he addressed them, *never* daring a full-faced glance.

The book of Esther also adds to our understanding of the court of a king in antiquity. In the book by her name, we read that Esther was worried about going before the king lest his wrath rise against her for coming into his presence unbidden. She rightfully feared losing her very life. When contrasted with the open-faced acceptance portrayed in the Aaronic benediction, we get a very different picture of the God we serve. The mental imagery of an audience with our King, who is God Almighty, and is smiling in favor upon us, then becomes strengthening and reassuring.

By now, the picture of Jesus' farewell to his disciples becomes even more encouraging and uplifting. Actually, you can look at it as a sealing of His beloved disciples for the work ahead of them. The passage in Luke reports that the disciples returned to Jerusalem joyfully. Why joyfully? After all, losing your Teacher, Mentor, Master, and Savior would not be an occasion for joy. But, these men, by Jesus' benediction, had God's seal put on them. The succeeding weeks, months, and years in their lives were going to be times of incredible change and trials. Reciting this ancient blessing upon His disciples, Jesus was leaving them with God's name, invoking His empowerment upon their lives.

This exemplifies the richness of the system of Biblical interpretation by the Jewish people, known as PaRDeS. We will approach the book of Daniel with this in mind. Throughout the book, we are going to see the God we serve in contrast to the gods of the surrounding nations.

The Magnitude of the Book

The book of Daniel stands head and shoulders above most other Old Testament books. The quality of vision it provides of history, coupled with revelation and augmented by its portrait of the character of God, makes the book without rival. The circumstances surrounding the events of Daniel provide the perfect environment to showcase God's inner heart for His people.

When, by all rights, we should be reading a book about God's displeasure and punishment of disobedience, we are instead reading of God's protection and promotion of His chosen people. We have the opportunity of being audience while the drama of Daniel unfolds in a foreign setting of great splendor—the powerful Babylonian Empire.

The book of Exodus showed us God in direct confrontation with the gods of Egypt. The Great "I AM" stood exalted above the Egyptian pantheon. Daniel shows us God Almighty, "El Shaddai" once again, this time confronting the gods of the Babylonian Empire, and a spectacular panorama of history unfolds.

The Old Testament has often been viewed as documentation on the wrath of God against a people who strayed from Him. Those who relegated the Old Testament to a treatise on wrath also ascribed all grace and forgiveness to the New Testament. This view's logical conclusion is that the New Testament superseded the Old in priority of study. If this has been your concept of the Old Testament, you will be encouraged as we explore Daniel and refer to other books, such as Isaiah and other prophets' writings, which shed further light on Daniel. The character and heart of God is revealed for us in ways that only this time period in history can provide. God can only turn His heart to wrath for so long before you see the dark clouds break and the sun shine through in glorious rays.

Daniel, Jaffa Oranges, and Olive Tree Roots

The book of Daniel lies masterfully wrapped in rich secondary resources. These supporting prophets' writings yield some of the most powerful, moving, and loved sections of Scripture. Some of our most stirring songs, as well as the promises that we cling to, are here waiting for us to discover how they relate to Daniel's experiences in Babylon—long before the Israelites were exiled to Babylon. We will *"soar on wings like eagles"* and *"run and not grow weary"* (Isa. 40:31); as well as being kept in *"perfect peace"* (Heb. *shalom, shalom*) if our minds are stayed on Him (Isa. 26:3). Isaiah also promises, *"The desert and the parched land will be glad; the wilderness will rejoice and blossom. Like the crocus, it will burst into bloom"* (Isa. 35:1). Modern Israel is living testament to the fulfillment of this Scripture. Another reference in Isaiah, even more specifically, calls to mind the present-day export of Jaffa oranges to all the world:

> *In days to come Jacob will take root, Israel will bud and blossom and fill all the world with fruit.*
>
> 27:6

Even more incredible, God promises to make Jerusalem *"the praise of the earth"* in the end of time. The appointed watchmen on the walls are exhorted to *"give yourselves no rest, and give him no rest,"* proclaiming His purposes for Israel (Isa. 62:7).

Directly pointed at the exiles to Babylon, Isaiah promised that God would be with them as they passed through waters and rivers (perhaps referring to their long march to Babylon, when they would have to ford the Euphrates several times enroute) and when they walked "through the fire," that the flames would not set them ablaze (43:2).

The book of Daniel is Jewish, the people about whom the book is written are Jewish, the story chronicles the events of the Jewish nation. This understanding is foundational. We sometimes forget that the roots of our Christian faith are in the fertile soil of Judaism. We gain security as we see the longsuffering nature of God and His covenantal character dealing with a people in spite of their perfidy.

As believers in Yeshua the Messiah, our faith is also strengthened to know the faithfulness of the God of the Old Testament who continues to fulfill His promises to Israel in the New Testament. Romans chapters 9,10, and 11, are one of the most important didactics to the church anywhere on our relational view of Israel. The common thread in both covenants is, *"I will never leave you nor forsake you"* (Deut. 31:6 and Heb. 13:5): The faithfulness of God's promises to His people continues in spite of their waywardness. God intends to fulfill His covenants through His people.

The message of Daniel, then, becomes a king's banquet compared to fast food when placed back in its own time period and explored with an eye to the context of when and to whom it was written.

The Stage is Set—Phase One

The stage was set for Daniel's story when the kingdom of Israel began to fall apart. It was not until the division of the kingdom that the major prophets were called forth. God's message seemed to be clear: *This is not how I want you to run the kingdom.* Seers and prophets who gave divine words of knowledge and wisdom to the leaders of the nation prior to the division were common. The books of Isaiah, Jeremiah, Ezekiel and Daniel signal a paradigm change.

These prophets were always called forth from among their own people. They came from the nation of Israel. They were not sent from some obscure nation or from across the ocean. These prophets were known by their own people, and they were given oracles of God to deliver to those people. God would give them the solution to their problems, and if they followed He would bless them; if they did not follow the solution, the consequences waited.

The Wickedness of the Assyrians

The book of II Kings records for us an attack of the Assyrians against Israel (the northern ten tribes). Israel and Judah are still intact at this time. Israel has not yet been carried away and King

The Final Kingdom

Hezekiah is ruling over the nation.

> *Then Eliakim son of Hilkiah, and Shebnah and Jonah said to the field commander, "Please speak to your servants in Aramaic, since we understand it. Don't speak to us in Hebrew in the hearing of the people on the wall." But the commander replied, "Was it only to your master and you that my master sent me to say these things, and not to the men sitting on the wall—who, like you, will have to eat their own filth and drink their own urine?"*
>
> *Then the commander stood and called out in Hebrew: "Hear the word of the great king, the king of Assyria! This is what the king says: Do not let Hezekiah deceive you. He cannot deliver you from my hand. Do not let Hezekiah persuade you to trust in the LORD when he says, 'The LORD will surely deliver us; this city will not be given into the hand of the king of Assyria.' Do not listen to Hezekiah. This is what the king of Assyria says: Make peace with me, and come out to me. Then every one of you will eat from his own vine and fig tree and drink water from his own cistern, until I come and take you to a land like your own, a land of grain and new wine, a land of bread and vineyards, a land of olive trees and honey. Choose life, not death! Do not listen to Hezekiah, for he has been misleading you when he says, 'The LORD will deliver us.' Has the God of any nation ever delivered his land from the hand of the king of Assyria? Where are the gods of Hamath, and Arpad? Where are the gods of Sepharvaim, Hena and Ivvah? Have they rescued Samaria from my hand? Who of all the gods of these countries has been able to save his land from me? How then can the LORD deliver Jerusalem from my hand?"*
>
> *But the people remained silent and said nothing in reply, because the king had commanded, "Do not answer him." Then Eliakim son of Hilkiah the palace administrator, Shebnah the secretary, and Jonah son of Asaph the recorder went to Hezekiah, with their clothes torn, and told him what the field commander had said.*
>
> II Kings 18:26-37

Some of the Israelites spoke Aramaic and some of the Assyrian soldiers spoke Hebrew. Therefore, we take it that some interchange with Babylon and Assyria had to have been already taking place. Most of the regular population did not speak

Aramaic, as we see from the watchmen's request: *"Please speak to your servants in Aramaic, since we understand it. Don't speak to us in Hebrew in the hearing of the people on the wall."*

The report of the watchmen troubles King Hezekiah greatly. He sees that the Assyrian army is about to overtake and destroy the northern tribes of Israel and, therefore, he becomes fearful for his people. The Assyrians were exceedingly cruel to those they took captive in battle. Their fearsome reputation preceded them. Some of the best vignettes of history have been left for us by the Assyrians in frescoes and sculptured wall reliefs on the royal palace at Nineveh.

If captured by the Assyrians in battle, it would be better for you to die at their hands than to go with them as a prisoner of war. Carved on the walls of their palaces are grisly records of the conquest and capture of neighboring nations. Lion hunts stand side by side with these in these palace wall reliefs. Assyrian kings were avid lion hunters. These lion hunts were focused battle-training exercises. They were cruel to the animals. Wall reliefs record Assyrian kings thrusting long spears down the throats of the lions during the hunt to kill them.

Upon capture of a prisoner of war by the Assyrian army, they pierced either the prisoner's jaw or lip with a heavy ring, then tied him to the back of a horse. If he could not keep up, he was dragged to death or his lips were torn off. If he succeeded in arriving at Nineveh, other appendages were cut off—thumbs and large toes—making the captive even less than a slave for the rest of his life. Humiliation of prisoners of war was the Assyrians' method of breaking the will of conquered nations.

Nineveh's wickedness was renowned. It is easy to understand why Jonah took a ship in the opposite direction when he was asked by God to go and proclaim His intentions to this great city. A modern comparison would be to have God ask you to travel to Baghdad, capital of Iraq, or Tehran, capital of Iran, to inform Saddam Hussein or the Ayatolla that God was about to judge his kingdom and destroy him!

Hezekiah brings his fears before the Lord.

Hezekiah received the letter from the messengers and read it. Then he went up to the temple of the LORD and spread it out before the LORD. And Hezekiah prayed to the LORD: "O LORD, God of Israel, enthroned between the cherubim, you alone are God over all the kingdoms of the earth. You have made heaven and earth. Give ear, O LORD, and hear; open your eyes, O LORD, and see, listen to the words Sennacherib has sent to insult the living God. It is true, O LORD, that the Assyrian kings have laid waste these nations and their lands. They have thrown their gods into the fire and destroyed them, for they were not gods but only wood and stone, fashioned by men's hands. Now, O LORD our God, deliver us from his hand, so that all the kingdoms on earth may know that you alone, O LORD, are God."

II Kings 19:14-19

God immediately sends Isaiah to Hezekiah to tell him that his prayer was heard and to prophesy the downfall of Sennacherib. God indeed did deliver Hezekiah from Sennacherib, and the Assyrians did not conquer Jerusalem. Hezekiah and his kingdom continued on until the time of his illness. He was even healed of his illness and fifteen years were added to his life.

What About the Lost Ten Tribes?

An interesting point should be inserted here. Before we see the scattering of the northern ten tribes by the Assyrian assault, some of the Israelites who dwelt there decided to return to Judah and Jerusalem.

The priests and Levites from all their districts throughout Israel sided with him. The Levites even abandoned their pasturelands and property, and came to Judah and Jerusalem because Jeroboam and his sons had rejected them as priests of the LORD. And he appointed his own priests for the high places and for the goat and calf idols he had made. Those from every tribe of Israel who set their hearts on seeking the LORD, the God of Israel, followed the Levites to Jerusalem to offer sacrifices to the LORD, the God of their fathers. They strengthened the kingdom of Judah and supported Rehoboam son of Solomon three years, walking in the ways of David and Solomon during this time.

II Chronicles 11:13-17

This sheds light on the theory of the "lost ten tribes." There may be a remnant of the "ten tribes" that are still somewhere scattered among the nations, but there are also those who returned back to Judah and Jerusalem. All of those ten tribes were accounted for even back during that time. They were accounted for during the captivity when they were led away to Babylon. According to the Jewish people they are still accounted for today among the Jews that are home in Israel.

Luke records for us that Anna the prophetess was from the tribe of Asher.

> *There was also a prophetess, Anna, the daughter of Phanuel, of the tribe of Asher. She was very old; she had lived with her husband seven years after her marriage.*

> Luke 2:36

James, as well, addresses his epistle to *"the twelve tribes scattered among the nations"* (James 1:1). This may seem to stand in opposition to my point but it is not addressed to the *"ten tribes"* but rather to the *"twelve tribes."* In those synagogues and meeting places scattered throughout the then-known-world were representatives of *all* the twelve tribes. All were still accounted for even in New Testament times.

These facts aid us in setting the scene for the time of trouble coming upon the Jewish nation. A time of real trial and testing for Hezekiah is about to give us a cross-section of the king's heart. Hezekiah, having been spared and healed, was told that judgment would bypass him and fall at a later date. Rather than repent for his people, Hezekiah breathes a sigh of relief that the judgment would not fall during the days of his reign.

Hezekiah's Weakness

The following instance does not involve Assyrians, but occurs later when the northern ten tribes have already been taken away by the Assyrians. Suddenly, Babylonian envoys come to visit King Hezekiah in Jerusalem.

> *At that time Merodach-Baladan son of Baladan king of Babylon sent Hezekiah letters and a gift, because he had heard of Hezekiah's illness. Hezekiah received the messengers and showed them all that was in his storehouses —the silver, the gold, the spices, and the fine oil—his armory and everything found among his treasures. There was nothing in his palace or in all his kingdom that Hezekiah did not show them.*

> *Then Isaiah the prophet went to King Hezekiah and asked,*

23

The Final Kingdom

*"What did those men say, and where did they come from?"
"From a distant land," Hezekiah replied. "They came from
Babylon." The prophet asked, "What did they see in your
palace?" "They saw everything in my palace," Hezekiah said.
"There is nothing among my treasures that I did not show
them."*

*Then Isaiah said to Hezekiah, "Hear the word of the LORD: The
time will surely come when everything in your palace, and all
that your fathers have stored up until this day, will be carried
off to Babylon. Nothing will be left, says the LORD. And some
of your descendants, your own flesh and blood, that will be
born to you, will be taken away, and they will become
eunuchs in the palace of the king of Babylon."*

II Kings 20:12-18

This message from Isaiah to Hezekiah had an surprising effect
on the king. In verse 19, Hezekiah consoles himself that at least
personally he will not have to suffer judgment. This turn of events
must have been like throwing cold water on Hezekiah after all he
had been through.

Perhaps Hezekiah was arrogantly thinking, *I have had envoys
visit me from Babylon. Now I'm playing ball with the big boys.*
Hezekiah was terrified of the Assyrians. If Hezekiah were
successful in striking an alliance with someone as powerful and
important as Babylon, he would be safe if war were to break out
with Assyria again.   This, of course, constitutes an unholy
alliance, as God expected the kings of Israel and Judah to depend
upon Him alone for their protection and not look to ungodly
nations for assistance. Unfortunately, Hezekiah followed through
in this false assurance, and consequently set himself and all of
Israel up for a great defeat. Truly, his pride and self-reliance led
the way.

*"The word of the LORD you have spoken is good," Hezekiah
replied. For he thought, "Will there not be peace and security
in my lifetime?"*

v. 19

Even in all this, God was faithful to His people.

We have seen the objective of the Assyrians and the captivity of
the remainder of the northern ten tribes who were carried away to
Assyria. The end result would be the actual fall of Jerusalem.

Just prior to the seige of Jerusalem, there were false prophets

24

who were advising that God would not allow the city to fall. They reasoned that God would not possibly do that to His own people. These prophets mocked Isaiah's and Jeremiah's words that warned the Babylonians would be coming to take them captive. The false prophets' advice was to ignore the doomsayers.

Obviously it was a critical time of decision for the populace of Jerusalem. I am sure they were asking themselves, *whom should I believe?* and *how can we know which of the messages are from God?*

The captivity and destruction and rebuilding of the Temple in Jerusalem are documented in II Chronicles:

The LORD, the God of their fathers, sent word to them through his messengers again and again, because he had pity on his people and on his dwelling place. But they mocked God's messengers, despised his words and scoffed at his prophets until the wrath of the LORD was aroused against his people and there was no remedy. He brought up against them the king of the Babylonians, who killed their young men with the sword in the sanctuary, and spared neither young man nor young woman, old man or aged.

God handed all of them over to Nebuchadnezzar. He carried to Babylon all the articles from the temple of God, both large and small, and the treasures of the LORD's temple and the treasures of the king and his officials. They set fire to God's temple and broke down the wall of Jerusalem; they burned all the palaces and destroyed everything of value there. He carried into exile to Babylon the remnant, who escaped from the sword, and they became servants to him and his sons until the kingdom of Persia came to power.

The land enjoyed its Sabbath rests; all the time of its desolation it rested, until the seventy years were completed in fulfillment of the word of the LORD spoken by Jeremiah.

In the first year of Cyrus king of Persia, in order to fulfill the word of the LORD spoken by Jeremiah, the LORD moved the heart of Cyrus king of Persia to make a proclamation throughout his realm and to put it in writing. "This is what Cyrus king of Persia says: 'The LORD, the God of heaven, has given me all the kingdoms of the earth and he has appointed me to build a temple for him at Jerusalem in Judah. Anyone of His people among you—may the LORD his God be with him, and let him go up.'" II Chronicles 36:15-23

Prophetic Warnings   •

God warned His people, detailing for them what was soon to come upon them, even the following promise to keep them safe from three things: *waters, rivers, fire.*

> *When you pass through the waters, I will be with you; and when you pass through the rivers, they will not sweep over you. When you walk through the fire, you will not be burned; the flames will not set you ablaze. For I am the LORD your God, the Holy One of Israel, your Savior. . .*
>
> Isaiah 43:2,3a

It would have been highly beneficial during that particular time to learn to hear from God for yourself. Conflicting interpretations of God's word and purposes by various prophets were as real for them in their day as they are for us in our day. In a time of great confusion, undoubtedly the message of ease was preferred.

The three young men that were thrown into the blazing fiery furnace later in Babylon no doubt hung on to Isaiah's words like a lifeline of promise. Isaiah was the kind of prophet that made sure that these instructions were engraved upon the people's hearts. His masterful use of the Hebrew language, his grand vocabulary and ability to arrange that vocabulary into heart-arresting prose and poetry, assured the Israelites that those promises would accompany the captives to Babylon like guardian angels.

God's warnings to His people abounded. Jeremiah declared:

> *While Nebuchadnezzar king of Babylon and all of his army and all the kingdoms and peoples in the empire he ruled were fighting against Jerusalem and all of its surrounding towns, this word came to Jeremiah from the LORD: "This is what the LORD, the God of Israel, says: Go to Zedekiah king of Judah and tell him, 'This is what the LORD says: I am about to hand this city over to the king of Babylon, and he will burn it down. You will not escape from his grasp, but will surely be captured and handed over to him. You will see the king of Babylon with your own eyes, and he will speak with you face to face. You will go to Babylon.*
>
> *Yet hear the promise of the LORD, O Zedekiah king of Judah. This is what the LORD says concerning you: You will not die by the sword; you will die peacefully. As people made a*

26

funeral fire in honor of your fathers, the former kings who preceded you, so they will make a fire in your honor and lament, "Alas, O master!" I make myself this promise, declares the LORD.'"

Then Jeremiah the prophet told all this to Zedekiah king of Judah, in Jerusalem, while the army of the king of Babylon was fighting against Jerusalem and the other cities of Judah that were still holding out—Lachish and Azekah. These were the only fortified cities left in Judah.

Jeremiah 34:1-7

A Bedouin Object Lesson

Further on in Jeremiah, a bedouin tribe becomes the audio visual tool which God used to teach an important lesson of obedience. The Racabites obeyed a simple word of good advice from an ancestor and it became tradition to them—transcending generations. In contrast, the Israelites, in possession of the "Holy Word" from Heaven, would not even obey God Almighty, who had delivered them from enemies time and time again. Thus, they were to be led away captive to Babylon.

This is the word of the LORD that came to Jeremiah from the LORD during the reign of Jehoiakim son of Josiah king of Judah:

"Go to the Racabite family and invite them to come to one of the side rooms of the house of the LORD and give them wine to drink."

So I went to get Jaazaniah the son of Jeremiah, the son of Habazziniah, and his brothers and his sons—the whole family of the Racabites. I brought them into the house of the LORD, into the room of the sons of Hanan son of Igdaliah the man of God. It was next to the room of the officials, that was over that of Ma'aseiah son of Shallum the doorkeeper. Then I set bowls full of wine and some cups before the men of the Racabite family and said to them, "Drink some wine."

But they replied, "We do not drink wine, because our forefather Jonadab son of Racab gave us this command: 'Neither you nor your descendants must ever drink wine. Also you must never build houses, sow seed, or plant vineyards; you must never have any of these things, but must always live in tents. Then you will live a long time in the land where you are nomads.' We have obeyed everything that our forefather Jonadab son of Racab commanded us. Neither we nor our wives nor our sons and daughters have ever drunk wine or built houses to live in or had vineyards, fields or crops. We have lived in tents and have fully obeyed everything our forefather Jonadab commanded us.

"But when Nebuchadnezzar king of Babylon invaded this land, we said, 'Come, we must go to Jerusalem to escape the Babylonian and Aramean armies.' So we have remained in Jerusalem."

Then the word of the LORD came to Jeremiah, saying: "This is what the LORD Almighty, the God of Israel, says: Go and tell the men of Judah and the people of Jerusalem, 'Will you not learn a lesson and obey my words?' declares the LORD. 'Jonadab son of Racab ordered his sons not to drink wine and this command has been kept. To this day they do not drink wine, because they obey their forefathers command. But I have spoken to you again and again, yet you have not obeyed me. Again and again I sent all my servants and prophets to you. They said, "Each of you must turn from your wicked ways and reform your actions; do not follow other gods to serve them. Then you will live in the land I have given you and your fathers." But you have not paid attention or listened to me. The descendants of Jonadab the son of Racab have carried out the command their forefathers gave them, but these people have not obeyed me.' "Therefore, this is what the LORD God Almighty, the God of Israel, says: 'Listen! I am going to bring on Judah and on everyone living in Jerusalem every disaster I pronounced against them. I spoke to them, but they did not listen; I called to them, but they did not answer.'"

Then Jeremiah said to the family of the Racabites, "This is what the LORD Almighty, the God of Israel, says: 'You have obeyed the command of your forefather Jonadab and have followed all his instructions and have done everything he ordered. Therefore, this is what the LORD Almighty, the God of Israel, says: "Jonadab the son of Recab will never fail to have a man to serve me."'"

Jeremiah 35:1-19

It is amazing, but bedouins—the descendants of these nomadic people—still follow the advice of their ancestor about wine and living in tents. This was an important lesson about God's requirement of absolute obedience to His word.

Through Jeremiah, the Lord spoke to the populace telling them to go to meet the Babylonians in surrender and not try to stay in Jerusalem. The warning was that if they disobeyed and stayed inside the city, which would be besieged, they would wind up losing their lives.

> *Furthermore, tell the people, 'This is what the LORD says: See, I am setting before you the way of life and the way of death. Whoever stays in this city will die by the sword, famine or plague. But whoever goes out and surrenders to the Babylonians who are besieging you will live; he will escape with his life. I have determined to do this city harm and not good, declares the LORD. It will be given into the hands of the king of Babylon, and he will destroy it with fire.'*

> Jeremiah 21:8-10

In fact, God told His people through Jeremiah that they were to "settle down" in Babylon and make a good life for themselves. He even instructed them to work for the "prosperity" of the community and nation of Babylon while they were there.

Jeremiah's letter to the exiles in Babylon reads:

> *This is what the LORD Almighty, the God of Israel, says to all those I carried into exile from Jerusalem to Babylon: "Build houses and settle down; plant gardens and eat what they produce. Marry and have sons and daughters; find wives for your sons and give your daughters in marriage, so that they too may have sons and daughters. Increase in number there; do not decrease. Also, seek the peace and prosperity of the city to which I have carried you into exile. Pray to the LORD for it, because if it prospers, you too will prosper."*

> 29:4-7

Zedekiah's Cave

Not every person was taken captive by the Babylonians. In order for Babylon to exact taxes from conquered nations, peasants and workers were left to continue to farm the conquered areas with Babylonian governors over them. Zedekiah was ordained

The Final Kingdom

king of Judah by Nebuchadnezzar to oversee these operations. In the ninth year of King Zedekiah's reign, he rebelled against the occupying authority. Second Kings chapter 25 tells us that Zedekiah fled from the city toward the *Arabah*, the desert, but that the Babylonian army overtook him in the plains of Jericho. The legend of Zedekiah fleeing the city involves a cave that still lies under the Old City of Jerusalem.

The cave, on the north side of the Old City walls of Jerusalem, is known as Zedekiah's Cave. The cave burrows underneath the Old City from the north wall, tunneling south. This cave is one of the larger caves in Jerusalem proper. It is believed that much of the stone used for the building of Solomon's Temple was taken from this cave. The distinct marks of ancient quarrying techniques can still be seen there.

Some three hundred feet inside, the cave opens into a monumental cavern. The roof and walls distinctly bear the tool marks of very skilled ancient stone masons.

Once, out of curiosity, I paced off the depth of the cave. First, I walked the length underground and then, resurfacing, I entered the Old City through Damascus Gate and paced off the same footage above ground.

I was rather amazed at the extent of the cave. Pacing the same number of steps on the secondary street leading from Damascus Gate, which runs from the north to the south, I wound up exactly on the Via Dolorosa. This is the street which cuts the Old City in half.

From the back of Zedekiah's cave you can see other caves branching out in other directions. The municipal authorities of the city of Jerusalem have blocked off access to those caves. Apparently previous explorers have been lost there and died. That would indeed lead you to believe that those offshoots of the main cave are extensive, giving validity to the legend about Zedekiah.

The legend says that King Zedekiah, in seeking to escape from the Babylonians, disappeared into this cave. There is a story from Jewish Midrashic sources that say that the king followed the cave all the way down to where it resurfaces in Wadi Kelt—a valley that heads from Jerusalem to Jericho through the desert. Zedekiah would have exited many miles from Jerusalem. The story says that God caused a gazelle to follow the kings footsteps above ground, leading the Babylonian army right to him when he came out in Wadi Kelt. The Babylonian army captured King

Zedekiah there in the valley and took him away. The extent to which God goes to make sure that His will is carried out is amazing.

How Daniel Differs

The book of Daniel differs greatly from the other major prophets. He is indeed counted among the major prophets, but typical earmarks of other prophetic works are not found in this book.

There are no proclamations in the name of the Lord as there are in the other major prophets. Daniel is not specifically historical; it is *eschatological*—a Greek word meaning "endings," dealing in some detail with the end of the age. It is also apocalyptic, containing visions and revelations of things to come in the end of time. It does not deal only with Israel—its scope is worldwide. Other biblical prophetic writings concern themselves with other nations, but that concern is on the basis of that particular nation's relationship to Israel. Daniel prophetically covers issues concerning the entire world system—from beginning to end.

The book of Daniel was actually forbidden by Marxist governments because the view of the last days proved that all government systems ultimately fail, including communism. The book of Daniel was not allowed to be printed, read, or possessed in communist nations. It was too pointed. Communist doctrine did not know how to cope with the fact that the "everlasting kingdom" they were trying to build would be struck at its feet by a stone and crumble to dust.

Babylon's Grandeur

Babylon was one of the great wonders of the world in its day. The Greek historian Herodotus wrote in the fifth century B.C., "In magnificence, there is no other city that approaches it." The walls of the city were actually walls nested inside walls. There were four city walls and they towered somewhere between 100 and 300 feet in height. A full four-horse chariot could easily be turned around on the tops of those broad walls.

The Euphrates River was controlled by the walls of the city. The gates on the north and the south part of the city could be opened or closed. This allowed the water to flow through the city in low stage, and in flood stage the closing of the gates diverted the river water around the outside of the city, making Babylon a virtual island.

The Final Kingdom

A 400-foot long bridge on the east side of the city spanned the river in its high stage. The city was massive. It stood as the capital of a major world empire. The rule and influence of the Babylonians as a world empire stretched from India to Europe. Their reputation differed from that of the Assyrians. Unlike the cruel Assyrians, the Babylonians were more gentle and well-educated. Governmental administration of conquered lands included satraps, or governors, who were appointed to rule over administered territories. These reported to headquarters in Babylon. They excised taxes for local purposes as well as imperial taxes which would benefit Babylon itself.

The Babylonians believed in a multiplicity of gods. Each satrap was to make sure that the worship of each region's local gods continued undisturbed. This meant that the captive Israelites would have been allowed to worship their God without persecution. This is also why it was not out of the ordinary for King Cyrus to issue a decree to rebuild Jerusalem and its Temple. We do not know what motivated the Babylonians to besiege Jerusalem, but we do know that the disobedience of the Jewish people motivated God to have them besieged. The rebuilding of the city was in the hands of God, and His imposed 70-year period of rest for the land had to be completed before the king's heart was moved to issue a decree that would undo what had been done.

The Babylonian kingdom rose up over a period of about 260 years to its ultimate glory. The city with its hanging gardens became one of the wonders of the world. With all her conquered territories, Babylon ruled one of the largest kingdoms in the history of mankind.

Nevertheless, 260 years later, Babylon completely disappeared under the sands of time for over 2000 years. The city vanished so totally that scholars thought Babylon to be only a legend until recent excavations proved otherwise.

This is a sobering thought to nations today who view themselves as world powers. Russia's communism came and went within a period of seventy years. This is a short period in the realm of ancient world powers. The United States of America is only just over 220 years old.

The study of Babylon's emergence as a nation helps us get a better idea of what Daniel and his contemporaries faced in the land of their captivity. The background information sets the scene in which Daniel dwells. The drama then unfolds with deeper meaning. The lessons of the book are more rich when we are thus equipped with this understanding.

Judaism Returns From Babylon

Babylon brought about changes in First Temple period Judaism. The religion that departed with the Jewish people to Babylon was altered forever when it returned to Jerusalem seventy years later. Those changes, from the time spent in Babylon, are still with us to this day.

Though there are varied ideas, it is plausible that the synagogue originated among the exiles in Babylon, who on foreign soil, and unable to continue with their sacrificial ritual, developed a more spiritual form of worship. Prayer and study took the place of offerings, and the synagogue became a substitute for the destroyed temple.

Without the Temple as a visible symbol of deity to lend sacredness to a specific place, and without propitiation by sacrifice or a privileged clergy to mediate or intercede for the comman man, the public worship held in the synagogue, both spiritual and democratic throughout, permitted anyone, anywhere, to commune with God.

The synagogue became not only a place of worship but the focus of the religious, social, and intellectual life of the Jews. It served not only as a place of public worship, but also as elementary school, law-court, communal center, and even a hotel for strangers.

Synagogue services world-wide now have customs that date back to the Babylonian time period. Both Orthodox and Conservative synagogues bear the remnants of that time. Each *Shabbat* (Sabbath), in every synagogue around the world, a portion of the first five books of Moses is read. This section of the Scriptures is called in Hebrew the *Torah*. The reading of the Torah scroll during the Shabbat service is a good example of these changes that took place.

Synagogue Torah scrolls are written in Hebrew on rolls of parchment, sometimes hundreds of feet long. They are rolled on beautifully carved wooden rollers and covered in a soft velvet cloth for their protection and preservation. They are stored before and after the reading in a specially made closet at the front of the synagogue called the *Aron HaKodesh,* meaning the "Holy Ark," (not to be confused with the Ark of the Covenant). The Aron HaKodesh is considered "holy" due to the fact that it houses God's Word, which is holy. In close proximity to the Ark, is a large table that sits on a platform called the *bimah.* Each Shabbat, several congregants are called forward to read or aid in the preparation for the Scripture reading from the Torah scroll.

During the reading, the designated reader of the actual Torah scroll is not allowed to look up at the congregation. A second reader, standing beside him, who reads in the language of the congregation is not allowed to look down at the Torah scroll. The one reading in the language of the congregation, be it English, French, or any other language is called the *meturgeman,* meaning "translator." This word is derived from the Hebrew word *targum.* A targum is a translation of the Torah into another language. The first *targumim* were Aramaic translations from the Hebrew.

The reason for the tradition concerning the attitude of the eyes stems from a supersensitive, but justified caution about the absolute authority of the Torah. What was read in Hebrew must never be confused with what was read from the translation. The Hebrew was and is considered the *Word of God*—from His own lips. The Jewish people have taken great pains to preserve the purity of the Word of God for millenia. That which is in another language may be more loosely translated and can be misinterpreted. The meturgeman's job was more or less "quality control" over what was understood from the reading of the Torah scrolls. This tradition has its roots in the Babylonian exile.

Changes in the "Oral Law"

The Jewish people teach that God gave the *written law* and along with it, He gave the *Oral Law*. The Oral Law was transmitted to the succeeding generation by word of mouth.

On several different occasions the Israelite community's existence was threatened with extinction. Sages finally deemed it necessary that the teachings which had been handed down by word of mouth should be written to keep them from being lost. These writings became known as the *Talmud*. The word actually means "the study." The Talmud is still used throughout the Jewish world.

Introduction

This voluminous collection is the field guide on how to live out the commandments given at Mount Sinai to Moses and the children of Israel. This "living out" is called *halacha*, from the Hebrew verb meaning "to walk." Throughout Scripture God tells His people "to walk" in His ways.

Even though the Talmud was not codified during the captivity in Babylon, the change of locale and the destruction of the Temple set into motion the necessary considerations for change in the Oral Law. The finished versions came into being many centuries later but there are certain *halakhot*—"rules of behavior"—which the Talmud itself attributes to the period of Nehemiah, that is, the beginning of the Second Temple era.

The Talmud—the achievement of Jews both in ancient Israel and in Babylonia—is recorded in two editions. The history of the book has parallel origins. The *Palestinian* version, compiled around A.D. 400, is known as the *Jerusalem Talmud*, or "*Yerushalmi*." Oddly enough, it is not widely studied or translated into English. The Babylonian edition, known as the "*Bavli*," was not completed until around A.D. 500; it has become the normative text in traditional Jewish education, especially in rabbinical training.

The Bavli edition dealt with the practice of Judaism outside of Israel in a time period when there was no Temple standing. The Yerushalmi edition held much that dealt with Temple sacrificial regulations as well as the 613 laws of the Torah that a Jewish person was expected to keep. But a great number of those laws cannot be kept in light of the fact that for a second time in history there is no Temple. The Babylonian edition did not deal with Temple-based issues as did the Jerusalem edition. Therefore, the Jewish community of the *diaspora* (Jews scattered to lands outside Israel), read the writings of the rabbis and the codification of the oral traditions from the Bavli edition. These could be applied in the nations where they lived and in the cultures where they had been scattered.

The Talmud is a complex forerunner of our modern day legal systems and codes of law. The Scriptures were understood as the inspired Word of God—from His own mouth—while the Oral Law is concerned with how to make those laws work in everyday life, to the minutest detail. The core of the Talmud is the *Mishnah*, which is an early collection of laws and rulings compiled by Rabbi Judah the Prince, Yehudah Hanasi, around A.D. 200. The early teachers were known as *Tana'im*.

The *Gemara* is another section of the Talmud. It is a commentary on the Mishnah, and was produced by scholar-teachers known as *Amora'im*, who lived from A.D. 200-500. The complete compilation of the Talmud took centuries. So together, the Mishnah and the Gemara comprise the Talmud. Modern editions of the Talmud also include later medieval commentaries which are printed in the margin. If you open an edition of the Talmud, you will find it a bit maze-like. Its central section is surrounded by other sections which are commentary, then in turn those commentary sections are surrounded by yet other commentary sections. The Midrash and Gemara exist there as the central sections, and all of the surrounding texts are commentaries on them. One of the traditionally renowned rabbis, Rashi, who has his own section in the Talmud, even has his own style of Hebrew writing and his own alphabet. The mass of documents is divided into *tractates* (compiled categories), according to subject matter. There are six categorical orders of tractates.

The discussions of the rabbis can be divided into narrative material known as *hagadah* (meaning "the telling")—treatment of Scripture and *halakhah* or "how to walk out the law."

The Talmud is the major repository of Jewish learning to survive from antiquity and represented for Jews their definitive link with the Bible itself. Taken as a whole, the Talmud can be thought of as the early rabbis' commentary on Scripture and wisdom for subsequent generations.

Falasha and Karaite Judaic Traditions

Various sectors of Judaism place varying degrees of authority upon the Talmud. The Ethiopian Jews, known as the *Falasha*, do not place as much emphasis upon the Talmud. The Falasha form of Judaism progressed, hermetically sealed away from the rest of Judaism-at-large because of their great distance from Israel and the simplicity of their culture. They maintained Jewish practices as they had taken them from King Solomon's time, prior to the Babylonian captivity. They depict themselves as descendants of King Solomon and the Queen of Sheba's son, Menelek.

Another exception to the authority of the Talmud are the Karaites who also hold only to the Torah. They came back to modern Israel from the region of southern Russia, and now have a synagogue inside the Old City of Jerusalem. Their rejection of the Talmud and other sources of Judaic literature is a controversial issue among the Jews of Israel. Some of the more orthodox strains of Judaism do not consider them to be Jewish, but the Karaites stringently hold to their convictions and faithfully practice their traditional form of Judaism. It is interesting to observe the differences in their practices of Judaic worship.

The captivity in Babylon began the changes that progressed over the centuries. The language of Babylon was Aramaic. Over the seventy year period they were captives, the Jewish people adapted to a whole new language. Not only just in daily life, but slowly even the language of their religious services changed to Aramaic, due to Babylonian influence.

The Topography Sets the Physical Stage

The topography of Israel and her surrounding nations should be considered as we begin to examine the book of Daniel. The Bible states on many occasions that Israel was attacked from the north. In fact, the description of the Babylonian invasion is described as coming from the *north*. This is confusing since Babylon lies southeast of Jerusalem.

It would have been impossible for the Babylonians to invade Israel from the east. Even though an easterly approach would seem most likely, the geography and topology of the area make it prohibitive.

A straight line from the city of Babylon to Jerusalem would traverse the most tortuous desert punctuated by the mountainous region of Moab and Edom. For an army it would have meant certain death. The forces would expend all their energies just making the journey to the battle ground.

The Fertile Crescent is a broad strip of land that follows the Tigris and Euphrates Rivers from Babylon northward toward modern Turkey. Just before it reaches the Turkish border, it turns west and travels toward the Mediterranean Sea. This route is relatively flat and well-watered. Populations amassed close to the rivers; therefore there were towns and villages along the way in which travelers or invading armies could get provisions. When the crescent arrived at the sea, the route then turned southward along the coastal plain and into Israel, leading all the way south to Egypt. This abundance of water and populations to provide supplies and other necessities laid the foundation for a superhighway through the Middle East.

It must be said though, that it was not impossible to cross the desert. As a matter of fact, camel caravans did so regularly. The fact was that camel caravans were more adapted to desert regions. They were the semi-trucks of that time period and most trade and commerce was delivered by camel. But these camel caravans were not expected to wage a battle at the end of their journey. Rather they could lie down exhausted, unlike a warring army, and not lose their lives for it. Messages though, had to travel quickly.

History books tell us that messages were sent from Jerusalem to Babylon in a most unusual manner. The beginning of Jewish biblical feasts were set by the visual observance of the cycles of the moon as viewed from Jerusalem. Obviously, it was necessary to get these messages from Jerusalem to Babylon quickly. The several month trip it took to physically travel the Fertile Crescent was out of any realm of feasibility. For these messages to travel quickly, a chain of bonfires was used on mountain tops! The first bonfire would probably have been set on the Mount of Olives, as it faces east into the Judean Desert. A long string of mountain-top bonfires followed in succession, traveling eastward to the city of Babylon.

Someone had to be positioned on those mountain peaks at those particular times. The history is scant on information regarding those who tended these fires. Reason says that they had to arrive there in enough time to find wood to burn—in a desert wasteland where no trees grew—and drag it to the tops of the designated mountains and wait for the signal. On the feast days when those bonfires were lit, there would be a continual bonfire signal straight to its destination—the Jews living in Babylon, with Daniel.

Through the Garden Gate

We now have enough background to enter that aforementioned citrus grove and begin to search the book of Daniel for its secret treasures. Too often this book is read in order to unlock the mystery of the "last days" schedule of prophetic events—to the minute! Indeed, the book has much to tell regarding last days—but if we seek only that from this great book, we will miss important lessons to be gained here. The smell of citrus blossoms is in the air.

Like these good figs,
I regard as good the
exiles from Judah,
whom I sent away from
this place to the land of
the Babylonians.
My eyes will watch over
them for their good,
and I will bring them
back to this land.

I will build them up
and not tear them
down; I will plant them
and not uproot them.
I will give them a heart
to know me,
that I am the LORD.
They will be my people,
and I will be their God,
for they will return to
me with all their heart.

Jeremiah 24:4-7

Palace wall relief uncovered by archaeologists depicts Jewish captive
with tzitzit (fringes) in his garment

The Characters Emerge

Character development is a vital part of good literature. God, through the writer of the book, develops the characters of Daniel and his fellow captives, Hananiah, Mishael, and Azariah, desiring that we identify with them. The expectation is undoubtedly that we should take on the attributes of these young men in our own lives.

If disobedience and rebellion sent the Jewish people into exile, why then, did God protect those whom He sent into captivity? Other times in the history of the Jewish nation, as when the Israelites wandered in the wilderness for forty years, God threatened to destroy the people and birth a new nation. In Exodus, Moses' intercession changed God's mind and He spared the people (Exodus 32). Yet, in the time period before the Babylonian invasion we see, again, a long duration of disobedience.

Jeremiah has inside information on how God felt about His people at this time of their history.

> Then the word of the LORD came to me: "This is what the LORD, the God of Israel, says: 'Like these good figs, I regard as good the exiles from Judah, whom I sent away from this place to the land of the Babylonians. My eyes will watch over them for their good, and I will bring them back to this land. I will build them up and not tear them down; I will plant them and not uproot them. I will give them a heart to know me, that I am the LORD. They will be my people, and I will be their God, for they will return to me with all of their heart.'"

> Jeremiah 24:4-7

Long before the Babylonian captivity, God foresaw that the Jewish people would return to Him again with all of their hearts. He also knew that there were lessons to be learned during their captivity in Babylon. Secondarily, but not of any less importance, there were things that the presence of the Jewish people would teach the very nations who were instrumental in their captivity and suffering. They would, in fact, contribute to Babylon's well being during their residence there. God's promise to Abraham to "bless all those who bless you" and "all nations of the earth will be blessed through you" would stand as truth (Gen. 12:3, 18:18).

41

The Final Kingdom

Who are Daniel, Hananiah, Mishael and Azariah?

Then the king ordered Ashpenaz, chief of his court officials, to bring in some of the Israelites from the royal family and the nobility—young men without any physical defect, handsome, showing aptitude for every kind of learning, well informed, quick to understand, and qualified to serve in the king's palace. He was to teach them the language and literature of the Babylonians.

Daniel 1:3,4

These verses from the first chapter tell us that these men were from the royal family line. They were the nobility of the nation of Israel. Several other characteristics are recorded for us about these young men. Their ages were probably between eighteen and twenty years; they were without any kind of physical imperfection; they were good-looking young men. We are also told that they had an intrinsic ability for learning—not just any kind of learning, but more specifically, *every* kind of learning.

The Isaiah Connection

These four young men resembled Isaiah, in that they had great potential for learning. The book of Isaiah, like the book of Daniel, surpasses other prophetic writings in many ways. Isaiah is embellished with both prose and poetry whose beauty is unsurpassed by other books of the Old Testament. Isaiah's broad vocabulary stands at some 2,200 words which exceeds any other Old Testament writer by at least twenty-five percent. Isaiah was an educated noble of the nation of Israel.

The book of Isaiah begs to be read along with Daniel. Many passages detail the plight of the Jews who would be carried away to Babylon. The uniqueness of Isaiah's writing was with definite purpose and must be mentioned. The Israelites were about to be carried out of their comfort zones, and, most likely, separated from their Scriptures for a time. Isaiah's method of writing made it easy to remember what you had heard. It sunk down into one's soul and found a place to dwell.

Isaiah's poetry might not fit today's description of poetry. Rhyming words at the ends of sentences, as we are most familiar with, were rarely used in Hebrew poetry. There were interestingly different approaches to poetry among the Hebrew writers.

Hebrew Poetry

Assonance, the use of similar sounding words, was often used by writers of the Hebrew Scriptures. A good example is Isaiah 5:7, where the Lord says that He looked for *mishpat* (justice), and found *mishpach* (bloodshed). In the same verse it is also recorded that He sought *tzadaka* (righteousness), and found instead *tza'akah* (an outcry). The "outcry" of the people because of injustice which was overpowering the land, is uniquely embodied in the similarity of the sounds of the Hebrew words used. It is not exactly a play on words, but a play with word sounds.

Onomatopoeia, a word which imitates the sound that an object makes, was another poetic tool often used by the Hebrews. A good example is the word for fly (the insect) in Hebrew, *zvoov*, which makes a buzzing sound when pronounced correctly. Another example is the word for bottle, *bakbuk*. The sound of liquid pouring from a bottle, *bak-buk-bak-buk-bak-buk*, plays with the ear pleasantly. Hebrew poetry is successful in creating a rhythm pleasing to the ear, stimulating imagery to the brain, and most important of all, saturating the spirit for the sake of memorizing Scriptures.

In a time period when individuals did not possess their own physical copies of the Scriptures, many different methods of memorizing the Word of God were utilized. Poetry was one of those methods.

As far as memorizing is concerned, Psalm 119 is an example of a very simple memory aid. Psalm 119 is written in twenty-two sections of eight lines each. Each of the lines, in each section, begins with one of the letters of the Hebrew alphabet. The first section of this Psalm begins with the first letter *aleph* "א"and each succeeding section progresses to the last Hebrew letter *tav* "ת". Using this method, those sections are more easily remembered by someone who may have no access to a copy of the book of Psalms.

Isaiah's use of poetry brings us some of the most beautiful sections of Scripture in the Bible. Isaiah chapter 24, verse 16 gives us an idea of the scope of the prophet's poetry. In English it says:

From the ends of the earth we hear singing: "Glory to the Righteous One." But I said, "I waste away, I waste away! Woe to me! The treacherous betray! With treachery, the treacherous betray! Terror and pit and snare await you, O people of the earth."

Granted, in English the rhythmic sound of the words is intriguing, but in Hebrew the assonance creates a rhythm that is even more penetrating:

> *Razili, razili,*
>
> *Oy-li, bogadim, bagadou, ouveged.*
>
> *Bogadim, bagadou,*
>
> *Pahad v'fahad v'fach, aleiha yoshev ha'aretz.*

The importance of the message Isaiah was trying to get across to his people needed this captivating rhythm that seems to pick you up and take you with it. It could almost have become a song in their spirit. It was the tool God used to cause His people to take to heart His message.

When we read Amos or similar prophets who were simple men, we see that they did not use such sophisticated language as Isaiah. They delivered a more straightforward message. Both kinds of prophets were inspired by God. Both were filled with the Holy Spirit for inspiration when they wrote the Word of God, which we believe is infallible. So how is it Isaiah wrote poetry like this, while Amos wrote a letter?

God uses each one of our own individual characters in the things He calls us to do for Him. We are not stamped out of a mold. We each have wonderful gifts that have been delivered to us. When the Holy Spirit anoints us and inspires us and works through us, He uses all our God-given giftings so that we may fulfill His call. Isaiah may have had a natural inclination to poetry and Amos to farming. The Lord uses the character that He created us with to accomplish His goals.

The young men whose characters are being developed in the first chapter of the book of Daniel are of similar quality as Isaiah.

Assimilation into Babylon

We now know that Daniel, Hananiah, Mishael, and Azariah, were from royal lineage, from nobility, and that they were godly young men, with good attitudes; now, they were going to be taught the language, culture, and literature of the Babylonians.

> *Then the king ordered Ashpenaz, chief of his court officials, to bring in some of the Israelites from the royal family and the nobility—young men without any physical defect, handsome, showing aptitude for every kind of learning, well informed,*

quick to understand, and qualified to serve in the king's palace. He was to teach them the language and literature of the Babylonians. The king assigned them a daily amount of food and wine from the king's table. They were to be trained for three years, and after that they were to enter the king's service.

Daniel 1:3-5

I am sure that if you were to inform your pastor that you were going to spend three years learning astrology, the depths of magic, dream interpretation, and an ancient language closely related to those crafts, he would counsel you against it. It would be fairly certain that at the end of that three-year period you would end up being polluted and influenced by the powers of darkness, having compromised your spiritual walk. Undoubtedly, your pastor would tell you that to follow such a path would be fraught with danger.

At the hands of their captors, these young men were going to be forced to go through a three-year period of learning both the Aramaic and Chaldean languages. They were to be trained in the dream interpretation of the Chaldeans. Volume upon volume of material was involved. The archaeological library in London where these ancient artifacts are kept records some 96,000 cuneiform tablets on these particular subjects.

The Babylonians, Assyrians, and Elamites practiced foretelling the future by reading extracted animal organs. The extracted liver from a goat or a sheep was checked for various characteristics which these people believed were indicators of future events. One purpose of these readings was to foretell events on a national scale when performed by the king's elite wise men.

This training was not just a simple introduction into the way of Babylonian thought. Chaldeans took lifetimes to learn such information and yet these young Hebrew captives would be forced to serve in the palace of the king of Babylon in the capacity of wise and learned men. This was a crash course and all was planned to be completed in a three-year time period.

These young men would also be introduced to the gods of the Babylonians. Babylon, and most other surrounding nations of the time, practiced worshiping a multiplicity of gods. The pantheon of the gods of Babylon was complex. In the *Emunah Aliesh*, a piece of literature about the Babylonian god Marduk, we learn that Marduk was the god at the top of the Babylonian pantheon. Marduk's history, however, goes back further than Babylon. His origin is Akkadian—a people who believed him to be the god of cosmic order.

The story of his climbing the social ladder in the pantheon of Babylonian gods was written down in a seven-tablet epic which contains the story of creation and the flood story, as well.

What's in a Name?

One of Babylon's first acts of subduing their newly acquired palace aides was to change their names. The Israelites named their children with purpose. At times, Hebrew names told the story of a child's desired future. But, as we shall see, it was not only the Israelites who purposefully named their children. We see that Babylonian names had meaning and purpose as well. Names were also given by Babylonians for a characteristic that the parents felt a child had, or would have, or that they wanted him to have. The significance of Babylonian names is that they generally incorporated the names of the Babylonian gods in hope of an earthly representation of that particular deity through their child.

The Hebrew names of these four young men are fundamental to the chapter.

Daniel means "God is my judge"—*Dani* (my judge)—and then -*el* (God) tacked onto the end of it. It seems also to mean, by the end of the book, that God would use Daniel to deliver His judgments to the Babylonian people.

Hananiah means *"gift of God."* Hananiah does not end in *"el,"* it ends in -*iah*; the Hebrew letters would be pronounced, *"yah."* It stands for the first two letters of the name "YaHWeH," God's name in Hebrew יְהֹוָה *yod-hey-vav-hey*—which means, *"I am that I am."*

Mishael means "who is like God?"—*mi* meaning "who," -*sha* meaning "is like" and -*el* meaning "God," or more literally, "Who is what God is?"

Azariah - *Azar* or *Ezra* is the first word, meaning "help," and -*iah*, or "yah" meaning God, thus meaning, "The Lord is my help."

The new names that the Babylonian king were now ascribing to these young men served to replace the name of God with the name of a Babylonian god in each case.

Belteshazzar - Daniel's new name consisted of *Bel* being another name for the god Marduk. The name *Belteshazzar* means "May god protect his life."

46

Shadrach - In Hananiah's new name the last -*ach* is another form of *Achu*, the Sumerian moon god—a lesser diety in the pantheon of Babylonian gods. Interestingly, his symbol was a moon crescent. We see a lot of moon crescents still in use in the Middle East today by Islam. Their most important Islamic feast, *Ramadan*, is scheduled and celebrated when the moon lies straight on its back in crescent form in the night sky.

Meshach - In Mishael's new name, as well, the -*ach* on the end of his name also indicates the god Achu, and one notices the -*me* or -*mi* meaning "who" and the -*sha* meaning "is like." His name means, "Who is like Achu?"

Avednego - Azariah's new name consists of *Aved* meaning "servant" -*nego* means "of Nebo." The name then means "the servant of Nebo." The same word *aved* still exists in Hebrew today. Sometimes in modern Hebrew a form of it is used as a name. *Nego* is another name for Nebo or Nebu, after whom *Nebuchadnezzar* is also named.

The ultimate objective of the Babylonians, therefore, was to change the character of the Israelites brought into the service of the Babylonian king, by changing their names. The power of a name was highly respected. In a nation given almost wholly to metaphysics, the idea that a name change could alter Daniel and his compatriots' characteristics was not extraordinary.

But in all of this, the desire to turn these Hebrews into Babylonians never worked. God remained in them and with them through all the depths to which they had to descend. These young Israelite nobles remained faithfully devoted to God, even in the midst of tremendous opposition to God's ways.

The Babylonian Gods

The Babylonian pantheon of gods tells us a lot about worship in Babylon. Understanding who these gods were may also shed light on the idolatrous practices the Israelites adopted from their neighbors. God confronted the Babylonians and their gods in the presence of their Israelite captives to solidify His universal sovereignty in their minds as well. Listed here are some of the many gods worshiped in the capital city and throughout the empire.

The Final Kingdom

Marduk

Babylonian/Akkadian—god of all creation.

The known period of worship was from 2,000 B.C. to 200 B.C. Marduk was the chief diety of Babylon. His parents were Enkai and Damgalnuna, also known as Ia and Damkina. His consort (wife) was the goddess Zarpinatu, with whom his marriage was reenacted in an annual New Year's festival in Babylon.

The symbol of Marduk is a triangle. This device resembled an agricultural tool known as a *mar* and was used all over Mesopotamia. The principal Marduk festival was called the *Akitu* and was performed at the New Year. This ceremony was performed by the Persian ruler Cambyses in 538 B.C. and observance of the ritual continued up to as late as 200 B.C.

Marduk's sanctuary in Babylon was a separate temple known as the Esagila, which was a large temple structure located close to the city's ziggurat. The ziggurat was a huge many-leveled, stacked structure like a pyramid. This ziggurat towered high above the massively high walls of Babylon. According to historical sources, the ziggurat was some 300 feet high and sat on a base 300 feet on each side. The courtyard surrounding the ziggurat was a quarter of a mile square. The walls of Babylon, estimated by some at 100 to 300 feet high, combined with the towering ziggurat, were an ominous structure, at least 400 to 600 feet high.

The topmost structure of the ziggurat, built differently from the other levels, was actually the sanctuary of Marduk, delineating his preeminence over the other Babylonian gods. The stairs leading up to each of these platforms resembled the Aztec pyramid-like temples that were uncovered by archaeologists in Latin America in the last century.

Bel

Another name for Marduk.

The name Bel later served as a generic title meaning "lord." Interestingly, the word for "lord" in Hebrew is *baal*, a form of *bel*. It does not mean God Almighty in Hebrew however; it means "lord" in the sense of "lord of a manor" as in Victorian England. Still today, in the ranks of the nobility of England, some men are called lords. There are still "gentlemen" in England who proudly wear the title. It does not mean they are trying to make themselves out to be gods.

For example, when renting an apartment here in Jerusalem, the landlord is called *baal ha-beit*, meaning "house-lord" or "land-lord." This word has come down through Akkadian and Aramaic. Both Hebrew and Arabic are sister languages, whose mother is Aramaic.

Nabu

Nabu, or *Nebo*; the god of wisdom and writing.

The source is Babylonian/Akkadian. He was the son of Marduk and Zarpinatu.

Nabu is symbolized by the writing stylus or writing pen. Nabu held the office of major deity in Babylon from the eighth century B.C. onward. Borsippa, near Babylon, was the site of his important sanctuary, known as the Ezita. Nabu was considered the god of mountainous regions and described as the firstborn son of Marduk. His image is closely involved in the New Year festival, the Akitu Festival.

Nabu's reputation for wisdom and writing is put in perspective by the amazing archaeological find at *Serabit el-Khadim* dating some six hundred years before Nabu arrives on the scene. Serbit el-Khadim was a Sinai desert cave mined by Hebrew slaves under the control of the Egyptians about 1500-1300 B.C.

Up to this time language was written in pictographs, not actual letter forms. Hieroglyphics were pictures that made sounds but an actual alphabet was yet to be invented and used. Amazingly, preserved by the arid Sinai Desert, inscriptions in real alphabetical lettering, not cuneiform or pictographs like hieroglyphics, were found on cave walls. This marks a quantum leap in the civilization of mankind and his communication skills.

The inscriptions were scant but clear. One inscription reads, "You shall give to Abubu eight portions." Another one said simply, "God is eternal." We therefore know that the reputation for the creation of a real alphabet enabling the progress of communication does not belong to Nabu.

Tutu

Tutu was the local god of Borsippa near Babylon. He was worshiped during the reign of Hammurabi in the old Babylonian period. Tutu was later superceded by Nabu/Nebo.

The Final Kingdom

Sammas

The sun-god, patron deity of the cities of Sipar and Larsa.

His consort is the mother goddess Ai. Sammas derives from the god Utu in the Sumerian pantheon of gods. He is associated with justice. His symbol is the sun disk and a star radiating sunbeams. He may carry a single-headed scimitar embellished with a panther head.

His name is Sammas in the Babylonian language. Noteworthy is that the word for "sun" in the Hebrew language is *shemesh*, and *sammas* in Arabic, an obvious derivative of the sun god Sammas. This is a good example of things that have trickled down from Babylon, through Aramaic, into Hebrew and Arabic.

Tammuz

The god of the fall season.

It was believed that Tammuz died in the fall, went underground, and was resurrected in the spring, bringing life back with him. Tammuz was a popular god among the farmers. Life for crops in an agricultural society is a serious matter. Without a successful agricultural season people would die. Purchasing provisions to make up what you did not raise was rare outside the huge cities, therefore worshiping the appropriate god seemed vital.

Israel was influenced by the nations surrounding her and had a propensity to adopt their customs and idolatrous religious practices. Israel's close association with Tammuz and resulting condition just prior to the Babylonian captivity is recorded.

> Then he brought me to the entrance of the north gate of the house of the LORD, and I saw women sitting there, mourning for Tammuz. He said to me, "Do you see this, son of man? You will see things that are even more detestable than this."
>
> He then brought me into the inner court of the house of the LORD, and there at the entrance to the temple, between the portico and the altar, were about twenty-five men. With their backs toward the temple of the LORD and their faces toward the east, they were bowing down to the sun in the east.
>
> Ezekiel 8:14-18

Here Israel's fall into idolatry is portrayed for us by Ezekiel. Women performed ceremonial rites in the fall, going to the Temple to weep for Tammuz, believing that their tears aided his resurrection in the spring and would thereby insure a good harvest. Weeping for Tammuz was a cultic ritual.

Contrary to popular teaching, idolatry was not so much about admiration for an object as much as it was fear! The fear that God could not provide their needs. Therefore, the Israelites felt that they needed to add something to their religious ceremony as insurance against poverty should their crops fail. At the same time, most of the Israelites also continued to celebrate the feasts established by Moses. In spite of their idolatry, they considered themselves worshippers of the Most High God—El Shaddai.

Ezekiel was appalled as he observed Israelite women who placed themselves before the Temple of God Almighty, the God of Israel, and yet, at the same time, engaged in an ancient Babylonian rite. The men, as well, with their backs turned away from God, waited for the rising sun that they might worship it.

Serarah

Goddess of the Persian Gulf.

In creation mythology she is given charge over the waters of the Persian Gulf by the god Enki.

Sin

God of the moon.

Derived from the older Sumerian model of Nana, who was the god of the moon. His consort is Nical. He is symbolized by the new moon and perceived as a bull whose horns are the crescent of the moon. Cult centers are identified at Ur, Haran, and Nerab, which indicates that his worship was rather widespread and ancient.

When Abram and his father Terah lived in Haran and Ur of the Chaldees, they lived in the area under the influence of the moon god.

There is an interesting Midrashic legend about Abram in regard to this. Jewish sources tell us that Abram's father, Terah, made his living creating various-sized idols for the local populace.

Abram was a boy of deep thought and reasoned within himself, "Surely the sun can't be god because it comes up and goes down, and the clouds come and hide the sun from me. So why should I worship the sun?" Likewise he reasoned, "The moon can't be god because it waxes and wanes and it is never the same and it throws our calendars off. How then can I worship the moon as god?"

In his search for God he did something rash. While his father was away from the shop one day, he took a huge club and beat all the idols to pieces except a large one, and then he put the club in the hand of the largest idol, the only one left standing.

When his father returned, he became angry with Abram because he had smashed all the idols. Abram said to him, "I didn't do it. He did it, the one with the club in his hand." His father said, "Don't be stupid! Do you think I'm going to believe that this mute piece of wood took a club and beat all these others to pieces? This is how I make my living. What are you trying to do, pull the wool over my eyes?" Abram said to his father, "If you don't believe that he is a real god, then why do we do this, and why do we worship him? We must find the true God."

This legend sheds light on Abram and his father as well as the city Ur of the Chaldees. The idolatry of Ur may have been a factor in Abram's exit from Haran. Abram's search obviously led him to where God could say to him, *Leave this place, leave your family, and go to a land that I will show you, because in that land that I will show you, I will reveal Myself to you,* and Abram would have been willing to obey.

In the beginning, Abram did not know God as we are privileged to know him today. Abram knew that He had spoken, but he did not know God's characteristics. He did not understand the fullness of *El Shaddai*, God Almighty. At that time he did not even know Him by that name. But, he knew he had to leave Haran, and believed that God would show him where to go and what to do.

Now, understanding the Sumerian moon god, Sin, it is interesting to note that the worship of this moon god predates Islam by about 1,600 years. If you asked a Moslem if he worships the moon god he would tell you "No!" He would tell you that he worships only one god—Allah. An important point though, is that the symbol of Islam is the crescent moon lying on its back. This same symbol from ancient times has been adopted by Islam and tops every mosque in the world. It is, in fact, a very ancient god— the one Abram rejected in his search for the True God.

In Judges 8:21, there are hints at the presence of this moon god. Gideon, after having killed the treacherous Midianite kings, Zebah and Zalmunnah, took the "ornaments off their camels' necks." Commentators say that these were moon crescents. It was popular during that time to place this symbol around camels' necks, most likely as a talisman for safety on journeys, which these kings no doubt believed.

Another example of this practice tells of the vain women in Jerusalem who were wearing moon "crescent necklaces."

Therefore the LORD will bring sores on the heads of the women of Zion; the LORD will make their scalps bald. In that day the LORD will snatch away their finery: the bangles and headbands and crescent necklaces, the earrings and bracelets and veils . . .

Isaiah 3:17-18

During Isaiah's time, Israelite women were concerned more with their vanity and looks than the condition of their nation. These were women who symbolized the spiritually-depressed state of Jerusalem, dressing up and primping, walking with "mincing steps," and filled with pride.

Ungodly relationships with the nations around them— Elamites, Akkadians, Assyrians, and Ur of the Chaldeans—led the Israelites to idolatrous practices and to their eventual doom.

As we can see, Babylon truly served a multiplicity of gods. There were many local deities as well. Every city had its own local deity or a host of varied deities. A city might have as many as fifty local deities and a pecking order by which they ruled humankind.

Each of these local gods had its specialty. Some were gods of the mountains. Some were gods of the plains. It is interesting that the Philistines were terrified to go up to try to conquer the Israelites in the mountainous areas. They presumed that Yahweh, the God of the Hebrews, was a god of the mountains. For this reason, they continually tried to engage the Israelites in battle on the coastal plain. Evidently, they thought that Yahweh could not protect the Israelite population if they succeeded in coercing them out of the mountains.

Daniel Sets the Boundaries

Daniel, and his friends agreed to reeducation and to new names, but rejected the Babylonian dietary fare (Dan. 1:8-16). It seems that Daniel and his captive friends were steadfastly dedicated to not defiling themselves with the king's food. There were several reasons Daniel and his friends drew the line at what entered their mouths.

The first portions of these foods were regularly offered to Babylonian gods. Also, the Babylonians took meat from ceremonially unclean animals. Not only were the animals ceremonially unclean but meat could have well come from tribes that practiced religious ceremonies involving bestiality with animals. Daniel was careful to observe the dietary laws given to Moses and the Israelites at Mount Sinai.

The Israelites knew enough about the practices of the nations that surrounded them that the decision was simple—they could not eat what they were being served. They knew vegetables were safe. They also understood that God would honor their decision.

The ten-day test turned out in their favor. Daniel's negotiation abilities proved that he was not acting out of rebellion to the king's order but for conscience's sake. The overseer could discern that he could cooperate with Daniel (if it did not get him into trouble) because of Daniel's sincere heart and spirit. The young men's success at this stage is tantamount to the stamp of God's approval on their lives, for holding fast to their convictions.

Though Daniel and his friends were required to be instructed in Chaldean dream interpretation literature, it is incredible that they turned out to be "ten times better" than their counterparts. Chaldean expertise in magic, omens, incantations, prayers, hymns, and their advancement in other areas did not dampen God's plan in sending His chosen elite into their midst. The Chaldean's were adept in scientific knowledge, glassmaking, mathematics, astrology, and astronomy. All these were areas in which Daniel and his friends received instruction.

Daniel served in the Babylonian palace through the rule of King Cyrus. At the time of the beginning of the reign of Cyrus, Daniel may have been as old as sixty-six.

There is no concrete evidence that Daniel and his friends ever returned to Israel. Their names are not mentioned in any of the lists of those who returned. There may be a reason for this.

Under the umbrella of the chief servant of the king of Babylon, who is described as "chief of the eunuchs," the four young men may also have been made eunuchs. A Levitical law states that any male cut or damaged in his genitals cannot enter into the Temple of God (Deut. 23:1). Some commentaries suggest that a number of the men held captive in Babylon were made eunuchs. A few commentators even include Ezra in the ranks of those made into eunuchs; however, that is less likely since we see him later in a leadership role, reading from the scroll of the law at the Water Gate back in Jerusalem (Neh. 8:1-6, 8:18).

Daniel's position in the kingdom of Babylon was more important than that of Ezra or Nehemiah in Babylon. It seems that if he had returned to the city of Jerusalem he would have played an important role in the rebuilding and reestablishing of Jerusalem and would have reappeared in the books that chronicle the return. Daniel, Hananiah, Mishael, and Azariah may therefore have simply lived out the rest of their lives in Babylon.

The Nations Surrounding Babylon

From an insignificant city among many great cities in the ancient Middle East, Babylon grew to world-power status after Nabopolasar, Nebuchadnezzar's father, conquered Assyria. Nebuchadnezzar's vision in Daniel chapter 1 suggests that God placed His seal of value on the empire since the "head"— symbolizing Nebuchadnezzar's reign—was described not just as gold but as "fine" gold.

This honored position is surprising in the face of the powerful peoples that surrounded Babylon and the heights to which they rose. Granted, in later years Babylon exhibited a ruthlessness. But the early years of this empire must have held qualities that God viewed as precious. There was a distinction between Assyria and Babylon in many ways. How so?

The reputation of Assyria was one of might coupled with cruel power. The character of Assyria and the character of Babylon issued forth from the hearts of their rulers. Strength of imperial might was evident in Babylon but, unlike Assyria, a sense of compassion toward their subjects existed that was absent with the Assyrians.

God used two nations, with two very different personalities, to bring judgment on His people. In the division of the kingdom of Israel, the crimes of Israel and Judah against God and their fellowmen were different. Israel was the rebellious child, tired of a theocracy where God ruled as king, and bent on violence toward their fellowmen. Later, Israel even conspired with heathen kings to attack Judah, their own brothers. God called for Assyria to be the scourge against Israel. A less harsh punishment was meted out for Judah—a time of protected banishment—for those whose rebellion was of lesser degree.

Babylon attacked and carried Jerusalem and Judah away captive because they refused to become subservient to the growing power of the Babylonian Empire. But, from a heavenly perspective, the captivity was because of Judah's refusal to submit to the might and power of God's Empire. Two very different reasons came together to accomplish God's will for His people. The captivity served as a tool used by God to bring about obedience in a disobedient people.

Information gleaned as Israel used the threshing floors of the Canaanites proved disastrous and paved the way for her impending doom. An important prerequisite for a threshing floor was a large slab of smooth bedrock. This was then surrounded by a low stone wall about three feet in height. Since not everyone had a large slab of bedrock on their property, those who did rented out their threshing floors to the surrounding community members during harvest time. Thus, Israel adopted customs from the people surrounding her that were opposed to the laws of God. What appeared as harmless insurance against starvation became Israel's undoing as she adopted their idolatrous practices.

It was not that the Israelites wanted to throw God away. Rather, it was out of their fear that they would not be able to make ends meet from one year's harvest to the following year's harvest. Seeing that those whom they had conquered worshiped local deities by placing fertility goddesses in niches in their threshing floor walls, the Israelites did likewise with a "just-in-case" attitude. The god of the wheat field and the god of the barley harvest seemed to produce the desired results for the Canaanites. I am sure they thought, *Why not give it a try?*

In those days a quick trip to the supermarket if supplies ran short was not a possibility. Trusting God's ability to provide from one season to the next was vital; actually, it was an integral part of making ends meet. Idolatry then turns up a new face. It was not just desire for an object, or a new worship practice, but fear that God would not be able to provide His people's needs. Do we then have to wonder that the prophets reminded the Israelites again and again to "trust in the Lord with all your heart?"

A nearby neighbor, the Philistines, attacked the Israelites at harvest time with good purpose. As a *thalassocracy*, meaning a "seafaring people," they were not adept at growing their own food. Being maritime nations both the Phoenicians and Philistines were occupied with ship building and neglected gaining agricultural prowess. Their cities were on the coast.

A great deal of Israel's agricultural area was then, and is today, the *shephelah*, or coastal plain, between the Mediterranean Sea and the mountains in which Jerusalem is nestled. It is difficult to grow good harvests in the mountains. The shorter growing season, rocky terrain, and cold winter nights make agriculture less productive. The Israelites had to continually trust God not only to provide for them agriculturally, but also to keep them strong against enemies who sought to ravage them for their own provisions.

With this we can understand the insidiousness of idolatry—to cause us to trust in something or someone other than God Himself. Again and again the Lord is beckoning us to "put away our idols"— as He did the Israelites—and place our trust in Him alone.

Babylonian Chronology Unreliable

An attempt to present an accurate chronological history of Babylon is a difficult thing, as even the Babylonians knew little about their history and seem to have been given to fabulously exaggerated stories about their background. Incredible stories abound, particularly regarding the time period before the flood in Noah's time. One such story records the reign of ten kings lasting some 456,000 years. Another records the reigns of eight kings lasting 241,000 years. Obviously, these figures are an example of recounting history via embellished storytelling.

The Reliable History

Then, of course, there are more reasonable historical chronologies. Some of the most important of these historical accounts will serve us here. One of preeminence is the reign of a king by the name of Urukagina who ruled in the city of Lagash. The city lay almost exactly between the Tigris and Euphrates Rivers in the area where Babylon would later emerge. There were three moments in the history of mankind when the giving of a code of law would change society historically. King Urukagina was one of these. In a kingdom riddled with serious abuses all the way from the priesthood to government officials, Urukagina set to work to abate these abuses.

The Final Kingdom

The earmark of a great king was one who could overcome the power that such a position gave a man. King Urukagina strove to compassionately take into consideration his people. He strove to make sure the working class was not abused by more powerful men of wealth. King Urukagina made the lives of the peasants safe in his kingdom. He actually comprised a code of law which spelled out trangressions against a fellow man and detailed punishments for them.

Other kings followed in embellishing a working code of ethics such as Hammurabi. He is the one most often given credit for the first code of ethics. The old Babylonian Empire reached its peak during his reign, and he is actually considered its founder. It declined after his death, but the capital city Babylon remained a great cultural center for more than a thousand years.

Hostile states battled to control the Babylonian Empire and greater Mesopotamia in the centuries following Babylonia's decline. An alliance between Egypt in the south and Mitanni, a kingdom which had sprung up in the area which is now northern Iraq, stopped the advance of the warmongering Hittites who inhabited the east sector of what is now Turkey. At this time, Babylon itself was ruled by a Kassite kingdom. During the Kassite reign, thirty-six kings ruled for 576 years. A small view into their culture and history is afforded us by the Tel-el-Amarna tablets excavated in the last century. We learn also of correspondence that took place with Amenhotep III, the King of Egypt.

In the 7th century B.C. a small part of the Mitanni kingdom separated itself from the greater kingdom and became one of the most formidable kingdoms to dominate the earth—Assyria. The Assyrian Empire spread itself in a monumental crescent from the Persian Gulf north to what is now Turkey, then turned west and descended in a wide swath, swallowing most of Israel and all of Egypt.

The last great power in Mesopotamia, the empire of Nebuchadnezzar II, arose in Babylonia after the break-up of the Assyrian Empire at the end of the 7th century B.C. It lasted until 539 B.C. when Babylon fell to the Persians.

The following years are a tug-of-war between Assyria and Babylon, with such kings as Shalmaneser V, Sennacherib, and Esarhaddon of Assyria trouncing Babylon in wars and skirmishes. Ashur-bani-pal ruled over both Assyria and Babylon between 668-626 B.C. Sin-shar-ishkun then reigned after him. His twin sons created a long-lasting civil war which weakened the Assyrian Empire. Nabopolassar came to the throne of Babylon under the rule of Ashur-bani-pal as a proxy king. His son Nebuchadnezzar was married to the daughter of Cyaxares, king of Media. Upon realizing that the twin sons of Sin-shar-ishkun had weakened the Assyrian kingdom to a critical point, Nabopolassar and Nebuchadnezzar invaded Nineveh and the Assyrian capital fell in 612 B.C., never to rise again, as Jonah had prophesied some two hundred years before. Zephaniah also foretold that it would be a pasture for flocks. Today the *tel* is called "mound of many sheep." Tel number two is called *Tel Nebi Ynis*—the prophet Jonah's tel. Nineveh's king, Sin-shar-ishkun, was burned to death in his palace. With the demise of Assyria, Babylon became independent and Nabopolassar established an army and strengthened his capital.

This chronology brings us to Daniel's sojourn in Babylon. Nebuchadnezzar, a new king, is determined to put his empire on the map. His world has been in turmoil. With Assyria out of the way and no longer a threat, he is looking to make Babylon a city of major world importance.

Sit in silence, go into darkness,
Daughter of the Babylonians;
no more will you be called queen of kingdoms.
I was angry with my people
and desecrated my inheritance;
I gave them into your hand
and you showed them no mercy.

Even on the aged you laid a very heavy yoke.
You said, "I will continue forever—
the eternal queen!"

But you did not consider these things or
reflect on what might happen.

Isaiah 47:5-7

*Rosette patterns, symbols of royalty, embellished the crowns and clothing of the
mighty kings of Mesopotamia.*

# The Bond of Dreams

A common thread binds chapters two and three together. Two statues unveil the wisdom of the heavens and, in turn, the degradation of earthly pride: one statue alive only in vision, the other, a man-made dream made reality. The meaning of the second statue stands in diameteric opposition to the first.

Often in life men benefit from heavenly wisdom and later allow the blessing of that wisdom to turn into a curse. Where once there was holy bowing before God Almighty—forger of all nations—a degrading prostration before an idol takes its place. According to Shakespeare's Sonnet 12, *"mercy is mightiest in the mightiest."* Likewise, foolishness shows itself most degrading when embraced by kings.

Déjà-vu

Here, the book of Daniel echoes the life of Joseph in the book of Genesis. God's gift given to Joseph, enabling him to interpret dreams, was not the same as occult practices of dream interpretation. God handed to Joseph, by His Spirit, the gift of knowledge and with comfortable familiarity he was able to come into His presence—with his requests—for the leadership and future of Egypt.

It is certain that Daniel was well aquainted with the record of the life of Joseph. Finding himself in similar circumstances, Daniel probably took courage from the story, realizing that this had all happened before. He knew that God did miraculous things on behalf of His people. Very difficult situations have presented the men and women of God with incredible challenges in the past, yet we have the written record of their victory over them through a personal encounter and relationship with the Almighty. These records afford us encouragement that we, too, can overcome the enormous difficulties that we face in life.

The Israelites coming out of Egypt had to trust God blindly, not having the benefit of biblical accounts of men of valor from the past. I am sure God took that into consideration and provided them with visible signs and wonders to assure them of His presence with them. We, on the other hand, have the *Torah* (the first five books of Moses), the *Prophets and Writings* (Joshua to Malachi), and *Ha-brit Ha-hadasha* (the New Testament), all packed with faith-building encounters with *El Elyon*—God Most High.

Lingua Franca—Aramaic

The text of Daniel from chapter 2:4 through the end of chapter 7 is no longer Hebrew but Aramaic. The Aramaic section could be viewed as local news for the people of Babylon. For the most part, it concerns what was happening at that time. It is only logical for it to be written in their language. The other sections of Daniel are more global. They deal with the world at large, other kingdoms, the future of the Jews, the future of the world right up to the time of the end of the age—in a sense, world news.

Foaming at the Mouth

Nebuchadnezzar has had a dream but is unwilling to tell the contents to his usual brood of magicians. Preoccupation with dreams was common in Mesopotamia, as evidenced by the abundance of tablets having to do with their interpretation unearthed by archaeologists in the area, presently housed in the British Museum.

There were dreams, and then there were dreams with the weight of Heaven on them. The king was acting peculiarly in chapter two, hinting that this particular dream had him emotionally upset (Dan. 2:1). His unwillingness to tell the dream may indicate that he was frightened by the content and wanted to avoid the usual bantering back and forth by many interpreters. His test was to ferret out a genuine teller of dreams so he could be assured he had the real meaning of the dream. Anger became the mode of the day as his test angers his aides, and in turn, their inability to soothe him angered him.

In a rather bold stroke, the astrologers answer the king. It was like pouring vinegar on baking soda:

> *There is not a man on earth who can can do what the king asks! No king, however great and mighty, has ever asked such a thing of any magician or enchanter or astrologer.*

> Daniel 2:10

It is very unusual for them to upbraid the king even though what he was asking was impossible. We have enough wisdom literature at our disposal to know that kings held the power of life and death in their hands.

The magicians' answer sends the king into a wild rage, in which he threatens to kill them all. The Aramaic words used to describe his anger are picturesque. He is described as being angered—*banas,* and enraged—*ketsef sagee. Katsefet,* which is the Hebrew word that has come to us from the Aramaic root *ketsef,* means "cream," as in whipping cream. If you have ever milked a cow, you know the cream comes rushing to the top of the milk pail. *Sagee* means "excessively" or "greatly." This picture of the king so angry that he is "foaming at the mouth" is a rich stroke of the author's pen (Dan. 2:12).

It is not surprising that in this upbraiding of the king his usual group of aides received exactly what he had promised them—the death sentence. Arioch, it is interesting to note, must not be one of the "wise men" because he is not being rounded up with the other wise men of the kingdom. Arioch plays a minor but interesting role when he comes into the picture (2:14-16).

Worship Opens Heaven's Gates

The harsh decree is issued and Daniel, in fear, returns to his house to pray and seek the face of the Lord with his friends (2:17,18). This reveals the power of intercessory prayer and the bond that praying friends have one with another. We see this attitude of relying wholly on God in the life of Joseph in his time of dire need as well.

Daniel properly takes opportunity to worship God for giving him wisdom and interpretation of the king's dream in the visions of the night.

Then Daniel returned to his house and explained the matter to his friends Hananiah, Mishael, and Azariah. He urged them to plead for mercy from the God of heaven concerning this mystery, so that he and his friends might not be executed with the rest of the wise men of Babylon. During the night the mystery was revealed to Daniel in a vision. Then Daniel praised the God of heaven and said:

The Final Kingdom

"Praise be to the name of God for ever
and ever;
wisdom and power are his.
He changes times and seasons;
he sets up kings and deposes them.
He gives wisdom to the wise
and knowlege to the discerning.
He reveals deep and hidden things;
He knows what lies in darkness,
and light dwells with him.
I thank and praise you, O God of my
fathers:
You have given me wisdom and
power,
you have made known to me what we
asked of you,
you have made known to us the
dream of the king.

vv. 17-23

Daniel's prayer is no longer intercessory—it quickly turned to high praise. He began by using the personal pronoun "He," but soon it turned to "You," a more intimate way of praying or praising the Lord. It was direct communication with God, face to face. Proclamation of the name of God and the character of God came close to taking a prophetic tone, acknowledging God who "changes times and seasons" and "sets up kings" and deposes them. It seems that Daniel could see what was on the horizon for Babylon and he responded in lavish praise to his God who ordains these things.

Two things should be noted here. What God showed to Nebuchadnezzar in a dream of the night He showed to Daniel in a *vision* while awake. Desperate petitions for mercy and high praise coupled together are powerful. Daniel is a man of humility. He thanks God for revealing the dream to the group corporately, never once taking credit for some great gift God had bestowed upon him. Daniel was a spiritual giant—a man upon whom God could call to do His bidding.

Daniel was being used by God as a prophet to predict the outcome of the statue vision. I have experienced that in seasons of high praise, the Holy Spirit moves through a person in a prophetic vein. Praise has the ability to lift one into the heavenlies to see situations and circumstances from God's perspective—after all, spiritually we are seated with Him.

> And raised [us] up together, and made [us] sit together in the heavenly [places] in Christ Jesus.
>
> Eph. 2:6 (NKJV)

The very essence of worship is dynamic when it is sincere and heartfelt. It is the place where you know you have entered the very presence of God. The role of the Holy Spirit is one of teaching each believer the depths of God and constantly exposing to us a new facet of His character. It is during these times that the Holy Spirit can also bring to the surface all kinds of forgotten issues and reveal wonderful solutions to problems.

The most common venue to describe this experience is a congregational worship service. While the worship leader is leading the congregation into the presence of the Lord, it is possible to be reading the words to the songs being sung and singing with all your concentration. Meanwhile, unhindered by all this, the Holy Spirit is teaching, refreshing, and revealing facets of the Heavenly Father which you may have never noticed before. Soon, many people find tears in their eyes at the most gentlemanly quality of the Spirit of God as He is leading you into a fuller understanding of our Heavenly Father.

Undoubtedly, Daniel and his friends experienced such a night with God, desperately seeking answers from His hand for their dilemma. We can guess that the prayers of Daniel and his friends were intense because their lives were at stake. This kind of intercession bears fruit. We see the results—God revealed to Daniel and company the dream of Nebuchadnezzar.

Cross Section of the Heart of an Intercessor

Daniel now seeks out Arioch to relate to him the solution to the king's demand. Daniel begs that the execution of the wise men of Babylon be stopped and that he be taken to the king (Dan. 2:24). In the development of the characters of the book of Daniel, it is noteworthy that the initiative to search out Arioch is Daniel's. Arioch's character is revealed as we see in his introduction to the king: Arioch takes credit for finding Daniel—the man who could tell the king his dream—when actually Daniel found Arioch.

> *Then Daniel went to Arioch, whom the king had appointed to execute the wise men of Babylon, and said to him, "Do not execute the wise men of Babylon. Take me to the king, and I will interpret his dream for him."*
>
> v. 24

Character development is vital. God wants us to identify with the men and women who people the pages of His Book. Many times in the books of I and II Samuel we discern a heartwarming cross-section of David's innermost being. We see his conscience overwhelm him for cutting off the fringes of Saul's garment.

God tunes us in to David's theology when he calls Saul "The Lord's anointed." A king who wished to see David dead is publically lauded and honored by David himself. In just a few chapters King Saul tried to kill David over a dozen times—the obvious attempts to kill him with his javelin and the less obvious plots to set him in impossible battle situations to cause him to lose his life. David's character only reflected the goodness of his Heavenly Father in respect for King Saul's position. The true heart of a person comes through in instances where injustice reigns, as it did under the reign of Saul.

The Scriptures do not reveal King Saul's heartfelt emotions to us as clearly as they do David's. We are left to deduce his spiritual state from his actions. The Holy Spirit reveals the hearts of like-minded men from whom we can vicariously appropriate spiritual lessons.

These character lessons serve also to bring us hope. We see in the servants of God the same weak links in their innermost hearts that exist in ours. Many times in the war of light against darkness, darkness *seems* to win. But we are comforted by the lives of these men because they verify that light indeed overcomes darkness.

The Hem of a Man's Garment

David's hem-snipping deed in the cave in I Samuel 24 is more serious than it first appears. In our day and age, a hem is just the end of someone's clothing, but the "hem" of someone's garment in David and Saul's time was the essence of the person himself. In the ancient Middle East, as far back as Ur of the Chaldees, the hem of a man's garment was equated with the character, identity, and in some cultures the spiritual reflection, of the man himself. It served several purposes. In some kingdoms in varying time periods, the impression of a man's hem in the wet clay of a merchant was like his Visa card. A garment's ornate design varied enough so that the hem would serve as a unique identification piece for a person. It represented his authority and his status in society as well.

Therefore, for David to cut off the "hem" of Saul's garment was as provoking as a divorce contract. David was saying to Saul, *I am finished with you—I reject your God-given authority.* God then gives us an inner glimpse of David as his heart smote him for what he had done. God probably said something to David like, *I am not ready for you to cut ties with Saul yet. I know he is a wicked man and a wicked king. It's true, he is not doing My will. Instead, he is doing unlawful things like stepping into the priesthood and offering sacrifices, totally against everything I have ever taught him. Nevertheless, I am not ready for you to make this kind of separation from Saul.*

No doubt David was reminded of other vivid historical examples of God putting one ruler down and raising up another. It appears that David is content to wait for God's perfect timing to bring him to the throne. David obviously discerned that this was *not* God's time and rejected the urging of his companions to take the throne.

When the showdown came, David undoubtedly was standing high up on the cliffs above the desert spring of Ein Gedi, near the Dead Sea. David must have shouted down to Saul in the valley. Saul recognized that David must be feeling guilt for what he had done. Saul's comment to David revealed that there was some measure of reconciliation in Saul's heart. Saul shouted back in the presence of his soldiers:

When David finished saying this, Saul asked, "Is that your voice, David my son?" And he wept aloud. "You are more righteous than I," he said. "You have treated me well, but I have treated you badly. You have just now told me of the good you did to me; the Lord delivered me into your hands, but you did not kill me. When a man finds his enemy, does he let him get away unharmed? May the Lord reward you well for the way you treated me today. I know that you will surely be king and that the kingdom of Israel will be established in your hands."

I Samuel 24:16-20

The Final Kingdom

Saul finally recognized the importance of the situation at hand as they stood in a face-off in the wilderness of Ein Gedi.

Judaism later designates the "hem" of a man's garment as a portion of a man's prayer shawl. The Torah (first five books of Moses) records in Numbers 15:37-41 that men should wear *tzitzit* (or fringes) in the hem of their garments. The purpose of the fringes was to remind the Israelites that they should be mindful of all the commandments of God. These fringes were actually tied in knots depicting the name of God in the manner in which the knots were tied. Because the Hebrew letters each have a numeric value, the four letters of the name of God (יְהֹוָה *yod-heh-vav-heh*) are portrayed in the number of the knots in the fringes. The fringes are tied in this series of knots: *yod* = 10, *heh* = 5, *vav* = 6, and *heh* = 5.

This unveils a new facet of the Gospel account of the woman with the issue of blood. This woman bent all the laws of the day in order to touch Jesus' cloak (Mark 5:25-34). Her desperation drove her to physically touch a man in public (a forbidden act by Jewish standards). It may well have been that she grabbed his cloak in the area of the fringes where she knew the name of God was symbolized. Her desperation drove her to put aside social taboos and reach out for healing from Yeshua. As we know, the Lord rewarded her bold faith and she was healed.

The Dream

Returning to chapter two of Daniel, we get a glimpse into Arioch's heart.

Arioch took Daniel to the king at once and said, "I have found a man among the exiles from Judah who can tell the king what his dream means."

v. 25

Arioch takes credit for finding Daniel and arranging the situation for the king. He was self-serving in his plan to magnify himself in the eyes of the king.

Credit Where Credit is Due

King Nebuchadnezzar then questions Daniel: *The king asked Daniel (also called Belteshazzar), "Are you able to tell me what I saw in my dream and interpret it?"* (v. 26). I love Daniel's answer.

He could have said, *Yes, I can tell you. I am going to tell you what you cannot even tell other people.* Daniel could have taken credit for knowing the interpretation of the king's dream and magnifying himself, as Arioch was attempting to do. He did not.

> *Daniel replied, "No wise man, enchanter, magician or diviner can explain to the king the mystery he has asked about, but there is a God in heaven who reveals mysteries. He has shown King Nebuchadnezzar what will happen in the days to come. Your dream and the visions that passed through your mind as you lay on your bed are these."*

vv. 27, 28

Daniel's answer is carefully worded to make a point: "No wise man can tell you, but there is a God in heaven who can." You could skip over this easily and not get the important message that Daniel is delivering to King Nebuchadnezzar: there is a God in *Heaven*, in contrast to the god in the ziggurat down the road that you carry from one place to another on the annual New Year's festival. This is God, the One True God of *Heaven*.

Daniel was making it clear that this was not a *local* god. Remember, the theology of the Babylonian Empire was a multiplicity of gods. Different local gods inhabited every city. There were even local gods directing the river that runs through Babylon. The hierarchy led to the top of the ziggurat where Marduk was worshiped. Daniel is making a major differentiation between his God and the god of the Babylonian ziggurat. With the location of Daniel's God established, the point is driven home that this God is a revealer of mysteries and dreams, in contrast to Babylon's gods.

A Statue for all Time

Daniel relates the king's dream:

> *As you were lying there, O king, your mind turned to things to come, and the revealer of mysteries showed you what is going to happen. As for me, this mystery has been revealed to me, not because I have greater wisdom than other living men, but so that you, O king, may know the interpretation and that you may understand what went through your mind. You looked, O king, and there before you stood a large statue—an enormous, dazzling statue—awesome in appearance. The head of the statue was made of pure gold, its chest and arms*

69

of silver, its belly and thighs of bronze, its legs of iron, its feet partly of iron and partly of baked clay.

vv. 29-33

The ominous statue of King Nebuchadnezzar's vision was an allegory of empires, with he and his kingdom standing in first position. The dream-statue depicts successive empires down through the ages to the end of time—the head of fine gold, chest and arms of silver, belly and thighs of bronze, legs of iron, and feet comprising an iron and clay mixture.

O Head of "Fine" Gold

We know Nebuchadnezzar had wide-ranging power and influence. Babylon depicted as a "head of fine gold" might be surprising in light of the latter-day stigma placed on Babylon. The truth of the matter is that mankind, beasts, birds, and the world of that day were fed and gained sustenance from Nebuchadnezzar's empire.

It is thought-provoking that when Babylon resurfaces again in the end of the ages, it is not depicted just as a city but rather as a symbol. It resurfaces as the epitome of wickedness, spiritual degradation, and deprivation.

If I were going to choose an empire to symbolize wickedness, on first consideration I would choose Assyria, and I would have the book of Revelation filled with allusions to the Assyrians [infamous for their wickedness and cruelty], rather than to the Babylonians.

The plausible reason for Babylon's characterization as the epitome of wickedness in the book of Revelation is her quick slide back into the degradation of *idolatry*. We witness Babylon brought to the Throne of God several times as God confronts each leader to deal with his sin. Each time the revelation is powerful enough to evoke an imperial decree that the God of the Hebrews ought to be worshiped alone. Yet, shortly after each turning point, there is another return back into idolatry.

A Shared Kingdom

The "chest and arms of silver" represented the Medo-Persian Empire, which was comprised of two kingdoms in close physical proximity, Media and Persia. These kingdoms lay north-northeast of Babylon. At the time of our story, a military campaign by the

Persians resulted in their being ruled by one king—Darius, whom we will hear much more about later.

Master Conqueror

The "belly and thighs of bronze" depict the Greek Empire. Alexander the Great, 330 B.C., the powerful Greek ruler, comes virtually bursting through the pages of the book of Daniel. Aggressive is a mild word to use for Alexander. Ambition drove him. He determined to rule the world. In Greece, in his time, people sought wisdom and spiritual guidance from certain women called *oracles*. Alexander visited the *Oracle of Delphi*. In other societies she would have been known as a prophetess. Alexander wanted her to prophesy great things about him. She told him, "I have nothing to tell you."

In anger, he grabbed her and dragged her into the temple, where she blurted out, "You shall rule the world!"

Alexander elevated her words to the stature of oracular decree and marched off to a place called Gordium, of which, at one time, the famed Midas was king. The people of Gordium were given to riddles, rhymes, and puzzle solving. In the palace of Gordium hung a huge knot, attached to a chariot, known as the Gordion knot. The legend of the Gordion knot stated that whoever could successfully untie the knot would "rule the world." Alexander simply hacked it in half with his sword.

The chariot was a very special chariot. Legend declared that whoever could untie it would use this chariot to conquer the world. The viability of the legend is uncertain, but Alexander the Great did conquer the world and was the ruler of the world by the age of twenty-five, and as his story goes, after accomplishing this goal, he wept because there was nothing left to conquer.

Alexander's legacy constitutes one of the bright and shining stars of the history books. Regardless of how ambitious or how aggressive or ruthless, conquering the world by the age of twenty-five deserves some of the honor Alexander received. There are no horror stories about his ruthlessness or cruelty as there are about the Assyrians, but history, nevertheless, tells us he was aggressive in his passion to rule the world.

Ruthless Rome

As we descend the statue to the "legs and feet" we arrive at the Roman Empire. Rome's history was one of conquering and forcing conquered kingdoms into submission. The iron-fist of Rome grew ever more ruthless as the empire matured. Reasonable in the beginning, Rome progressed to insane despotism before its demise.

Composed of iron, symbolizing the strength of the Roman Empire in its early days, it then progresses to iron mixed with clay. The physical attributes of these two items do not mix. The heat needed to bake clay would melt iron into a puddle. The vision is indicative of the state of affairs from the end of the Roman Empire right up to our present time. The weakness of the world governing system just before the stone strikes the feet of the statue is a fair assessment of our world today. There were no other kingdoms weighty enough to make it into Nebuchadnezzar's vision.

The Rock of Anointing

Daniel now continues with the wrap-up of Nebuchadnezzar's vision, saying:

> While you were watching, a rock was cut out, but not by human hands. It struck the statue on its feet of iron and clay and smashed them. Then the iron, the clay, the bronze, the silver and the gold were broken to pieces at the same time and became like chaff on a threshing floor in the summer. The wind swept them away without leaving a trace. But the rock that struck the statue became a huge mountain and filled the whole earth.
>
> vv. 34-35

Living in the last days presents some serious problems. The dilemma of how to effectively pray for a world that is assured of getting progressively worse before the stone hits the feet and all blows away into dust can cause some consternation. I do not see us fixing the world before Messiah returns to make things right. This vision flies in the face of that theology. Like Daniel, staying closely tuned to God's Spirit is the key to know *how* to pray.

Nebuchadnezzar now sits spellbound, realizing that Daniel has some amazing gift of insight. Daniel relates to him the wisdom of the universe, handed to him "for such a time as this" from God on high. He relates:

> This was the dream, and now we will interpret it to the king. You, O king, are the king of kings. The God of heaven has given you dominion and power and might and glory; in your hands he has placed mankind and the beasts of the field and the birds of the air. Wherever they live, he has made you ruler over them all. You are that head of gold.
>
> After you, another kingdom will rise, inferior to yours. Next, a third kingdom, one of bronze, will rule over the whole earth. Finally, there will be a fourth kingdom, strong as iron—for iron breaks and smashes everything—and as iron breaks things to pieces, so it will crush and break all the others. Just as you saw that the feet and toes were partly of baked clay and partly of iron, so this will be a divided kingdom; yet it will have some of the strength of iron in it, even as you saw iron mixed with clay. As the toes were partly iron and partly clay, so this kingdom will be partly strong and partly brittle. And just as you saw the iron mixed with baked clay, so the people will be a mixture and will not remain united, any more than iron mixes with clay.

vv. 36-43

Daniel, in a few sentences, telescopes history into a simple story. The end of mankind's attempts to unify the earth are futile. There will never be unity between earthly kingdoms.

Daniel concludes by saying:

> In the time of those kings, the God of heaven will set up a kingdom that will never be destroyed, nor will it be left to another people. It will crush all those kingdoms and bring them to an end, but it will itself endure forever. This is the meaning of the vision of the rock cut out of the mountain, but not by human hands—a rock that broke the iron, the bronze, the clay, the silver and the gold to pieces. The great God has shown the king what will take place in the future. The dream is true and the interpretation is trustworthy.

vv. 44, 45

The "rock that is cut out without hands" is the Messiah. The kingdom of the Messiah will come in the end of time and destroy the kingdoms of the world, breaking them down and turning them to chaff, which will blow away as chaff does in the wind of the threshing floor.

Unearthly Promotion

Nebuchadnezzar is undone. He, being a king, does a very unkingly thing:

> Then King Nebuchadnezzar fell prostrate before Daniel and paid him honor and ordered that an offering and incense be presented to him. The king said to Daniel, "Surely your God is the God of gods and the Lord of kings and a revealer of mysteries, for you were able to reveal this mystery."
>
> vv. 46, 47

Throwing himself down in front of a palace servant and ordering incense to be brought as an offering tells us that King Nebuchadnezzar thought Daniel was a god. Something so new to King Nebuchadnezzar caused him to make a declaration of devotion to Daniel's God. He must have thought, *The gods have come down to us in flesh, and we must offer up something.* This is echoed in the book of Acts at Lystra where Paul heals a lame man.

> When the crowd saw what Paul had done, they shouted in the Lycaonian language, "The gods have come down to us in human form!" Barnabas they called Zeus, and Paul they called Hermes because he was the chief speaker. The priest of Zeus, whose temple was just outside the city, brought bulls and wreaths to the city gates because he and the crowd wanted to offer sacrifices to them.
>
> Acts 14:11-13

When the power of God is manifested, it makes those who do not really have a connection with God see the heavenly kingdom, but often they see it erroneously. They perceive it in the form of a man and not in the proper form of a kingdom that is yet to come.

God's plans now go into effect. Daniel and his men have been appointed to this specific time in history and God has orchestrated a vision for Nebuchadnezzar that will act as the springboard to set things in motion.

> Then the king placed Daniel in a high position and lavished many gifts on him. He made him ruler over the entire province of Babylon and placed him in charge of all its wise men.

Moreover, at Daniel's request the king appointed Shadrach, Meshach and Abednego administrators over the province of Babylon, while Daniel himself remained at the royal court.

2:48,49

Promotions are in order and God's prophetic mouthpieces are now being dispersed into the fabric of Babylonian society. Daniel was promoted to an extraordinarily high position—second in command to King Nebuchadnezzar of the empire of Babylon.

Bel bows down, Nebo stoops low;
their idols are borne by beasts of burden.
The images that are carried about are burdensome,
a burden for the weary.

They stoop and bow down together;
unable to rescue the burden, they themselves go off
into captivity.

Listen to me, O house
of Jacob,
all you who remain of
the house of Israel,
you whom I have
upheld since you were
conceived,
and have carried since
your birth.
Even to your old age
and gray hairs
I am he,
I am he who will
sustain you.
I have made you
and I will carry you . . .

Isaiah 46:1-4

On the plain of Dura, Nebuchadnezzar set up his golden statue for all to worship.

Idol of Pride

The time period between chapters two and three must have been one of introspective brooding for Nebuchadnezzar. I am certain he spent time analyzing Daniel's revelation of his dream. Head of Gold! Heady stuff. His kingdom is the best that there will ever be: high and lofty, held far above all other earthly kingdoms. The revelation of the God of heaven in the midst of Nebuchadnazzar's ordeal is quickly forgotten in the powerful light of the egotism that emerges in this leader of a major world power.

We do not know how much time passed between chapters two and three. Some Bible commentators guess as much as sixteen years lapsed between the two. However long the time period, the Scriptures state:

> *King Nebuchadnezzar made an image of gold, ninety feet high and nine feet wide, and set it up on the plain of Dura in the province of Babylon.*
>
> Daniel 3:1

The plain of Dura lay outside the city walls of Babylon in a wide and open area. Other sources note its being called Durushakurabe.

At Nebuchadnezzar's bidding, the vision of the statue, symbolizing earth's kingdoms, now takes physical shape in the hands of his craftsmen. It was not enough that the king of Babylon had been shown that he was the golden head. The erecting of this statue was not an attempt to visually play out his dream. There was no silver, or iron, or clay in it. The whole statue was wrought in gold. Ninety feet of massive splendor sat on the plain of Dura. This giant statue must have been a visual wonder. Babylonian artisans were of extraordinary talent. Relics of their workmanship can be seen in some of the palaces that have been unearthed in recent times by archaeologists.

Burdensome Idolatry

In the context of time and place, the mention of a statue would naturally make you think of idolatry. Nebuchadnezzar's statue in the plain of Dura is different. Indications are that this statue's purpose was not idolatry. Being erected on the plain of Dura and not in the city ziggurat is a strong clue. Because of its height, it would not fit in any known ziggurat. The magnitude and purpose of this statue was new to the populace of Babylon. Political motives may have driven Nebuchadnezzar to have the statue built in order to show his importance as the ruling king of greater Babylon. The ceremony at which it was unveiled and subsequent ceremonies echo the festive ceremonies of the idol gods in the ziggurat. Isaiah describes these festivals in a poetic and descriptive tongue-in-cheek manner. During the New Year festivals and other festivals, the gods were taken out of their temples and transported by human labor in a great parade. These idols were incredibly heavy, burdensome, and a great hardship to carry. Isaiah paints the picture perfectly.

Bel bows down, Nebo stoops low; their idols are borne by beasts of burden. The images that are carried about are burdensome, a burden for the weary. They stoop and bow down together; unable to rescue the burden, they themselves go off into captivity.

Listen to me, O house of Jacob, all you who remain of the house of Israel, you whom I have upheld since you were conceived, and have carried since your birth. Even to your old age and gray hairs I am he who will sustain you. I have made you and I will carry you. I will sustain you and I will rescue you.

To whom will you compare me or count me equal? To whom will you liken me, that we may be compared? Some pour out gold from their bags and weigh out silver on the scales; they hire a goldsmith to make it into a god, and they bow down and worship it. They lift it to their shoulders and carry it; they set it up in its place, and there it stands. From that spot it cannot move. Though one cries out to it, it does not answer; it cannot save him from his troubles.

Remember this, fix it in mind, take it to heart, you rebels. Remember the former things, those of long ago; I am God, and there is no other; I am God, and there is none like me. I make known the end from the beginning, from ancient times, what is still to come. I say: My purpose will stand, and I will do all that I please.

From the east I summon a bird of prey; from a far-off land, a man to fulfill my purpose. What I have said, that will I bring about; what I have planned, that will I do. Listen to me, you stubborn-hearted, you who are far from righteousness. I am bringing my righteousness near, it is not far away; and my salvation will not be delayed. I will grant salvation to Zion, my splendor to Israel."

Isaiah 46

It is obvious that God is comparing the burden of idolatry to the true worship He established for His people. According to this chapter in Isaiah, idolatry resulted in a wearing down of Babylon's populace. Heavy expectations took its toll on the Babylonians and may have led to an undercurrent that ripened into a rebellion during Belshazzar's reign.

God also establishes that His purposes are higher than the crown of any king and their designated idols. His ultimate intention for Israel is her salvation.

Eternal Queen?

Isaiah chapter 47 further develops the picture, spelling out the destruction of Babylon by a man whom He will raise up. Babylon, who claimed the title "Eternal Queen" and thought that she could never suffer loss, will stand judged for her sorceries, magic spells, idolatry, and oppression of the aged, among a long list of other offenses against God and her people. The warning of these two chapters of Isaiah was given to the Jewish people long before the Babylonians appeared on the horizon to carry them away captive. The message was clear for them that they would be entering a civilization of idolatry to the point of backbreaking burdens.

All Fall Down

With the successful erection of Nebuchadnezzar's statue, every provincial administrator was summoned to participate in the ceremony. This too hints at a political motive for the building of the statue.

He then summoned the satraps, prefects, governors, advisers, treasurers, judges, magistrates and all the other provincial officials to come to the dedication of the image that he had set up. So the satraps, prefects, governors, advisers, treasurers, judges, magistrates, and all the other provincial officials assembled for the dedication of the image that King Nebuchadnezzar had set up, and they stood before it. Then the herald loudly proclaimed, "This is what you are commanded to do, O peoples, nations and men of every language: As soon as you hear the sound of the horn, flute, zither, lyre, harp, pipes and all kinds of music, you must fall down and worship the image of gold that King Nebuchadnezzar has set up. Whoever does not fall down and worship will immediately be thrown into a blazing furnace." Therefore, as soon as they heard the sound of the horn, flute, zither, lyre, harp and all kinds of music, all the peoples, nations and men of every language fell down and worshiped the image of gold that King Nebuchadnezzar had set up.

3:2-7

Seven levels of governmental representation were required to be present at the ceremony and are listed in these verses.

In a society accustomed to a multiplicity of gods, varied cult ceremonies, and diverse manners of worshiping, the only people to take offense by bowing down to an idol, however grand it was, would have been the Jewish people.

If Nebuchadnezzar had been acquainted with Daniel and his men for any length of time, it would have come as no surprise to him that they would refuse to bow to his new statue. This may be a plus on the side of those who argue that the time period between the vision of the statue of chapter two and the construction of the statue of chapter three might not have been so long. In a kingdom as complex as Babylon, the king may not have been fully acquainted with the rituals of his Jewish captives. The Jewish people might even have been exempt from worship of Babylon's other pantheon of gods. But when refusal to bow to his statue had became political defiance to the king, the politics became a vise grip, with Daniel and his fellow travelers held fast. In a much earlier but similar event, the Tower of Babel was not really a ladder to reach heaven as some suppose. It was to create an artificial unity so that the people of the earth would not be scattered. Likewise, this maneuver by Nebuchadnezzar seems to have been an attempt at unification of his populace in some manner. In effect, both events were attempts to usurp God's rightful place. In these two situations headquarters was no longer heaven but instead the Tower of Babel and the plain of Dura.

At this point, in an elementary school tactic, astrologers arrive at the palace bearing news that the Jews are refusing to bow down to the statue during the ceremonies on the plain of Dura (3:8-2).

Into a Ceramic Kiln

Furious with rage, Nebuchadnezzar summoned Shadrach, Meshach and Abednego. So these men were brought before the king, and Nebuchadnezzar said to them, "Is it true, Shadrach, Meshach and Abednego, that you do not serve my gods or worship the image of gold that I have set up? Now when you hear the sound of the horn, flute, zither, lyre, harp, pipes and all kinds of music, if you are ready to fall down and worship the image I have made, very good. But if you do not worship it, you will be thrown immediately into a blazing furnace. Then what god will be able to rescue you from my hand?"

vv. 13-15

In effect, King Nebuchadnezzar had set up an idolatrous worship service. When his intentions were rejected, his heart changed toward those he had so greatly esteemed before.

The three answered boldly that their God would rescue them from Nebuchadnezzar's furnace. Their resolve, though, did not depend upon rescue. They held fast their allegiance to their God even if that meant death. This is very bold, to inform the king that you have no intention of doing what he asks you to do.

This attitude is also echoed in the book of Revelation in the description of the souls of those who had been beheaded for their faith. The irony is remarkable—the antichrist repeating history almost letter for letter—setting up an idol to be worshiped in a city called Babylon, and referred to as "O great city" as well (Rev. 18:10).

And I saw the souls of those who had been beheaded because of their testimony for Jesus and because of the word of God. They had not worshiped the beast or his image and had not received his mark on their foreheads or their hands. They came to life and reigned with Christ a thousand years.

Revelation 20:4b

The Final Kingdom

Nebuchadnezzar now goes into action against his perceived enemies.

Nebuchadnezzar was furious with Shadrach, Meshach and Abednego, and his attitude toward them changed. He ordered the furnace heated seven times hotter than usual and commanded some of the strongest soldiers in his armies to tie up Shadrach Meshach and Abednego and throw them into the blazing furnace.

3:19, 20

The awe-inspiring Ishtar Gate of the city of Babylon and its wondrous construction have been a marvel for thousands of years. This gate was comprised of high-fire, kiln-baked bricks with a striking blue glaze. The gate has lasted for some 2,600 years. In order to achieve this sophisticated difficult process the Babylonians had to have been very skilled craftsmen in the art of ceramics, brickmaking, and the chemistry of ceramic glazes. If one can make a glaze that would withstand the harsh desert elements for millenia, they must have been adept at the craft. A kiln hot enough to bake bricks and melt silica and the chemistry used to make glazes is a furnace hot enough to make glass. To heat this furnace (kiln) seven times *hotter*, it is not surprising that the men who threw the three Hebrews in, were instantly killed.

If You Can't Stand the Heat . . .

Being acquainted with ceramic kilns from my college days makes this section of Scripture come to life. The kilns of our ceramics department were the size of a small bathroom. The kilns were carefully loaded with pottery to be fired over a period of two weeks. When the thick door was finally closed, a small hole held three special firing cones where one could easily see them. During the intense heat of a kiln firing we needed to stand halfway across the room but could still see the small cones from that distance. They are made to melt at different temperatures. When you see the first one droop over, you know that the kiln is up to a certain temperature. When the second one goes down, you know the kiln has reached another bench mark on the temperature scale. Finally, when the third one goes down, the kiln is turned down and the cooling process begun. The kiln is not turned off, but the heat is first reduced, to let the temperature come down for 24 hours. Only then is the kiln turned off and left to cool for a full day, or more, before opening. Babylon had to have an entire ceramics industry, with production control and sophisticated baking ovens.

Nebuchadnezzar's decree must have sent shockwaves through the ceramics industry of Babylon. To heat such an oven seven times hotter than normal would be unheard of—in any time period. I am sure brickmakers were not conscripted to throw Shadrach, Meshach, and Abednego into the fire. They were probably so aghast and confused by the king's urgent order that the military had to be called in to carry out his angry and unreasonable demand. Brickmakers, and those with knowledge of ceramics, probably went home sure that the king had lost his mind and that their method of livelihood would be ruined by such a rash decree. Undoubtedly, they thought the kiln would explode. Not even the ashes of a human body would be left in a furnace that hot.

Continuing on in the same chapter is a description of the attitude of the three doomed Israelites, the death of the soldiers who threw them in, and then finally the furnace itself.

> *So these men, wearing their robes, trousers, turbans and other clothes, were bound and thrown into the blazing furnace. The king's command was so urgent and the furnace so hot that the flames of the fire killed the soldiers who took up Shadrach, Meshach and Abednego, and these three men, firmly tied, fell into the blazing furnace. Then King Nebuchadnezzar leaped to his feet in amazement and asked his advisers, "Weren't there three men that we tied up and threw into the fire?" They replied, "Certainly, O king." He said, "Look! I see four men walking around in the fire, unbound and unharmed, and the fourth looks like a son of the gods." Nebuchadnezzar then approached the opening of the blazing furnace and shouted, "Shadrach, Meshach and Abednego, servants of the Most High God, come out! Come here!"*

vv. 21-26

Evidently, the king had his eyes opened and suspects that these are not normal people he has just thrown into the firey blaze. Except for the troublesome issue of the "fourth" man in the fire, there are actually some farfetched explanations for this event. According to ancient texts, both medical and magical, the blood of a salamander keeps flesh from burning in a fire. The cost of enough salamander blood to successfully cover three men would have probably built Nebuchadnezzar's ziggurat alone. And the ability to keep them safe in this kind of a fire is absurd. The presence of the fourth man, obviously an epiphany (an appearance of Yeshua), lifted this situation out of the sphere of the commonplace, and placed it in the realm of Heaven. Time must have seemed to stand still for the king.

> *So Shadrach, Meshach and Abednego came out of the fire, and the satraps, prefects, governors and royal advisers crowded around them. They saw that the fire had not harmed their bodies, nor was a hair of their heads singed; their robes were not scorched and there was no smell of fire on them.*

vv. 26b, 27

Clothing carries the smell of smoke very clearly for quite some time. For instance, after a barbeque, campfire, or just sitting next to someone smoking a cigarette, the aroma of smoke imprints itself on those close by. What a miracle of God's protection on these men's lives. The testimony to the king was obvious.

A Word to the Wise is Sufficent

God prepared the Israelites for this day. Through the prophet Isaiah, God gave a word for His people to cling to.

> *When you pass through the waters, I will be with you; and when you pass through the rivers, they will not sweep over you. When you walk through the fire, you will not be burned; the flames will not set you ablaze. For I am the LORD, your God, the Holy One of Israel, your Savior . . .*

Isaiah 43:2, 3

Here are terrifying elements that the Lord assures the Israelites that He would deliver them in: waters, rivers, fires and flames. Very clearly the Lord stated through Isaiah, "When you walk through the fire, you will not be burned . . ." No doubt these men walking into that fiery furnace that day believed God's word, and God remained faithful to them, to deliver them mightily.

On the route to Babylon, there were several major river crossings. Fear could easily have caused panic in the Israelites as they approached these forbidding obstacles. Many people of that day were not swimmers. God promised protection to those who had "ears to hear," not only from "water," but from "fire" as well.

This good news came from Isaiah before they ever went to Babylon.

Nebuchadnezzar's plan "backfired".

Then Nebuchadnezzar said, "Praise be to the God of Shadrach, Meshach and Abednego, who has sent his angel and rescued his servants! They trusted in him and defied the king's command and were willing to give up their lives rather than serve or worship any god except their own God. Therefore I decree that the people of any nation or language who say anything against the God of Shadrach, Meshach and Abednego be cut into pieces and their houses turned into piles of rubble, for no other god can save in this way." Then the king promoted Shadrach, Meshach and Abednego in the province of Babylon.

3:28-30

Nebuchadnezzar's motives are unclear, but it all goes awry and God receives the praise. The importance of his statue seems to fade into the background. We see the Babylonian Empire brought to the throne of God when Nebuchadnezzar makes his surprising decree.

This is a great feat for Daniel and his three compatriots to accomplish. God has been magnified publically in Babylon, a great king has been humbled before his subjects, and decrees have been handed down that the God of the captive Jewish population is of greater honor than any in the pantheon of Babylon's mighty local deities. Undoubtedly, among the Jewish population, news of this event spread and stood to underscore God's purpose for having them in Babylon. There are now promotions among the friends of Daniel from Jerusalem.

But God is not done with Nebuchadnezzar. All this prompts us to consider *why* Babylon becomes the symbol of all that is wicked in the end of time, when its beginning was depicted as a "head of gold," crowning all nations, even from Heaven's perspective. The tendency to pass a decree in a moment of passionate emotion, then let a bit of time pass and return to the old ways of idolatry, seems to have been the norm for Babylon's kings. Not seeing clearly enough to effect life changes is a dangerous road.

He sits enthroned above the circle of the earth,
and its people are like grasshoppers.
He stretches out the heavens like a canopy,
and spreads them out like a tent to live in.
He brings princes to naught
and reduces the rulers of this world
to nothing.
Isaiah 40:22-23

The mighty tree reached the heavens and seemed to disappear into the clouds.

How Big is Enormous?

As chapter four opens, a night vision of a tree of enormous stature shakes Nebuchadnezzar's world. How big is enormous to a king who built 300-foot ziggurats towering above city walls that were between 100 and 300 feet high? This tree could be seen to the ends of the earth, the Scripture tells us. This information lends the dream a decidedly political flavor. The tree is actually much more than a tree. This mighty tree, higher than any Sequoia or Redwood on earth, symbolized the might of Nebuchadnezzar's empire and how it fed and sheltered the peoples of the world of that day.

Why did the vision terrify Nebuchadnezzar? He had been the recipient of strange night visions before. There are dreams of minor importance wherein the subconscious seems to be trying to filter too much jumbled information. There are dreams that attempt to work out simple problems or, without rhyme or reason, create unfinished skits that make little sense. Then there are dreams that have the weight of Heaven attached to them. They seem to carry their own atmosphere—sometimes of fear, sometimes of dread—and usually serve as a wake-up call. Nebuchadnezzar responded in fear—he was terrified.

> *I, Nebuchadnezzar, was at home in my palace, contented and prosperous. I had a dream that made me afraid. As I was lying in my bed, the images and visions that passed through my mind terrified me.*

> Daniel 4:4, 5

In his terror, Nebuchadnezzar turned again to Daniel for help. The resources of cosmic wisdom at the king's disposal could not provide an interpretation to his fearful dream.

> *So I commanded that all the wise men of Babylon be brought before me to interpret the dream for me. When the magicians, enchanters, astrologers and diviners came, I told them the dream, but they could not interpret it for me. Finally, Daniel came into my presence and I told him the dream. (He is called Belteshazzar, after the name of my god, and the spirit of the holy gods is in him.) I said, "Belteshazzar, chief of the magicians, I know that the spirit of the holy gods is in you,*

and no mystery is too difficult for you. Here is my dream; interpret it for me."

vv. 6-9

The king's comment that the "spirit of the holy gods" was in Daniel indicates that Nebuchadnezzar's understanding of the nature of the God of the Hebrews was still elemental. The Aramaic word which he used, *Elahin* (meaning "gods" in the plural form), reveals his narrow vision. Surrounded by a pantheon of gods and goddesses, the king was living in a state of ignorance, most likely self-inflicted, which blinded his eyes to the true nature of God.

Plant a Tree

These are the visions I saw while lying in my bed: I looked, and there before me stood a tree in the middle of the land. Its height was enormous. The tree grew large and strong and its top touched the sky; it was visible to the ends of the earth. Its leaves were beautiful, its fruit abundant, and on it was food for all. Under it the beasts of the field found shelter, and the birds of the air lived in its branches; from it every creature was fed.

vv. 10-12

It is ironic in this situation that the vision likened the might of Babylon to a majestic tree, as trees have always been important to the Jewish people. God must have been extracting double meaning from the vision, firstly for Nebuchadnezzar and secondly for Daniel. Deuteronomy explains the importance of trees to the Jewish people.

When you lay siege to a city for a long time, fighting against it to capture it, do not destroy its trees by putting an ax to them, because you can eat their fruit. Do not cut them down. Are the trees of the field people, that you should besiege them?

Deuteronomy 20:19

The Jewish people, through the Jewish National Fund, upon return to the nation of Israel in our own lifetimes, have planted somewhere in the vicinity of 360 million trees with the intention of reforesting the desolated landscape. That is somewhere in the vicinity of forty-four trees for every person living in Israel. The Holy

88

Land had been denuded of its forests by the Islamic Turkish Ottoman Empire, from about A.D. 1517 until 1917. The reason is simple: The Turks taxed the trees of land owners. During their rule, whoever had trees on his land that did not bear fruit, feed his family, or add income, cut them down to avoid taxation. Millions of trees were hacked down during the centuries that the Turkish Empire ruled the Middle East. To this day Israelis regularly plant trees in the land. The forests of Israel are steadily being replenished.

The Jewish people understand that trees are very important to God. Trees are miracles. They are a wondrous work of creation. It is a fact that they do tremendous good for mankind. It is common knowledge that they provide oxygen as well as absorb carbon dioxide. Each tree assures us cleaner air. God says they should not be cut down. It is interesting that today in Israel you must get a municipal permit before cutting down a tree.

Mark Twain's travelogue, *The Innocents Abroad*, written in 1869, describes his travels through Europe, the Middle East and on to Egypt. Twain traveled from Damascus to Tiberias, then to Jerusalem, before going on to Egypt. He wrote that during the journey from Damascus to Tiberias he never saw a blade of grass, never saw a human being, never saw an animal—nothing but great wasted expanses of nothingness. He finally came to the conclusion that it was highly unlikely this land would ever play an important role in history again!

Now, only one hundred and thirty-three years later, if one travels between Damascus and Tiberias through the Golan Heights, it would be difficult to find a place of any size that is not growing something. Even the areas that are not cultivated are covered with wonderful growth.

Not long ago, I was in this region taking pictures for an article on the archaeological excavation at Hatzor and upon return I took the road heading from the north to the south of the Golan Heights. It was beautiful the entire distance, but just before dropping down from the heights at the Jordanian border, I came across a corn field. This was the corn field of all corn fields! It disappeared over the horizon in every direction. It was amazing. As an American, I thought, *Iowa! Look at this!* Hill after hill, filled with beautiful green corn—huge, tall stalks of corn. None of it was blighted or turning brown. I thought, *Mark Twain, you were wrong!*

There is a special day in the Jewish calendar for the planting of trees called Tu B'Shevat, which is very similar to American Arbor

Day. Tu B'Shevat also has what can almost be considered a *seder*. Passover, on the Jewish calendar, is celebrated with a memorial meal called a *seder*. The Hebrew word *seder* simply means "to make order of things." There is a seder as well for Tu B'Shevat— the day for remembering trees. The Jewish people bless the Lord by eating the fruits of the trees of the land of Israel. By celebrating this holiday in Israel they believe it to be a symbolic way to "heal the land."

What do they mean by that? They believe the indiscretion by Adam and Eve in the Garden of Eden, by partaking of the fruit which was forbidden, as having involved a *tree* and a fruit in this disobedience to the Lord. Reversing that process by partaking of fruit from a tree and being actively involved in planting trees is believed to be in some small way a step toward repairing this breach that happened so long ago. This is understood to be symbolic. Trees are planted all year long, but this particular ceremony is only observed on Tu B'Shevat.

Daniel's story now tells us that a holy messenger visits Nebuchadnezzar.

> In the visions I saw while lying in my bed, I looked, and there before me was a messenger, a holy one, coming down from heaven. He called in a loud voice: 'Cut down the tree and trim off its branches; strip off its leaves and scatter its fruit. Let the animals flee from under it, and the birds from its branches. But let the stump and its roots, bound with iron and bronze, remain in the ground, in the grass of the field. Let him be drenched with the dew of heaven, and let him live with the animals among the plants of the earth. Let his mind be changed from that of a man and let him be given the mind of an animal, till seven times pass by for him. The decision is announced by messengers, the holy ones declare the verdict, so that the living may know that the Most High is sovereign over the kingdoms of men and gives them to anyone he wishes and sets over them the lowliest of men.'

vv. 13-17

So that all the Earth may Know

An undetermined period of time delineated by the term "seven times" shall pass over the king before his restoration. Before considering the meaning of the tree being cut down, there are some vital points to raise.

The purpose of the visitation is clear. " . . . *so that the living may know that the Most High is sovereign over the kingdoms of men.*"

This theme threads itself through other sections of Scripture as well. When people come to visit Jerusalem, and I know they are going to visit the Western Wall, the only remaining wall of the Temple area, I often share with them an important section of Scripture—II Chronicles chapter 6. This scene was the dedication of King Solomon's newly-built Temple. On the day of the dedication he had a brass altar erected, not for sacrifice, but to serve as a platform. Stepping up onto the platform, King Solomon got down on his knees and lifted his hands in the air and out over the heads of the gathered Israelites. His voice rang out in a wonderful, lengthy prayer. It was a memorial for all that God had done, but then in verse 32 it took a new turn. He prayed:

> *"As for the foreigner who does not belong to your people Israel but has come from a distant land because of your great name and your mighty hand and your outstretched arm—when he comes and prays toward this temple, then hear from heaven, your dwelling place, and do whatever the foreigner asks of you, so that all the peoples of the earth may know your name and fear you, as do your own people Israel, and may know that this house I have built bears your Name."*

II Chronicles 6:32-33

This appears to be a blank check, drawn on the account of heaven, for Gentiles coming to the land of Israel. Solomon foresaw this situation thousands of years ago and asked God for special favor for *you*! Solomon is beseeching God to answer your prayers from this locale.

There's a reason for his request! *So that the Gentiles might know that the God of Israel exists.* People who visit here and see the wonders of Israel and soak it in, return to where they came from and to tell their friends what they have seen. In effect they are telling everybody that the God of Israel still exists. Whether or not the hearers are believers, they listen to these testimonies of what God is still up to in the Middle East. It is difficult to deny the modern-day miracle of Israel's existence.

This ties in to the message given from Heaven to Nebuchadnezzar. Daniel did not come to Babylon a famous man.

The Final Kingdom

He brought God's message to the Gentile empire of Babylon and he outlived three kings, leading each of those kings to the throne of God, not just personally, but on a level that affected the entire populace of greater Babylon.

Terror Strikes Daniel's Heart

Daniel interpreted this dream for the king.

"This is the dream that I, King Nebuchadnezzar, had. Now, Belteshazzar, tell me what it means, for none of the wise men in my kingdom can interpret it for me. But you can, because the spirit of the holy gods is in you." Then Daniel, (also called Belteshazzar) was greatly perplexed for a time, and his thoughts terrified him. So the king said, "Belteshazzar, do not let the dream or its meaning alarm you."

Belteshazzar answered, "My lord, if only the dream applied to your enemies and its meaning to your adversaries! The tree you saw, which grew large and strong, with its top touching the sky, visible to the whole earth, with beautiful leaves and abundant fruit, providing food for all, giving shelter to the beasts of the field, and having nesting places in its branches for the birds of the air—you, O king, are that tree! You have become great and strong; your greatness has grown until it reaches the sky, and your dominion extends to distant parts of the earth. You, O king, saw a messenger, coming down from heaven and saying, 'Cut down the tree and destroy it, but leave the stump, bound with iron and bronze, in the grass of the field, while its roots remain in the ground. Let him be drenched with the dew of heaven; let him live like the wild animals, until seven times passes by for him.'

This is the interpretation, O king, and this is the decree the Most High has issued against my lord the king: You will be driven away from the people and will live with the wild animals; you will eat grass like cattle and be drenched with the dew of heaven. Seven times will pass by for you until you acknowledge that the Most High is sovereign over the kingdoms of men and gives them to anyone he wishes. The command to leave the stump of the tree with its roots means that your kingdom will be restored to you when you acknowledge that Heaven rules.

"Therefore, O king, be pleased to accept my advice: Renounce your sins by doing what is right, and your wickedness by being kind to the oppressed. It may be then that your prosperity will continue."

4:18-27

This time it was not only Nebuchadnezzar who was terrified; Daniel was fearful as well. The Jewish people had been uprooted from the northern kingdom of Israel and then from Jerusalem in two different phases. Israel had been taken captive to Assyria, and later Jerusalem, Judah, and Benjamin to Babylon. They had been told by God, through the prophets, to go willingly to Babylon, settle down and raise families, to build houses, and to work for the good of the community of the city of Babylon where they were taken captive (Jer. 29:5-7). Now suddenly Nebuchadnezzar, who was the overshadowing security in a highly unstable time of history, had been given a vision by God of *his* impending destruction. We can fully understand Daniel's concern. *If God destroys Nebuchadnezzar, what will happen to my people? Where are we, the captive Jews, in the midst of all this?* The queen of kingdoms was about to topple, along with all those who depended upon her for sustenance.

Daniel was afraid, as well, that their relatively good life in Babylon might come to an end. This punishment will endure, Daniel says, until Nebuchadnezzar acknowledges that the Most High is sovereign. He uses an important phrase here at the end of verse 26—". . . that your kingdom will be restored to you when you acknowledge that Heaven rules." The term "Heaven rules" is a Hebraic epithet for "God." This made it clear to Nebuchadnezzar that Daniel was not talking about the gods of the ziggurat. He was talking about the God of Heaven, the God of all gods, Yahweh, the One who is King of kings and Lord of lords over all, even the "great Babylon."

God is patient. It did not happen immediately.

All this happened to king Nebuchadnezzar. Twelve months later, as the king was walking on the roof of the royal palace of Babylon, he said, "Is not this the great Babylon I have built as the royal residence, by my mighty power and for the glory of my majesty?" The words were still on his lips when a voice came from heaven, "This is what is decreed for you, King Nebuchadnezzar: Your royal authority has been taken from you. You will be driven away from people and will live with

93

the wild animals; you will eat grass like cattle. Seven times will pass by for you until you acknowledge that the Most High is sovereign over the kingdoms of men and gives them to anyone that he wishes." Immediately what had been said about Nebuchadnezzar was fulfilled. He was driven away from people and ate grass like cattle. His body was drenched with the dew of heaven until his hair grew like the feathers of an eagle and his nails like the claws of a bird.

At the end of that time, I, Nebuchadnezzar, raised my eyes toward heaven, and my sanity was restored. Then I praised the Most High; I honored and glorified him who lives forever.

vv. 28-34

Nebuchadnezzar's time out in the field may have been a time of mental illness. Some mental problems could be described by this list of symptoms. Something happened to Nebuchadnezzar during his period of banishment, for when he returned to power it was no longer, "O king live forever!" but rather "God, who lives forever." Then Nebuchadnezzar breaks forth in wonderful praise:

His dominion is an eternal dominion; his kingdom endures from generation to generation. All the peoples of the earth are regarded as nothing. He does as he pleases with the powers of heaven and the peoples of earth. No one can hold back his hand or say to him: 'What have you done?' At the same time that my sanity was restored, my honor and splendor were returned to me for the glory of my kingdom. My advisers and nobles sought me out, and I was restored to my throne and became even greater than before. Now I, Nebuchadnezzar, praise and exalt and glorify the King of heaven, because everything he does is right and all his ways are just. And those who walk in pride he is able to humble."

vv. 34b-37

Nebuchadnezzar's pride had blinded him to truth. God, exercising His authority over a king and kingdom unwilling to submit to His supreme Lordship, cuts down the tree that had symbolized Nebuchadnezzar's greatness and drives him to insanity.

The multiplicity of Babylon's gods was so much easier to tolerate than to try to effect religious change in such a powerful empire. Time, and following the path of least resistance, stole the reality of the moment of revelation from his eyes. Only when the passing of the heavenly-appointed time was accomplished did Nebuchadnezzar lift his eyes to Heaven and declare the majesty, and most important of all, the sovereignty of God Almighty. The results were an even greater kingdom restored back to him than he had ruled before.

Nebuchadnezzar's dream-tree was big—enormous in fact—but God's kingdom towers above it all. Dwarfed by the sovereignty of God, Nebuchadnezzar's issues were placed in proper perspective. Humility always restores us to a place of grace.

Thus says the LORD: Even the captives of the mighty shall be taken, and the prey of the tyrant be rescued; for I will contend with those who contend with you, and I will save your children.
. . . Then all flesh shall know that I am the LORD your Savior, and your Redeemer, the Mighty One of Jacob.

Isaiah 49:25-26
NRSV

Close to the lampstand the handwriting appeared on the wall.

# A Child on the Throne

Excitement and intrigue build in chapter five, bringing it close to the level of epic. Ironically, Darius plays the part of the hero. There is a bit of confusion about Cyrus and Darius during this time period, but Darius may have been appointed to govern Babylon or may actually be the throne-name of Cyrus of Persia himself. Only the wildest imagination could concoct a story stranger than the truth of Belshazzar's short reign. Playing movie director with the chapter, coupled with historical background insight, helps fill in the final days of the Babylonian Empire. Some theologians think chapters five and six are out of order chronologically and belong later in the book. Nevertheless, the story is rich with the atmosphere that sets the stage for the wrap-up of an era.

There are no words in either Biblical Hebrew or Aramaic for "grandfather" or "grandson;" Belshazzar was son of Nebuchadnezzar in a succeeding generation, much like the Scriptures speak of Jesus as the "son of David." Actually, Belshazzar was co-regent and the son of Nabonidus who may have been the husband of one of Nebuchadnezzar's daughters. In spite of the fact that King Nabonidus appointed Belshazzar regent of Babylon, he may have been too young or too immature and inexperienced to rule well. Nabonidus did not rule from Babylon but from Timma, several day's journey from Babylon in the Arabian peninsula.

Belshazzar's Last Party

Sometimes, the unexpected presence of an item, in striking contrast with its lack of mention before, demands a conclusion. The sudden appearance of the stolen Temple treasures at a massive banquet seemingly discloses a character quality of King Nebuchadnezzar that has up till now evaded us. Evidently, Nebuchadnezzar had either respect for, or fear of, the holy items from the Temple in Jerusalem and must have had them stored away out of everyday use.

We see in Isaiah 39:5 that when Hezekiah showed the emissaries from Babylon all the treasures of the Temple, the prophet told Hezekiah that they all would be taken away in the siege of Jerusalem. Now, according to the Word of God, the holy items appeared in the midst of a great feast given by Belshazzar, attended by all his leadership.

> *While Belshazzar was drinking his wine, he gave orders to bring in the gold and silver goblets that Nebuchadnezzar his father had taken from the temple in Jerusalem, so that the king and his nobles, his wives and his concubines might drink from them. So they brought in the gold goblets that had been taken from the temple of God in Jerusalem, and the king and his nobles, his wives and his concubines drank from them.*
>
> Daniel 5:2-4

A thousand of Belshazzar's nobles sat at a feast whose duration, customarily, was many days.

Belshazzar's character is documented by historians who remark on his impiety. One such documented incident was the mortal striking down of one of his nobles for beating him to the draw and killing the game during a hunt. At another banquet, he mutilated a courtier when a woman remarked on his good looks. Jealousy, insecurity, and self-indulgence marked his character.

Belshazzar's feast may have purposes that are not immediately apparent in the biblical account. There were struggles from time to time over which of the gods in the Babylonian culture should be on the top rung of the ladder. Babylon considered most gods valid, therefore, in such a cosmopolitan society, portions of the demographic mix brought preferences as to which god was the most awesome, the most worthy, the most protective, or perhaps even the most fashionable.

Outsiders and newcomers to the city may have been plotting some theological upsets. Some sources say that Belshazzar's feast may have been a celebration of one of the gods of the city. He may also have been making plans to usurp Marduk's authority by replacing him with the moon god Sin, and allotting to him the upper dwellings of the ziggurat. This feast may have had an underlying political plot brought to fruition by Sin's lobbyists.

Did God design this feast in order to bring down the increasingly corrupt Babylonian Empire, or did the corruption of the situation move God to bring down the kingdom? This is indeed a riddle without a certain answer, but we do know that God uses situations and circumstances to bring about His own will.

The Concept of Holiness

Belshazzar does not understand the Hebraic idea of "holiness" and "consecration to the Lord" as perhaps Nebuchadnezzar did. It may be that when Babylon beseiged Jerusalem, Nebuchadnezzar ordered the Temple items to be brought to Babylon by the Israelite priesthood. We do know that Nebuchadnezzar had a distant respect for foreign gods. It seems these items may have been carefully put away from harm's reach by Nebuchadnezzar.

Belshazzar did not understand the distinction between holiness and consecration and mere personal righteousness. I am speaking of the holiness described in Leviticus 6:14-18. This passage addresses regulations of the grain offering offered to the Lord by Aaron's sons. The procedure for priestly partaking of the offering ends by saying, *"Whatever touches them will become holy."* I think most people imagine that if they were to touch something holy, the holy item might be defiled by the touch of a less holy person. With ceremonies of the Temple, the opposite was the case. For this reason, the lay people were kept away from holy Temple items. Leviticus 6:27 also states that whatsoever "touches" the flesh of the sin offering "will become holy." This transference of holiness might have a very different effect than expected. This consecration to the Lord was for one of two purposes, either for service or for destruction. Both were consequences of becoming "holy to the LORD."

From all we can tell, Nebuchadnezzar had held the holy items taken from the Temple in Jerusalem in sacred esteem. Most likely, they were placed safely out of use because of his respect for the religious sensibilities of surrounding nations.

The Fall of a Moon God

Several theories concerning Belshazzar's motives are purported by various commentators. They range from ideas like raw rebellious independence to military diversionary tactics due to the fact that he knew that his father had been captured by Cyrus' forces. The allegation of raw rebellion does not seem to hold too much weight and Cyrus' movements may have been better served by waiting patiently for Belshazzar to "hang" himself. There may have been sectors of the population who were not in favor of changing the order of the gods. Religious fears and beliefs ran deep in an agricultural population who depended on the smiling favor of the gods to insure existence from harvest to harvest.

The layout of the city itself provided the stage for the coming invasion. The huge gates on the north and south sides of the city could be raised in varying degrees, allowing the Euphrates River to flow through the city in the summer time. When the water level was high in the winter, the gates could be closed to divert the water around the city. It is possible that the water gates were left open just enough, by inside agents, so that the invading army could enter the city. Those gates were not well defended and to breech the walls would have taken a great long-lasting battle.

Several days into the drunken orgy organized by Belshazzar, the dramatic moment of God's descending judgment arrives. The lights are low, guests are sufficiently bored with the festivities, and then in the glow of a palace lampstand near the wall . . .

Suddenly the fingers of a human hand appeared and wrote on the plaster of the wall, near the lampstand in the royal palace. The king watched the hand as it wrote. His face turned pale and he was so frightened that his knees knocked together and his legs gave way.

vv. 5, 6

Belshazzar's reaction was not amazement; he was terrified. His knees knocking together and his legs finally giving way under him underscores his level of fright. This supernatural, yet simple display of the power of God, may tell us that the tricks of the Chaldeans and magicians of the Babylonian realm were less than impressive. Witnessing the writing on the wall and not being able to read it, Belshazzar anxiously called for his magicians. His "cosmic wise men" could not tell them what it meant. He was probably used to omens and signs on a regular basis. The nature of this sign was unlike any he had ever experienced. Suddenly, his aides' magic was useless and the king was exceedingly troubled.

Belshazzar knows he has been drinking from the gold goblets of a foreign god and suspects that this may have a bearing on the mysterious writing on the wall. This frightens him even more. Heavy with wine, rich food, and feasting, Belshazzar's wits are failing him and terror overtakes him to the point that the queen's attention is captured. This queen is not Belshazzar's wife, but according to scholars, the wife of Nabonidus, Belshazzar's father.

Mother Knows Best

The queen, hearing the voices of the king and his nobles, came into the banquet hall. "O king, live forever!" she said. "Don't be alarmed! Don't look so pale! There is a man in your kingdom who has the spirit of the holy gods in him. In the time of your father he was found to have insight and intelligence and wisdom like that of the gods.

King Nebuchadnezzar—your father—your father the king, I say—appointed him chief of the magicians, enchanters, astrologers and diviners. This man Daniel, whom the king called Belteshazzar, was found to have a keen mind and knowledge and understanding, and also the ability to interpret dreams, explain riddles and solve difficult problems. Call for Daniel, and he will tell you what the writing means."

So Daniel was brought before the king, and the king said to him, "Are you Daniel, one of the exiles my father the king brought from Judah? I have heard that the spirit of the gods is in you and that you have insight, intelligence and outstanding wisdom. The wise men and enchanters were brought before me to read this writing and tell me what it means, but they could not explain it. Now I have heard that you are able to give interpretations and to solve difficult problems. If you can read this writing and tell me what it means, you will be clothed in purple and have a gold chain placed around your neck, and you will be made the third highest ruler in the kingdom."

Then Daniel answered the king, "You may keep your gifts for yourself and give your rewards to someone else. Nevertheless, I will read the writing for the king and tell him what it means."

vv. 10-17

By now, Daniel has gained a reputation of godly integrity, who walks in divine wisdom and giftings. The Queen Mother vividly remembers encounters with Daniel. Daniel has maintained a purity of motives over the years of service in Babylon. He could have used these heavenly gifts to his own personal benefit, but he chose rather to glorify God at every opportunity. We also see that he was not impressed or moved by worldly wealth and positions of power. Daniel now provides Belshazzar with a history lesson and describes in detail the results of pride.

O king, the Most High God gave your father Nebuchadnezzar sovereignty and greatness and glory and splendor. Because of the high position he gave him, all the peoples and nations and men of every language dreaded and feared him. Those the king wanted to put to death, he put to death; those he wanted to spare he spared; those he wanted to promote he promoted; and those he wanted to humble, he humbled.

But when his heart became arrogant and hardened with pride, he was deposed from his royal throne and stripped of his glory. He was driven away from people and given the mind of an animal; he lived with the wild donkeys and ate grass like cattle; and his body was drenched with the dew of heaven, until he acknowledged that the Most High God is sovereign over the kingdoms of men and sets over them anyone he wishes.

But you his son, O Belshazzar, have not humbled yourself, though you knew all this. Instead, you have set yourself up against the Lord of Heaven.' [Once again, Daniel makes the distinction between the Lord of Heaven, and the god of the ziggurat].

You had the goblets from his temple brought to you, and you and your nobles, your wives and your concubines drank wine from them. You praised the gods of silver and gold, of iron, bronze, wood and stone, which cannot see or hear or understand. But you did not honor the God who holds in his hand your life and all of your ways. Therefore he sent the hand that wrote the inscription.

vv. 18-24

Daniel was quick to point out that Belshazzar had chosen to follow the idols of Babylon instead of the one true God revealed to his father. He simply confirms the kings fears. He had violated the sanctity of the holy vessels of God's Temple. By this act, he dishonored God, and was subject to His judgment.

Purple/Blue—For God or King?

Daniel's promised reward for solving the riddle of the writing on the wall was that he would be clothed in purple. As well, he would receive the third highest seat in the kingdom.

The regent's offer of a purple robe is much more involved than what is mentioned here. The color purple runs like a thread throughout the Scriptures and has an intriguing aspect. It is first mentioned in the first two books of the Torah, Genesis and Exodus. The colors "blue" and "purple" are somewhat interchangable in the scriptural sense. This was the blue color mentioned in Numbers chapter 15 that would be tied into the *tzitzit* of the men in the corners of their garments. Both of these colors were extracted from sea snails by an arduous method. Only a few drops of dye per snail were able to be aquired.

Blue and purple were considered royal colors because of the expense and difficulty of aquisition. There are two words in Hebrew for blue or purple: *argamon* and *cahol*. Argamon is a red-purple. Cahol is similar, but a blue-purple. The color in the Jewish men's fringes or tzitzit is *techelet,* which is a form of the word *cahol*.

The color techelet is not a strong purple. It's a bluish purple—almost periwinkle blue. (From your childhood perhaps you will remember periwinkle from a box of crayons). That is a fair representation of the color *tachelet*.

Blue and the Rebellion of Korah

Judaic sources give more details to the story of the rebellion of Korah in the Sinai wilderness which is recounted in Numbers 16. These sources relate that Korah challenged Moses, accusing him of lifting himself up above the people. The Judaic sources relate that the item of contention was the color blue worn by all the men. It is said that Korah scoffingly told Moses to take a look at his own robe. "It's all blue," he chided. His derision seems to point to Korah's financial state of affairs. The cost of a whole cape in blue may indicate that Korah was wealthy. The inference was doubt cast on Moses' ability to rule the people based on his financial status.

The story of these colors travel down the ages of history and is documented in the pages of the Bible. Another instance referring to this valuable color is about a well-known woman named Lydia, who was a seller of purple (Acts 16:14). From this we deduce that Lydia was not a poor woman. To extract an ounce of purple dye from its source, the tiny murex snail, about 12,000 snails had to be crushed. These snails are almost exclusively found in the Mediterranean Sea or the Persian Gulf. One human being could never extract enough of the dye alone. Lydia must have had a fair-sized production operation going on to make a profitable living on the sale of the purple dye or dyed cloth.

When Alexander the Great conquered the Persian city of Shushan, he found approximately 270,000 pounds of purple dyed material that had been taken as booty from the royal treasuries of the Greek city of Hermione. It had been stored on the shelves of the treasury there for two hundred years and still had its fresh vibrant color.

The Jewish people used this rare color as a unifying factor. They would never have viewed it as something one would wear to distinguish his status from another. Every Jewish man had the right to wear purple in the fringes of his garment according to the scriptural tenent, regardless of his financial situation. This color not only proclaimed that the man had a connection with God, but that he had a connection with his community, in that they *all* wore the thread.

In view of this, it helps us to understand why Daniel responded that the king could keep his purple robe and gold chain. But, for Daniel to turn down offers of gratitude from a powerful king in this time period could have had grave consequences. With the understanding of the importance of the color to the Jewish people as a national identity and as a connection with their God, you can almost read Daniel's mind. He would not wear an item to lift himself up above his fellow captives in the Babylonian Empire, even if he were to enjoy the position of third in the kingdom. The fellowship of serving God Almighty was the mortar between the bricks that kept the Jewish people a nation within a nation. The color purple was one of the earmarks of that fellowship.

Over the centuries there have been some changes. Some Jewish prayer shawls today do not have blue or purple in their fringes but instead have a black stripe in the shawl itself. During the dispersion of the Jews in A.D. 70 from Israel, the exact technique of manufacturing this unique color was lost. Certainty of the shade of blue or purple was dubious. As the Jews migrated through Europe, they decided to substitute a black stripe to commemorate the destruction of the Temple rather than guessing at the correct biblical color of blue. This is one example of Jewish carefulness in attempting to maintain and preserve that which God gave to them through His word.

In A.D. 68 there was an imperial edict from Rome stating that only the emperor could wear purple. Therefore, Jews all over the world who were wearing the color purple in the tzitzit of their prayer shawls and their garments were suddenly forbidden to use this color! No longer could they purchase the dye. Perhaps Lydia's livelihood came to an end. Two years later came the Jewish rebellion against Rome. This edict from Rome may have served as the proverbial "straw that broke the camel's back." I can imagine that the Jews said, *We can no longer cooperate with Rome.* Every Jewish man who prayed to God had a purple cord in the tzitzit of his prayer shawl. In A.D. 70 the rebellion against Rome resulted in the scattering of the Jews from the city of Jerusalem and the fleeing of the "Zealots" to Masada.

Masada, the desert fortress that Herod built but never visited, became the stage for this monumental drama. High above the Dead Sea the Jewish resistance fled to the almost deserted fortress and set up their camp of resistance. It took the Romans three years to get to the Jewish hold-outs. Finally, Rome conquered Masada but victory was empty as over nine hundred Jewish men, women, and children had committed suicide to keep the Romans from abusing them. From that time on, the Jews were forbidden to come to the city of Jerusalem. The city was renamed "Aelia Capitolina" by Hadrian, the Roman emperor at the time. But the greatest loss to the Jews was that their Temple was destroyed in the seige.

Nickel, Dime, Dollar—Scatter

After declining the kings gift's, Daniel sets about to tell Belshazzar what the mysterious handwriting says. He relays God's message to him:

This is the inscription that was written:

MENE, MENE, TEKEL, PARSIN

This is what these words mean: MENE: *God has numbered the days of your reign and brought it to an end.* TEKEL: *You have been weighed on the scales and found wanting.* PERES: *Your kingdom is divided and given to the Medes and the Persians."*

vv. 25-28

Several possible interpretations present themselves for consideration. Were the wise men not able to read the message because they were simply words joined together that made no sense? If so, we might get the sense of their frustration by just translating what the words mean, although it must be stated that each of the words have several possibilities for translation. *Mene* or *mina* is an Aramaic monetary unit. *Tekel* can mean either to "weigh out," or "shekel" as in the coin. *Peres* means either "to divide," or a "half-shekel," or the nation of Persia.

For English speakers the riddle might sound like: "Nickel, dime, dollar—scatter." People would be able to read the words but who could say what it meant? The words of themselves are not hard but the underlying meaning is obscure. Daniel was able to relate not only what the writing said, but what it meant and Who was delivering the message to the empire of Babylon. This was holy wisdom coming down from Heaven.

And, and, and . . .

The structure of Aramaic and Hebrew differ from English or Greek on one important point. It is the prefix "U." In Aramaic the "u" tacked onto the front of the word, *parsin*, making it *upharsin*, simply means "and." This is a telltale earmark of a semitic language. Dr. Robert Lindsey, who pastored the Narkis Street congregation in Jerusalem from 1945 - 1988, wrote an interesting book about the New Testament before he died. He proposed that the New Testament was originally written in Hebrew, and not in Greek.

Dr. Robert L. Lindsey (1917 - 1995), pastor and Bible scholar, pioneered a new understanding of synoptic relationships. Lindsey was born in Norman, Oklahoma. He first came to Israel in 1939 in order to study Hebrew. He returned to live permanently in Israel in 1945. For the next forty-two years he served in Israel as a pastor and Bible translator. He, and his colleague David Flusser of the Hebrew University, developed a fresh approach to the Gospels. Dr. Lindsey's synoptic theories led to the founding (in 1985) of the Jerusalem School of Synoptic Research. Some of his most important published works include, *A Hebrew Translation of the Gospel of Mark*, *A Comparative Greek Concordance of the Synoptic Gospels*, and *Jesus, Rabbi and Lord: The Hebrew Story of Jesus Behind Our Gospels*.

The point that Dr. Lindsey makes in *A Hebrew Translation of the Gospel of Mark* is that there are "earmarks" in the New Testament of an underlying language. There are several chapters in some of the Gospels that contain the word "and" as many as thirty-six times. This is a very Hebraic way of linking together thoughts and ideas. Actually, it constitutes one very long run-on sentence. This was not a Greek way of writing or speaking but it certainly reflects typical Aramaic and Hebrew writing, as we see even in modern Hebrew.

The End is Near

Back at the Babylonian palace, things were wrapping up.

Then at Belshazzar's command, Daniel was clothed in purple, a gold chain was placed around his neck, and he was proclaimed the third highest ruler in the kingdom.

v. 29

Daniel's declining of Belshazzar's gifts seems to have been ignored and it looks like whether Daniel wanted to be clothed in purple or not he was, as well as being promoted to the position of third ruler in the kingdom.

Even as Belshazzar was making royal proclamations on behalf of Daniel, Persian troops were breaking into his city by stealth.

That very night Belshazzar, king of the Babylonians, was slain, and Darius the Mede took over the kingdom, at the age of sixty-two.

v. 30

Daniel and his compatriots slipped quietly from one imperial administration to another. God's man was not *on* the throne, but sat *next* to the throne. Through Daniel, God Almighty brought kingdom after kingdom to the foot of His holy throne in face-to-face confrontation. When the sun rose the next morning, a new day was dawning on the ancient kingdom of Babylon.

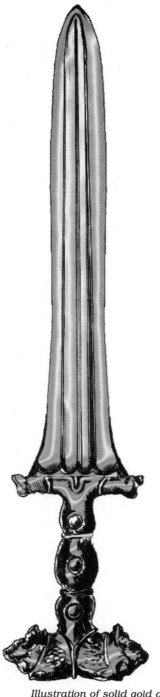

*I will raise up
Cyrus in my
righteousness:
I will make all his ways
straight.
He will rebuild my city
and set my exiles free,
but not for a price or
reward,
says the LORD Almighty.*

Isaiah 45:13

Illustration of solid gold dagger found by archaeologists in Babylon.

Cyrus Should Have Died

Initially in chapter six, not much information on Darius is given to us. Even the inauguration of the new Mesopotamian king is sidestepped. There is some confusion among scholars as several rulers were named Cyrus. "Darius the Mede" may have been Cyrus' throne name in Babylon.

A story is told by the ancient historian Herodotus that sheds important light on the life of Cyrus, who is likely one and the same with Darius. Even though we do not view Cyrus necessarily as God's man, God protected him until the time he had allotted to use him. The Lord often uses political leaders for His divine purposes.

Before Cyrus was born, the king of the Medes, Astyages (As-tie-ag-gis), had witnessed the defeat of his father's kingdom by the Scythians. They had conquered and ruled over Media for twenty-eight years. Their defeat and the re-establishment of the kingdom of the Medes was a monumental accomplishment. Upon ascending the throne after his father's death, fear of losing the kingdom again created an almost paranoiac state in Astyages. He dreamed that from his daughter Mandane a stream flowed that not only covered his capital but covered the whole of Asia.

Troubled by the dream, he went to the Magi who were known for interpreting dreams. They were people of one of the provinces of the Medes, from which scholars think the followers of Jesus' star may have come centuries later.

The interpretation of the dream terrified Astyages. He was told that a child born from his daughter's womb would usurp the kingdom from him. He therefore plotted to arrange circumstances so that his dream would not come to pass. Astyages would not give his daughters hand in marriage to a Mede. The Medes were known for their prowess in war and for their aggressiveness. Instead he would have her marry a Persian. The Persians, in contrast, were known to be of quiet temper and considered much inferior to Medes. He chose a particularly even-tempered Persian man named Cambyses.

Thus, Cambyses married Mandane and took her south to his home in Persia. In the very first year of their marriage, Astyages had a second dream. In his dream, a vine grew from the womb of his daughter and overshadowed the whole of Asia. According to the Magi, the second dream was a repeat of the first. In a fearful tremor, Astyages sent to Persia for his daughter, who was with child, had her brought to the royal palace, and set a watch over her. When she arrived she was near the time to deliver her first child. The plan of Astyages was that if the child to be born were male, it would be spirited away and murdered by Astyages' primary palace aide, Harpagus. Again, Astyages' terrifying dreams caused him to attempt to maneuver circumstances he deemed threatening to his throne.

A Son is Born

Mandane soon gave birth to Cyrus, her firstborn son. The baby was delivered to Harpagus who wrapped him in royal garments and, weeping, took the infant to his own hometown in the mountainous area of Media. Upon arriving home to his wife, he related the story of the king's intent to take the baby's life.

"What, then, is in your heart to do?" his wife questioned him.

"I will not be the man to work his will, or lend a helping hand to such a murder as this," he said. He therefore sent for a herdsman of the area whom he knew. He instructed him to take the baby and perform the will of the king.

The herdsman carried the baby into the mountains to his own home where his wife, in his absence, had just given birth to a stillborn male child. Uncovering King Astyages' daughter's baby and seeing what a beautiful boy he was, clothed in finery and gold, she begged her husband not to take the life of the living child but to replace their stillborn son in exchange for the living boy—which he did. Changing the clothing of the two babies, the herdsman carried his own dead child to the mountains, left him exposed for three days and returned to Harpagus' house with news that the child was now dead. Harpagus sent one of his most trusted bodyguards to accomplish three things: to witness that the child was indeed dead; to arrange for a burial; and to take news to the king that his will had been done.

Ten years later, child's play brought Cyrus before his grandfather and though the gears of heaven grind slow— nevertheless, they grind sure. In the small village where the herdsman lived, the child Cyrus (not yet known by that name) was playing with other village children who, in a game of make-believe, appointed Cyrus to be their "king." Cyrus was appointing some boys to build houses and palaces, while others were appointed to be the king's spies and guards. He then began to order them about, as kings were known to do, but one of the boys refused to be ordered by the pretend King Cyrus. He then had the guards seize him and he personally whipped him severely, leaving marks on his back.

The chastised boy happened to be the son of a distinguished nobleman of the village who in a rage took his son to King Astyages to complain about what the cowherd's son had done. The king sent for the cowherd and his son to hear the complaint fully. Upon their arrival the king set his eyes upon the boy and asked him if he was aware that he had abused the son of a nobleman of the village. Cyrus answered, "My lord, I only treated him as he deserved. I was chosen to be king in play by the boys of our village, because they thought me best for it. He himself was one of the boys who chose me. All the others did according to my orders; but he refused, and made light of them, until at last he got his due reward. If for this I deserve to suffer punishment, here I am— ready to submit to it."

The king was struck by the nobleness of his answer and his personal demeanor. At the same time, he thought he saw something in his face too much like his own to be coincidence. He also mentally tabulated that the boy was of the age to have been a baby when he had had his grandson left on the mountains to meet his fate. Quickly he dismissed the nobleman and his son with assurances that justice would be wrought, so that in fact he might question the herdsman alone.

Astyages had the boy Cyrus taken to an inner room and then he faced the herdsman alone. "Where did you get this boy?" the king queried.

"He is my own son, the child of my wife who is still alive and lives with me in my house."

The king had his guards apprehend the man roughly. "You are very ill-advised to bring yourself into such great trouble!" The guards then were instructed to haul the man off to the rack. Falling into a heap on the floor, the cowherd then told the story exactly as it had happened many years previously without concealing anything, ending with pleas and prayers to the king to forgive him.

The king's rage then turned upon Harpagus who was sent for. The king spared nothing in showing to Harpagus his rage at being disobeyed. Harpagus, knowing his life was on the line, recounted the story as it had happened and swore that he was certain that the child was dead even though he had not wanted to slay the boy with his own hands.

Astyages then softened, saying, "So, the boy is alive, and best it is, for the child's fate was a great sorrow to me, and the reproaches of my daughter went to my heart. Truly fortune has played us a good turn in this. Go home then, and send thy son to be with the newcomer, and tonight, as I mean to sacrifice thank-offerings for the child's safety to the gods to whom such honor is due, I look to have thee a guest at the banquet."

Harpagus then returned home with the news and obeyed, sending his son to help the boy, Cyrus, in the palace, as the king had requested.

King Astyages then went about wickedly to punish Harpagus for his disobedience of ten years ago. The king had Harpagus' son murdered, roasted, and served to him during the feasting of the banquet. Only Harpagus was to partake of the "special dish" and when done, the king asked how the meal had pleased Harpagus. Harpagus replied that he had enjoyed it excessively. Astyages then had servants bring out a covered basket with the head, hands and feet of Harpagus' son and presented it to him.

Steeling himself against the wickedness of the king and retaining his self-control, Harpagus took the remains of his son and buried them.

In a quandary about what to do with Cyrus, the king sent for the Magi once again. They convinced him that since the boy had "played" king and was brought to the palace for just that reason, the dream had probably already been fulfilled and Astyages had no further reason to fear the boy. He was advised to send him to his real mother in Persia and forget the omens. Since the boy was truly a Persian anyway and would, if allowed to come to the throne, treat the Medes as foreigners, it was indeed best to send him far away.

Cambyses and Mandane, upon receiving their long-lost son and hearing the story of how he had survived, gladly received him into their arms and lives.

When Cyrus was grown to manhood, he became known as the bravest and most popular of all his peers. King Astyages' palace aide Harpagus was bent on avenging himself for the horrible death of his son. He began to pay friendship tribute to Cyrus secretly with gifts and messages. Weaving a web of intrigue by befriending disgruntled Medes in the army and creating a network of potential revolt, Harpagus plotted against the kingdom of Astyages. He slowly convinced the Median nobles that they would find a kingdom much more suited to their good if they would find a way to place Cyrus at their head. Finally the day came to test the willingness of Cyrus himself.

Knowing the roads to Persia were patrolled by Median soldiers, Harpagus contrived a secret method of sending word to Cyrus that a revolt plan was in order. In the hands of a peasant huntsman Harpagus put a wild hare with instructions to take it to Cyrus, telling him to gut the animal himself. Inside the hare Harpagus had sewn a message with the desires of the rebels of Media. The letter read:

"Son of Cambyses, the gods assuredly watch over you, or never would you have passed through your many wonderful adventures —now is the time when you may avenge yourself upon Astyages, your murderer. He willed your death, remember; to the gods and to me you owe that you are still alive. I think you are not ignorant of what he did to you, nor of what I have suffered at his hands because I committed you to the cowherd, and did not put you to death. Listen now to me, and obey my words . . ." Thus Harpagus spelled out the plan to Cyrus.

Cyrus devised a plan to convince the Persians to revolt against Astyages. In a royal scroll, he read to his countrymen that Astyages had appointed him to be their general. He ordered them to bring all the reaping scythes they could find and report to him the next day. Showing them a huge field of thorns, he instructed that they should reap them before sundown.

The following day he had them report again—this time to a feast of banqueting and drinking all day long. At the end of the two days Cyrus questioned which of the days was more enjoyable to his compatriots. The resounding answer was the day of feasting. Cyrus then revealed the plan to revolt against Astyages' kingdom which had been symbolized by the field of thorns and to choose Cyrus as their king—symbolized by the day of feasting. Without question his people were ready to fight.

Meanwhile, back in Media, King Astyages, hearing of Cyrus' plans to attack and in a panic of forgetfulness of how he had injured Harpagus, appointed the latter general of all his forces to fight against Cyrus. In the battle, only a few Medes fought against Cyrus' forces. All the others knew the plan and the armies of Media were soundly defeated. Astyages was taken hostage and Cyrus set on the throne of the now Medo-Persian Empire.

Later, conquering Babylon much in the same way as he conquered the Medes, Cyrus was a tool in the hand of God. For God could successfully plant in the heart of Cyrus the decree allowing the Jewish people to return to Jerusalem. He would even help them rebuild their city and Temple. The time had come that God had ordained for Cyrus. Both of Astyages' dreams had come true.

A Change in the Wind

The story of Astyages and Cyrus helps us understand God's intervention in the affairs of Babylon from the heavenly standpoint.

Undoubtedly, the government of Babylon was in a time of great change. A new era was descending upon this region. From Babylon itself, the conquered territories would be administered by appointees of the king. One hundred and twenty governors would oversee the new laws of the Persian Empire. These one hundred and twenty would be overseen by three heads, one of which was a figure much like today's prime minister.

A plot fueled by jealousy sought to undo Daniel. Being acquainted with the childhood of Cyrus helps us to understand the king's reaction to the plot conjured up to make an end of Daniel. Cyrus spent a night of anguish while Daniel sat in the lions' den. That must have brought back the memories of King Astyages' plot to end his own life.

The demographics of Babylon are almost certainly diverse by this time. It is fairly certain that a cosmopolitan mix peopled the city. I doubt, therefore, that the hatred of Daniel was nationalistic in nature. Hatred of the Jews may have already been growing. This theme threads its way down through history, documented in the pages of the Bible, i.e., the Book of Esther, as well as outside the pages of the Bible.

Different time periods have served as the backdrop for various dramatic episodes of antisemitism. Some of the characteristics that the Jewish people have been blamed for have been the fruits of intense anti-Jewish sentiment. In Europe, the Catholic Church used the Jewish people to loan out money at interest because they believed it to be against their biblical principles to do so. The Jewish people were generally very good at what they did. Some of the first banks that were ever set up were established and run by Jewish people and became very successful endeavors. Because of this the non-Jewish world became jealous, and they in turn accused the Jewish people of being "money hungry." The fact of the matter is that the livelihood the Church forced upon the Jewish people became cause for which to persecute them.

God blesses His people in spite of all oppressive efforts—both human and Satanic—to suppress them. As Germany grew closer to actualizing its "final solution" campaign against the Jewish people in the last century, constraints were placed upon the Jews in degrees. It took many years to harden the German people's hearts toward the Jews to the point that they would turn a blind eye to their cruel deaths.

Satan's evil intentions toward the Jewish people in Germany was unprecedented wickedness in any society. Out of that horror, and in many amazingly miraculous situations, God gave his people a homeland to which they could escape to safety.

Returning to the conspiracy of Daniel's co-regents, their evil plan wound up falling back on their own heads. They quickly decided that they would never find fault with him in the evaluation of his duties as a court administrator; therefore, they knew the plot must take a religious turn to be successful.

So the administrators and the satraps went as a group to the king and said: "O King Darius, live forever! The royal administrators, prefects, satraps, advisers and governors have all agreed that the king should issue an edict and enforce the decree that anyone who prays to any god or man during the next thirty days, except to you, O king, shall be thrown into the lions' den. Now, O king, issue the decree and put it in writing so that it cannot be altered—in accordance with the laws of the Medes and Persians, which cannot be repealed." So King Darius put the decree in writing.

vv. 6-9

The Satrap's Trap

The report to King Darius claiming that everyone had been consulted about the decree of loyalty to the king's sovereignty was a ruse. Not everyone had been consulted. The apparent strengthening of the king's throne constituted a veiled plot. The request of the administrators gives us an inside peek at Babylonian religious life—if the message between the lines is discerned. If no one was going to pray for thirty days, that must have meant that worship in the Babylonian pantheon of gods was cyclical and there was at least a thirty day period where no one else would fall into the satraps' trap.

Daniel had lived at the palace long enough for many to know the Jewish religious rituals, prayer times, and other ceremonies that he strictly observed. In this, the jealous and hate-filled palace employees knew that Daniel would play right into their hands. In this conspiracy, Daniel was the lightning rod for the potential extermination of his people.

The reference to the "law of the Medes and the Persians" reveals an interesting development in the book. Citing these laws shows us that the new rulers of Babylon had moved toward a philosophy of governing that would crop up later in many nations, that philosophy being the infallibility, and god-like character of the ruler. In the Roman Empire, this dogma matures and its emperors finally demand worship from the people they govern upon threat of death.

Now when Daniel learned that the decree had been published, he went home to his upstairs room where the windows opened towards Jerusalem. Three times a day he got down on his knees and prayed, giving thanks to his God, just as he had done before.

v. 10

Daniel is recorded as going home to pray. Normally, within Judaism, prayer took place in a group of ten men called a *minyan*. The number in a minyan was arrived at by the story of Abraham's negotiating with God over the salvation of Sodom if as few as ten righteous men could be found in the city. The negotiations ended at ten men; therefore, Jewish sources have considered corporate prayer sessions to take place in the presence of at least ten men. Synagogue services do not begin until a minyan is present.

The fact that Daniel went home to pray suggests that he may

have been trying to throw the spotlight off his prayer life and the lives of his friends in order to save life on that fateful day. Judaism views human life as a supreme blessing from God, and to pointlessly endanger one's life is to transgress God's command to populate the earth. The Judaic view of the sanctity of life would then suggest that any manner of behavior protecting human life would rank very high in God's view.

In Judaism, standing while facing Jerusalem, is the position of prayer. Daniel was probably in extreme distress. His personal prayer time would probably have been different than the corporate prayer that is done with a minyan. The Jewish concept of prayer differs somewhat from the Christian concept, but interestingly so.

In Jewish prayer, he who comes into the presence of God views his spirit like a candle flame. The Hebrew word for spirit is *ruach* which means "wind." Therefore, when one is coming into contact with the Holy Spirit of God, *Ruach HaKodesh*, that candle flame will be affected—it will move back and forth at the presence of the wind. In light of this, the movements of Jewish men at prayer in synagogues and at the Western Wall in Jerusalem makes sense. The rocking motion back and forth, while intent in prayer is communicating their inner feelings and hearts to God in body language.

There is a noteworthy concept regarding prayer among the Jewish people which is far removed from the Babylonian idea of worship. *Kavanah* is the Hebrew word for "direction" or "purpose." Unlike the Babylonians, vain repetition of prayers that become meaningless is forbidden for the Jews. The worship of the gods in Babylon's pantheon of deities was one of burdensome weariness.

Small idol-like dolls, called "votive idols," have been uncovered all over Mesopotamia. They were not idols that one worshiped though. Archaeologists discovered them to be stylized likenesses of the purchasers of the dolls, which were to be placed in the temples to take their place for prayers. Even today "prayer wheels" among eastern religions serve the same purpose. Talismans against impiety, these prayer wheels are turned and the written prayers are thought to ascend heavenward to appease the gods. Not so among the Hebrews. In contrast, kavanah, when in the context of prayer, means "praying with purposeful direction."

In light of the urgency of this conspiracy, Daniel is found beseeching God upon his knees.

The Final Kingdom

Then these men went as a group and found Daniel praying and asking God for help. So they went to the king and spoke to him about his royal decree:

"Did you not publish a decree that during the next thirty days anyone who prays to any god or man except to you, O king, would be thrown into the lions' den?"

The king answered, "The decree stands—in accordance with the laws of the Medes and Persians, which cannot be repealed." Then they said to the king, "Daniel, who is one of the exiles from Judah, pays no attention to you, O king, or to the decree you put in writing. He still prays three times a day."

When the king heard this, he was greatly distressed; he was determined to rescue Daniel and made every effort until sundown to save him. Then the men went as a group to the king and said to him, "Remember, O king, that according to the law of the Medes and Persians no decree or edict that the king issues can be changed." So the king gave the order, and they brought Daniel and threw him into the lions' den.

The king said to Daniel, "May your God, whom you serve continually, rescue you!" A stone was brought and placed over the mouth of the den, and the king sealed it with his own signet ring and with the rings of his nobles, so that Daniel's situation might not be changed. Then the king returned to his palace and spent the night without eating and without any entertainment being brought to him. And he could not sleep.

At the first light of dawn, the king got up and hurried to the lions' den. When he came near the den, he called to Daniel in an anguished voice, "Daniel, servant of the living God, has your God, whom you serve continually, been able to rescue you from the lions?" Daniel answered, "O king, live forever! My God sent his angel, and he shut the mouths of the lions. They have not hurt me, because I was found innocent in his sight. Nor have I ever done any wrong before you, O king." The king was overjoyed and gave orders to lift Daniel out of the den. And when Daniel was lifted from the den, no wound was found on him, because he had trusted in his God.

vv. 11-23

Daniel treated prayer, not as a routine formula to appease a far-away god, but as a window opening on a Living God's kingdom. Prayer for Daniel was not just a set of rules but a purposeful exercise, directed to the King of Heaven.

Ahuramazda and the Sacred Fire

Corporal punishment in previous chapters involved being thrown in a furnace of intense heat. Daniel's three friends experienced that penal system. Not so here. The changeover in the kingdom also brought new winds of worship and religious practice from the northeast. Now a Medo-Persian Empire was ruling Babylon under the rulership of Darius, also known as Cyrus. Zoroaster, the prophet of an ancient Persian god—Ahuramazda—and founder of the religion later known as Zoroastrianism, predated these kingdoms by centuries. One of the practices of the Zoroastrians was the worship of "fire." The Zoroastrians believed fire to be the celestial essence of the power of the universe. Therefore, to throw a human body into fire was, in effect, to pollute the universe. It would have been unthinkable by Persians. The Zoroastrians also viewed the earth as a holy entity. The burial of any body in the earth, as well, was a pollution of the universe.

The punishment of Daniel for disobeying the decree of the king fit the theology of the Zoroastrians perfectly. His being thrown into a den of lions followed the prescribed disposal of a dead human body. Tombs across present day Iran and parts of Iraq are tall rectangles of creamy limestone with the gabled tops open to the sky. The dead body was left uncovered in the open tomb to allow animals and birds of prey to come and dispose of the flesh of the body. Daniel being exposed to hungry lions was the manner of execution that did not result in the pollution of the earth with human flesh.

The king's reaction to Daniel's guilty verdict in the indictment of his co-regents is touching. Evidently the law passed by the king that could not be changed grieved him to the point of self-chastisement. He spent the night in what resembles prayer and fasting. His evident love and respect for Daniel sheds light on Daniel's character indirectly.

It is interesting in this dictatorial monarchy that the inner working of the government had a flavor of democracy. The edicts and decrees that could be put into motion by the council of all regents high and low guaranteed that a passed law could not be overridden, even by royalty. It is also evident by the punishment of Daniel's accusers that Daniel is unmarried. In Persian law, the family of the guilty were punished along with him, as in the book of Esther when Haman's ten sons were hanged on the gallows that he had built for Mordechai (Esther 4:13,14).

The next verse in chapter six reveals the king's fury directed toward these who initiated Daniel's punishment:

At the king's command, the men who had falsely accused Daniel were brought in and thrown into the lions' den, along with their wives and children. And before they reached the floor of the den, the lions overpowered them and crushed all their bones.

v. 24

We can see that Daniel's preservation was not because the lions were not hungry: God shut their mouths. It is now obvious to the king that Daniel is true and righteous in contrast to his satraps who now had to bear the consequences of "false accusers."

A ministering angel took care of Daniel (v. 22). When the real guilty parties were thrown to the lions, the beasts' hunger and natural instincts were put back into action by heavenly decree.

Another King Delivered to God's Throne

Chapter six fades with the God of the Israelites getting center stage and the recognition due Him under the rulership of Daniel and his compatriots once again.

Then King Darius wrote to all the peoples, nations and men of every language throughout the land! "May you prosper greatly! I issue a decree that in every part of my kingdom people must fear and reverence the God of Daniel. For he is the living God and he endures forever; his kingdom will not be destroyed; his dominion will never end. He rescues and he saves; he performs signs and wonders in the heavens and on the earth. He has rescued Daniel from the power of the lions." So Daniel prospered during the reign of Darius and the reign of Cyrus the Persian."

vv. 25-28

It is amazing that once again a king who ruled a city under the shadow of a pantheon of gods is actually declaring that the God of Israel reigns over the hierarchy of the Babylonian pantheon.

Through Daniel and his friends, Babylon has become a spiritual crucible where gods are brought to their knees. What Babylonian god could do the miracles we have so far been observing from the grandstands? The Kingdom of God dwelling in tabernacles of flesh was a catalyst for demonstrative change.

The Lord uses Daniel once again and causes a king to encounter the Living God, who by this incident is elevated and glorified before the whole kingdom. All the qualities that God placed in Daniel seemed to come together for just such a mission.

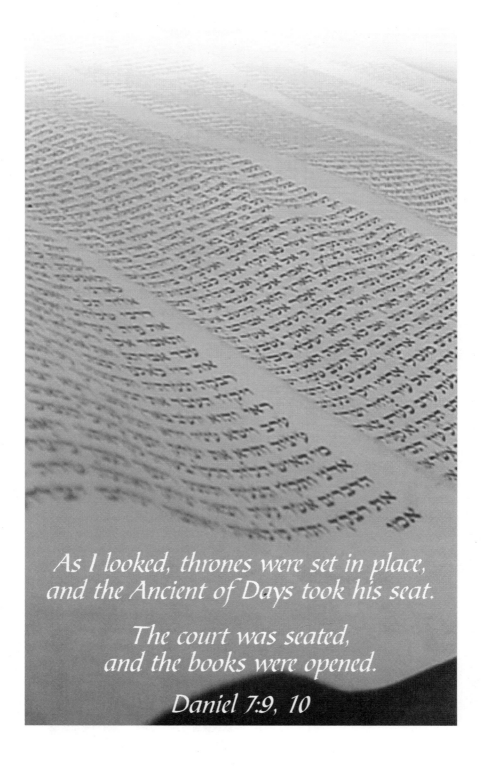

*As I looked, thrones were set in place,
and the Ancient of Days took his seat.*

*The court was seated,
and the books were opened.*

Daniel 7:9, 10

The Ancient of Days

According to Bible scholars, chapter seven precedes chapter five. The first two verses say:

In the first year of Belshazzar king of Babylon, Daniel had a dream, and visions passed through his mind as he was lying on his bed. He wrote down the substance of his dream. Daniel said: "In my vision at night I looked, and there before me were the four winds of heaven churning up the great sea."

Daniel 7:1,2

Prior to Belshazzar's downfall, Daniel himself is being enlightened by messages from on high.

Four great beasts, each different from the others, came up out of the sea.

The first was like a lion, and it had the wings of an eagle. I watched until its wings were torn off and it was lifted from the ground so that it stood on two feet like a man, and the heart of a man was given to it.

And there before me was a second beast, which looked like a bear. It was raised up on one of its sides, and it had three ribs in its mouth between its teeth. It was told, 'Get up and eat your fill of flesh!'

After that, I looked, and there before me was another beast, one that looked like a leopard. And on its back it had four wings like those of a bird. This beast had four heads, and it was given authority to rule.

After that, in my vision at night I looked, and there before me was a fourth beast—terrifying and frightening and very powerful. It had large iron teeth; it crushed and devoured its victims and trampled underfoot whatever was left. It was different from all the former beasts, and it had ten horns.

While I was thinking about the horns, there before me was another horn, a little one, which came up among them; and three of the first horns were uprooted before it. This horn had eyes like the eyes of a man and a mouth that spoke boastfully."

vv. 3-8

The Final Kingdom

These four beasts were symbolic of coming imperial administrations. The first looked like a lion with wings. To appreciate the weight of these beasts and the empires they represented, it helps to know where else a "winged lion" has been mentioned.

Greeting cards have often portrayed *cherubs* as baby-like angelic beings with tiny wings and whimsical expressions. Actually, a cherub is more like this winged lion of whom likenesses have been found in the palaces of Nineveh and Babylon. It was a cherub whose presence was fearsome enough to guard the path to the Garden of Eden after the expulsion of Adam and Eve (Gen. 1:24). The Hebrew word for "cherub" is *charuv*. These magnificent heavenly winged creatures were attached to the cover of the Ark of the Covenant (Ex. 25:18-22).

Later, when the Temple was constructed, larger *cherubim* were placed in the Holy of Holies to overshadow the Ark itself (I Ki. 6:23-28, Heb. 9:5). The physical presence of heavenly beings has been diminished in our present day and age to the point that we make light of them. Actually, upon beholding angels and other heavenly beings, the Scriptures document men falling face down in a death-like state. They actually have to be physically raised up by the angelic being and reassured not to be afraid. English translates *charuvim* [which is the plural form in Hebrew] as "cherubim". The "im" on the end of any Hebrew word delineates the masculine plural form of a noun. Therefore, it is not necessary to add an "s" to cherubim, i.e., cherubims, as this would create an unnecessary doubling of a plural.

This picture of fearsome heavenly beings overshadowing the Ark of the Covenant, not with expressions of anger but with the body language of awesome submission and adoration of God Almighty in Heaven, is powerful. The mental picture underscores the importance God places on "covering" and "protecting." *"He who dwells in the shelter of the Most High will rest in the shadow of the Almighty"* (Psalm 91:1). A wonderful picture of a protected place where one can abide in safety. This is diametrically opposed to the guarding cherub at the gates of the Garden of Eden. On this side of the atonement, provided by Messiah's crucifixion, we fear God—in the sense of reverencing Him, but He also means for us to enjoy Him.

Babylonian Empire

Daniel's vision of this "winged lion" was not exactly the biblical cherub, however. It is not an eternal being whose longevity of existence was ordained by God. According to these verses, this lion was defeathered, then the wings were ripped off. These acts were symbolic of the future of the Babylonian Empire. The picture was of Nebuchadnezzar's and Belshazzar's humbling, and the eventual loss of their kingdom.

Medo-Persian Empire

The "bear" is an appropriate symbol for the empire it represents. It is massive in size, slow in responsiveness, but determined and dangerous. The bear's position is important, though easily overlooked. If the bear is raising itself up on one side, that must mean there is "another" side. Lifting himself up on one "side," he is described as eating "three ribs (v. 5)." According to historians' documentation of the time period, the bear represents the Medo-Persian Empire which was comprised of two powerful kingdoms banded together to conquer the Assyrians, and later to become a mighty ruling world power.

Persia held the upper hand in the government of the combined empire. The "three ribs" represent the three major conquests of the Medo-Persians: Lydia, Babylon, and Egypt. The bear image well symbolizes the Medo-Persian Empire. Slow and heavy, with massive strength characteristic of a bear, the Medo-Persian Empire's armies, even on moderate expeditions, ranged from 300,000 to a full million men. Darius marched through the desolate regions of Scythia with 700,000 men, plus a fleet of six hundred ships carrying a naval force of 122,000 men. Xerxes, also of the same empire, came against Greece with 2,500,000 men. Artaxerxes brought an army against his brother, Cyrus the Younger, of 900,000 men, followed by 300,000—more who simply arrived late to the battle site. The Medo-Persian Empire outstripped all others in sheer quantities of fighting men.

Greek Empire

Size and massive strength might be held aloft as the ultimate goal and the last word in world-conquering empires. The described animal proves otherwise: a leopard—the animal

125

kingdom's darling of sleekness—with four wings. No excess fat adorns a leopard, just rippling muscle and flashing speed. Leopards have been clocked at over seventy miles per hour. They are beautiful animals to behold, and the one described here is a quadra-winged creature.

The leopard representation is another look at Alexander the Great. The four heads speak again of the four quadrants into which Alexander's empire was divided upon his death. Like a comet, he lit up the sky, stringing conquered cities like pearls on a necklace: Troy, Ancyra (Ankara in modern Turkey), Tarsus, Sidon, Tyre (in modern Lebanon), Memphis (Cairo), Alexandria, in the south; then on to Damascus, Opis (Baghdad), Babylon, Ecbatana, through Persia to the Far East—even as far as China.

Alexander's flame of fame glowed long after his demise. It is even thought that the custom of depicting Jesus with blonde hair and blue eyes came from early Christians ascribing the attributes of the world-conquering Alexander to him.

Final Beast of Terror

Alexander is now eclipsed in the symbolism by a terrible beast. This beast is so savage that there is no animal to depict it. The Scripture says it has ten horns and ten toes. This may or may not mean exactly the number ten. In Hebrew thought, number amounts are at times represented by round numbers. Hebrew thought differed from Hellenistic thought patterns. The Greeks and Romans were not comfortable unless "A" preceded "B" and "C" followed. Chronological thought processes are foreign to the Hebrew mental make-up. A good example is chapter seven of the book of Daniel preceding chapter five.

A word about "horns" is necessary. Michelangelo's incredibly powerful sculpture of Moses, adorning the tomb of Pope Julius II in Rome, wears horns on his head. A Latin Vulgate mistranslation of the Hebrew word *keren* is responsible. *Keren* has many meanings in Hebrew, of which "horn" is only one, and one that is more rarely used than others. *Keren* also means "principal" or "capital" (as in finances), "fund," a "ray of light," or "corner." It is also used to describe the "corner" of the altar—or the "horns" of the altar. It also can mean "angle." Therefore, we see that Moses coming down off the mountain (in the Hebrew mind [Ex. 34:29]) is glorious with rays of light (*karan*—horn) emanating from his head, while the Moses of Renaissance paintings is represented as a horned creature.

126

Hannah's prayer in I Samuel 2:1, says, ". . . *My horn is exalted in the Lord . . ."* (NKJV). She is not referring to a protrusion on her head. Here, it would most likely be translated as "my strength." There are many places in Scripture where *keren* is used. God uses this word of David in Psalm 132:17 when He says, *"There I will make the* horn *of David to grow. I will prepare a lamp for My Anointed"* (NKJV). In this passage it would no doubt mean his "rulership" or "kingship."

I remember an episode of an American television series called "Little House on the Prairie" where a Jewish cabinet maker moves to the Midwest and sets up his cabinet shop. Albert, the young man who was playing the part of the little boy adopted by Charles and his family, takes up with the Jewish man and they become close friends. For awhile, he becomes his assistant in the cabinet shop. One of the episodes deals with Albert trying to get the Jewish man to take his hat off, because he had heard that Jews had horns. Finally, the elderly Jewish man catches on to what Albert is doing and explains that it was a mistranslation from the Hebrew word. The answer solved Albert's whole dilemma.

Satan's "Final Kingdom"

Sensationalist methods of interpreting prophecy inhibit the more important aspects of Daniel. Using Daniel only to uncover the schedule of the coming of the Messiah misses the point of the book dramatically. It has a very important part but must stay embedded in the context and story line of the entire book.

In Daniel's vision, a "boastful" horn raises its head. This boastful horn is a prophetic foreshadowing of the coming antichrist. Prophecy is like heading across a broad plain to a mountain range on the other side. While crossing the plain you see the mountains as only a line of jagged purple on the horizon. For many miles, it looks like one large mountain. As you come closer to the mountain, you begin to see some distinction. The closer you get, the more obvious it becomes that it is not just one high mountain, but rather lots of little hills that compose the foothills of the mountains. Gradually the hills get larger, and finally the hills become almost mountains themselves before you can begin to make an ascent to the peak. Likewise, as we go through Daniel we will see things that look like the fulfillment of prophecies in the book. Oftentimes though, they do not quite meet the final exacting standards of the whole picture.

The Final Kingdom

One of the foothills of prophecy is the depiction of the "little horn"—Antiochus Epiphanes IV. In Greek, his name means "god in the flesh." The uprooting of three horns by the little horn describe him overthrowing Ptolemy Philometer, Ptolemy Evergetis, and Artarxia the King of Armenia.

While I was thinking about the horns, there before me was another horn, a little one, which came up among them; and three of the first horns were uprooted before it. This horn had eyes like the eyes of a man and a mouth that spoke boastfully.

7:8

Anyone bearing a name meaning "god incarnate" would certainly be a candidate for the office of "boastful person." At this juncture of history we have come to the place where rulers view themselves as deity.

The fourth beast, *"terrifying and frightening and very powerful,"* symbolizes the last world empire the Bible considers important enough to play a major role in history—Rome. Historically, Rome disappeared into the sands of time almost two millenia ago. But then again, maybe it did not.

John and the prophet Daniel have much in common: prisoners for the sake of their religious beliefs; held captive in places far from their homes; visions of such intensity that their physical bodies suffer illness. Parallelisms in their writings cannot be dismissed, and particularly at this point in our exploration they must be compared.

The "beast" of John's revelation has all the characteristics of Daniel's beasts combined.

And the dragon stood on the shore of the sea. And I saw a beast coming out of the sea. He had ten horns and seven heads, with ten crowns on his horns, and on each head a blasphemous name.

The beast I saw resembled a leopard, but had feet like those of a bear and a mouth like that of a lion. The dragon gave the beast his power and his throne and great authority.

One of the heads of the beast seemed to have had a fatal wound, but the fatal wound had been healed. The whole world was astonished and followed the beast.

Revelation 13:1-3

What was only hinted at and foreshadowed in Daniel is now out from under wraps and standing in full sunlight. The restraints are flung off and wickedness in all its gore is unleashed on the earth. Satan's attempt to establish a final kingdom is rivaled only by God's equally open and abrassive counterattack to this hellish challenge.

How did Rome change the world and what "leftovers" of the empire are still around today? In the book of Revelation we see a resurrection of a Roman-style government with many of the earmarks of this first empire symbolized as the woman on the "beast" (Rev. 17).

This chapter of Revelation is more than pertinent to the "last days" time period which we are entering. "Babylon the Great" sitting on a beast in the desert, is described as arraying herself in "purple" and "scarlet."

Then the angel carried me away in the Spirit into a desert. There I saw a woman sitting on a scarlet beast that was covered with blasphemous names and had seven heads and ten horns.

The woman was dressed in purple and scarlet, and was glittering with gold, precious stones and pearls. She held a golden cup in her hand, filled with abominable things and the filth of her adulteries.

This title was written on her forehead:

MYSTERY

BABYLON THE GREAT

THE MOTHER OF PROSTITUTES

AND OF THE ABOMINATIONS OF THE EARTH.

vv. 3-5

Her "purple" garments would seem an insignificant point if it were not for the previous detailing of the importance of purple. Crossing lines and disregarding rules seems to be standard for this symbol of that once great city. She has now become a "prostitute" astride a "beast" with "ten horns" (symbolizing ten kings), and has sunk to the title, "Abominations of the earth." A serious slide downhill.

It appears that "Babylon the Great" of Daniel's time—laden with excessive riches and power—has digressed and become the symbol of all that is anti-God. Portrayed here is Satan's valiant attempt to set up a look-alike kingdom through the antichrist, but this kingdom too will crumble and come to its demise through the final judgment of God (Rev. 18:10).

Today, we speak about the shrinking of our planet due to advanced methods of travel and communication. Rome initiated this phenomenon with the paved road, making travel from one nation to another faster than had been imagined. These paved roads are still being excavated in many areas of the world. Many of these same roads became our modern-day roads.

Rome also changed the calendar. "August" came from Augustus Caesar and "July" from Julius Caesar. The alphabet we use today was perfected by the Romans—not just the letters themselves but the magnificent craftsmanship with which the letters were inscribed. Worldwide, awe-inspiring Roman inscriptions can be found which exhibit a grace and style which, even with today's technology, are hard to emulate. The language in which those letters communicate, Latin, served as the basis for all Romance languages.

Rome sought to influence not only language, communication, and commerce, but religion as well. The restrictions on religion changed as Rome matured, moving from *tolerance* for conquered territories' religions to *intolerance*. Finally, by the time Roman Emperors declared themselves gods and demanded worship from the populace, devotion to another god could mean death. The residue of influence clung to Italy, the strongest of the Roman colonies. The Renaissance of the 16th century was a revival of Roman thought. This can be seen in many places. Paintings of Jesus with his mother Mary abound, showing the baby Jesus uncircumcised. The Jewish roots of Christianity had been smothered in Romanesque theology and culture.

Only in the last one hundred years or so has a widespread movement among Christians come into being recognizing the fact that Jesus was born Jewish and underwent *all* the ceremonies included in Judaism. He was circumcised on the eighth day, and on the fortieth day was taken to the Temple for the *Pideon HaBen*, meaning the "dedication of the firstborn son."

Simeon took him in his arms and praised God, saying:

"Sovereign Lord, as you have promised, you now dismiss your servant in peace.

For my eyes have seen your salvation, which you have prepared in the sight of all people, a light for revelation to the Gentiles and for glory to your people Israel."

Luke 2:21-32

Every firstborn son of Israel was taken to the Temple in Jerusalem and dedicated to the Lord.

Roman democratic-style government, much of which was good, still abides with us today. Many nations of the world operate with a senate or a parliament, where state issues are debated by members considered among the wise of the populace. The inherent danger is that when Rome resurfaces in the last days, the substructure is already in place.

The "fourth" beast's indefinable terror must come echoing down the ages to us from the corrupt Roman Empire. In its last days, all reason took leave from its rulers. Rome began to fall apart in A.D. 426, one colony after another. The fall of Rome was the result of political and moral values so corrupt that they could no longer be tolerated by God.

Now, the throne room of Heaven is opened and God's counterplan is detailed against Satan's earthly schemes.

The Ancient of Days

Descriptions of Daniel's vision of the throne of the Ancient of Days in chapter seven are inadequate in earthly terms. This is a decidedly heart-arresting revelation of the final Kingdom! The characteristics of God listed in these six verses are unrivaled in any literature, at any time, describing any god. White hair, white clothes, throne of fire with blazing wheels, river of fire, and ten thousand times ten thousand—one hundred million beings standing before the Ancient of Days in awe and worship. He shares no throne space with any earthly king. Glorious in appearance, yet delivering authority and power of such importance that worship is ascribed to One described as "a son of man [a term for Messiah] coming with the clouds of heaven" (v. 13). This is echoed again in the Gospel of Mark.

"I am," Jesus said. "And you will see the Son of Man sitting at the right hand of the Mighty One and coming in the clouds of heaven."

Mark 14:62

131

The Final Kingdom

John, in a parallel reference, and similar to Daniel's vision, describes this "son of man" for us in his revelation:

And among the lampstands was someone "like a son of man", dressed in a robe reaching down to his feet and with a golden sash round his chest.

His head and hair were white like wool, as white as snow, and his eyes were like blazing fire.

His feet were like bronze glowing in a furnace, and his voice was like the sound of rushing waters.

In his right hand he held seven stars, and out of his mouth came a sharp double-edged sword. His face was like the sun shining in all its brilliance.

Revelation 1:13-16

This authoritative "son of man" designation from the most High, reaches its zenith in the end of days. He appears in the heavens as an ensign for all nations of the earth to view.

At that time the sign of the Son of Man will appear in the sky, and all the nations of the earth will mourn. They will see the Son of Man coming on the clouds of the sky, with power and great glory. And he will send his angels with a loud trumpet call, and they will gather his elect from the four winds, from one end of the heavens to the other.

Matthew 24:30-31

Daniel's inimitable description of the throne room of the Ancient of Days is earthshaking.

As I looked, thrones were set in place, and the Ancient of Days took his seat. His clothing was as white as snow; the hair of his head was white like wool. His throne was flaming with fire, and its wheels were all ablaze.

A river of fire was flowing, coming out from before him. Thousands upon thousands attended him; ten thousand times ten thousand stood before him. The court was seated, and the books were opened. Then I continued to watch because of the boastful words the horn was speaking. I kept looking until the beast was slain and its body destroyed and thrown into the blazing fire. (The other beasts had been stripped of their authority, but were allowed to live for a period of time.)

In my vision at night I looked, and there before me was one like a son of man, coming with the clouds of heaven. He approached the Ancient of Days and was led into his presence. He was given authority, glory and sovereign power; all peoples, nations and men of every language worshiped him. His dominion is an everlasting dominion that will not pass away, and his kingdom is one that will never be destroyed.

7:9-14

Sovereignty is a weighty issue: limitless power, absolute dominion. This authority, once imparted, becomes an everlasting dominion—a kingdom that will *never* be destroyed—the *final* Kingdom!

What is different about this throne room from other descriptions of the throne of God elsewhere in the Bible? And why? It is a judgment scene, differing significantly from the judgment scenes in the book of Revelation (Rev. 22:1, 2). It is with purpose that this scene is different. When we see the throne room in Revelation and in the book of Ezekiel, a river of water flows out from the throne (Ezek. 47:1-6). Here, in this section of Daniel, the river flowing from the throne of God is a river of *fire*.

The revelation to Babylon, at this particular time, underscores the characteristic of God—making the message fit the time and place. God actually marries the message to the people to whom it is being delivered. Remember from the last chapter that the Babylonian kingdom, at this time, is being ruled by the Medes and Persians who were fire worshipers. God wants to meet the Medo-Persian rulership with an eye-opening revelation that He is the God of holy fire and not Ahuramazda, the god whom they worshiped. Secondarily, the beast is destroyed by being thrown into the "blazing fire" (Dan. 7:11) against the law of the Zoroastrians.

In a similar situation, Paul delivers the message of the Gospel through a familar legend. Paul went to Athens and told the Athenians that he had come to declare to them the "Unknown God."

For as I walked around and looked carefully at your objects of worship, I even found an altar with this inscription: TO AN UNKNOWN GOD. *Now what you worship as something unknown I am going to proclaim to you.*

The God who made the world and everything in it is the Lord

133

of heaven and earth and does not live in temples built by hands.

Acts 17:23, 24

Paul used the story of a Cretan philosopher by the name of Epimenides. In 600 B.C. Athens had been stricken with a plague. The Athenians sought the counsel of a very wise Cretan philosopher who advised them to let a number of hungry sheep graze on Mars Hill. If any of the sheep were to lay down in the grass at feeding time rather than grazing, as would have been usual, this was to be an indication that an unknown god—who would reveal himself at a later time—was acknowledging his presence and was asking for those sheep that had refused to graze to be sacrificed to him.

The legend says that some of the sheep did indeed lay down and were then sacrificed on altars built and dedicated to an "Unknown God." The plague broke, and from that day on there was preserved at least one altar in Athens dedicated to a benevolent god who had yet to reveal himself. Whether the story of Epimenides was true or not, the altar was there and the legend was used by Paul to lead the Athenians to God.

Paul knew the literature of the Greeks and their mindset on religious themes. God was able to wed His message to the people of Athens by using terms and mental images with which they were familiar.

Back in the heavenly throne room, "the *books* were opened." This is an important spiritual precept. The Scripture does not say *a* book was opened, but "books." When we think of the Day of Judgment, we think only of the Book of Life that will reveal our names inscribed for eternal life. But there are other books. And the tenderness of this Almighty Glorious Being revealed in the book of Malachi is disarming.

God's Scrapbook

Malachi 3:16 says, *"Then those who feared the Lord talked with each other, and the LORD listened and heard. . ."* In Hebrew, when a verb is repeated twice, or a close form of a verb is used, doubling the thought, it is for a very important reason. It is a Hebraic way of telling you, "Pay attention! Something very important is happening here!" *". . . the Lord listened and heard. A scroll of remembrance was written in his presence concerning those who*

134

feared the Lord and honored his name." God calls His heavenly scribe. I can almost hear Him saying, *Listen, these people who love Me have all gathered to talk about My goodness.* The scribe's job is to write down what is being said. This could be considered something like, "God's Scrapbook." God is having these conversations recorded in a scroll for the day when the books are opened. Verse 17 goes on to say, *"They will be mine, says the Lord Almighty, in the day when I make up my treasured possession. I will spare them, just as in compassion a man spares his son who serves him."*

What man gets up in the morning and decides whether to "spare" his son? No one I know, and hopefully no one you know. In modern life this seems preposterous, but in the days of the ancients, kings were the ones whose most vile enemies may have been members of their own families. In some places in the Scriptures, it is recorded that a king "strengthened his kingdom." That often involved putting members of his family to death who were rebellious and ambitious to wrest the crown from him.

The importance of this Scripture is the picture of the loving care that God has for His subjects. He is trying to say, *I care so much for you that I have written down even the words that you speak to each other about Me. I am going to gather you together as precious jewels to put into My treasure box. I am going to spare you as a king spares his son whom he sees has potential to follow him in the rulership of the kingdom.*

What a glorious picture of the opening of the books in the fiery throne room of God.

Daniel's Visions Make Him Ill

Daniel, who has been the interpreter of others' dreams, cannot interpret his own dream. Why? Because the gifts of God are not exclusive. God uses dreams to bring kings to His throne, to bring them to their knees, to elevate their kingdoms, to bring their kingdoms down, and now it is as if He is saying to Daniel, *I will give you a dream also, but I am Sovereign and you will not know what it means. Someone else will help you now. I have not handed you a gift that belongs exclusively to you to puff you up.* So, for the first time, Daniel has to call on someone standing by him in this vision to interpret its meaning.

I, Daniel, was troubled in spirit, and the visions that passed through my mind disturbed me. I approached one of those standing there and asked him the true meaning of all of this. So he told me and gave me the interpretation of all of these things: 'The four great beasts are four kingdoms that will rise from the earth. But the saints of the Most High will receive the kingdom and will possess it forever—yes, for ever and ever.'

Then I wanted to know the true meaning of the fourth beast, which was different from all the others and most terrifying, with iron teeth and bronze claws—the beast that crushed and devoured its victims and trampled underfoot whatever was left. I also wanted to know about the ten horns on its head and about the other horn that came up, before which three of them fell—the horn that looked more imposing than the others and that had eyes and a mouth that spoke boastfully. As I watched, this horn was waging war against the saints and defeating them.

Until the Ancient of Days came and pronounced judgment in favor of the saints of the Most High, and the time came when they possessed the kingdom.

7:15-22

The Ancient of Days comes and pronounces "judgment in favor of the saints of the most High." God is affirming His favor for you and me. When God says: *These are My people and I am in favor of them,* things change. It is, in fact, a vote against the kingdom of darkness. *"If God is for us, who can be against us?"* (Rom. 8:31). We have the promise of Yeshua as He said, ". . . *And surely I am with you always, to the very end of the age"* (Matt. 28:20).

The "beast" will come on the scene in the last days, opposing God in arrogant, boastful ways and will declare war on the saints.

And he shall speak [great] words against the most High, and shall wear out the saints of the most High, and think to change times and laws: and they shall be given into his hand until a time and times and the dividing of time. But the judgment shall sit, and they shall take away his dominion, to consume and to destroy [it] unto the end.

Daniel 7:25, 26 (KJV)

The saints of God will experience the worst kind of opposition ever known in the history of God's people. According to this section of Daniel (v. 21), and Revelation, Satan is waging war against them and is "defeating" them. He is literally wearing them

136

down in the hopes of ultimately being victorious over them.

He was given power to make war against the saints and to conquer them. And he was given authority over every tribe, people, language and nation.

All inhabitants of the earth will worship the beast—all whose names have not been written in the book of life belonging to the Lamb that was slain from the creation of the world.

Revelation 13:7, 8

God intervenes—He always does. In fact, we can count on the Ancient of Days exercising His judgment against this look-alike kingdom—false and satanically inspired.

Satan is known by his prideful manner and antichrist religious practices throughout history. The saints of God will of course oppose him and all that he stands for. Not unlike what Daniel and his compatriots experienced here in Babylon, God will empower these saints to endure until the end even though it costs them their lives. Even as the kingdom of Babylon in Daniel's day, God Almighty will be known as the Ruler of all kingdoms, while the "Great Babylon" and this final earthly kingdom and its rulers will fall. The Lord will be victorious over all the kingdoms in the final hour and His saints will possess the kingdom.

The visions that are shaking Daniel to his core continue with the angel's explanation:

He gave me this explanation: 'The fourth beast is a fourth kingdom that will appear on earth. It will be different from all the other kingdoms and will devour the whole earth, trampling it down and crushing it.

The ten horns are ten kings who will come from this kingdom. After them another king will arise, different from the earlier ones; he will subdue three kings.

He will speak against the Most High and oppress his saints and try to change the set times and the laws. The saints will be handed over to him for a time, times and half a time.'

7:23-26

The terrifying vision that overwhelms Daniel to the point of illness is another view of the antichrist of Revelation and his final kingdom—whose duration is "time, times and half a time" (three and a half years). The saints being handed over to this devourer is certainly instrumental in Daniel's mental state of being.

137

The Final Kingdom

But the court will sit, and his power will be taken away and completely destroyed for ever.

Then the sovereignty, power and greatness of the kingdoms under the whole heaven will be handed over to the saints, the people of the Most High. His kingdom will be an everlasting kingdom, and all rulers will worship and obey him.

This is the end of the matter. I, Daniel, was deeply troubled by my thoughts, and my face turned pale, but I kept the matter to myself.

vv. 26-28

Perseverance in the face of trouble yeilds great reward. The power and greatness of all earthly kingdoms is being reserved for the saints of God. History verifies that this is no common statement. There have been great empires throughout the centuries, but they will pale in the face of God's final kingdom and the rulership will belong to those who overcame.

This revelation made Daniel physically ill. I have not had many visions in my life, but I can imagine that a vision with the weight that this one carried could make you physically ill. Daniel simply held this vision in his heart. He did not run to tell the others what he had experienced. I am sure it took some days to sort out all the emotions of such an encounter.

And They Sat Down

Two phrases mentioned in these verses about the Ancient of Days make points which punctuate the heavenly vision majestically.

". . .thrones were set in place, and the Ancient of Days took his seat. . ." (7:9), and, "But the court will sit, and his power [the "beast"] will be taken away and completely destroyed forever" (v. 26).

Many times, ceremonies of the earthly Temple or even architecture and furniture were copied from heavenly visions or directives. Some earthly practices of ceremony seem to echo the picture of God's supreme court in Heaven. Sitting down in the Scriptures has deeper meaning than just taking your seat.

Yeshua teaching in the synagogue illustrates the point. He stood and read from the section of the scroll of Isaiah announcing that "the year of the Lord's favor" had arrived. Then he *sat* down.

Then he rolled up the scroll, gave it back to the attendant and sat down. The eyes of everyone in the synagogue were fastened on him, and he began by saying to them, "Today this scripture is fulfilled in your hearing."

Luke 4:20, 21

The ceremonial structure of the synagogue service during Yeshua's time, which came from Babylon, seems to imitate what Daniel saw in his vision. Synagogue services were conducted by one called the *darshan*, from the word *derash*, meaning to "seek out" or to "search out." He could be labeled Rabbi or Minister in modern terminology. The job of the darshan was to make the heavenly message from the Scriptures come to life and apply to the circumstances of the day, much like our modern sermons. The synagogue was called to order only when the darshan took his seat. Then all eyes were fixed upon him as he proclaimed the prepared exposé from the Scriptures.

Standing next to the darshan on the platform called a *bima*, was a man considered second-in-command. His job was to be well aquainted with all passages of Scripture and where they could be located in the scrolls. During the darshan's sermon, this man would bend close to the darshan and whisper the location of the passages from which the darshan was expositing. Men like these later came to be known as *Tannaim*. They were the sages who were authorities on the Scriptures.

Not far from the man who was second-in-command stood the *meturgeman*, who would "interpret" the message into another language, if there was a need to do so. In light of this, Yeshua was taking His rightful place as the darshan, in line with the synagogue service structure. His speaking as "one having authority," now makes sense.

They were amazed at his teaching, because his message had authority.

Luke 4:32

In the Jewish book *Parashiot Maagdot HaTannaim* there is a story that, in the end of time, God Himself will "sit down" in the Garden of Eden and give a *Torah Hadasha*, "new law," and that it will be delivered by the hand of the Messiah. Then Zerubbabel, from the royal line of David, and Joshua the high priest will say "Amen!" And all the earth will respond, "Amen!" Zerubbabel is also in the direct geneological line of the Messiah (Matt. 1:12).

The Final Kingdom

Zerubbabel's pronouncement of the "Amen" which all *must* respond to by saying "Amen" is actually part of a prayer that was recited at the end of each synagogue service. The prayer has come to be called the "Mourner's Kaddish" and is recited in modern synagogues as a memorial prayer for deceased loved ones. But the prayer was not always recited as a memorial prayer.

The Kaddish is actually a prayer of great adoration and praise for God Almighty, the most High, and was used at the end of teaching sessions in early synagogue services. There is probably no liturgical prayer anywhere with more declarations of worship for God or descriptive magnifying language than this one.

This is the prayer recited at the end of Steven Spielberg's movie about the Holocaust, *Schindler's List*. When Schindler called for two minutes of silence in memory of the slain millions of European Jews, the Jewish people gathered there in his factory allowed about fifteen seconds to pass out of courtesy for Schindler. However, Jewish people do not observe "silence" for the dead. Instead, they recite the Kaddish:

The Kaddish

Magnified and sanctified be His Great Name
In the world which He hath created according to His will.
May He establish His kingdom during your life
And during your days, yeah, and during the life
Of all the house of Israel, even speedily and soon.
    And all say Amen: Amen!

May His Great Name be blessed forever, to all eternity,
Blessed, and praised, and glorified, and exalted, and extolled,
And revered, and highly honored, and lauded
Be the Name of the Holy One, Blessed be He,
Beyond all blessings, above and beyond all hymns, and praises,
And consolations that are uttered in the world.
    And say ye Amen: Amen!

May there be total and abundant peace from Heaven
And life for us, and for all Israel.
    And all say Amen: Amen!

He who makes peace in the heavens,
He will make peace over us, and and over all Israel.
    And all say Amen: Amen!

I must mention the author Chaim Potok, who wrote *The Chosen* (also made into a movie), as well as *The Book of Lights*, as a brief explanation of the Kaddish. *The Book of Lights* is about Jewish scientists who were conscripted by the United States Government to create the atomic bomb. They agreed, convinced it would be used against Hitler's Nazi regime. They were horrified when it was used instead against the nation of Japan. The children of these nuclear physicists grew up under a great weight of guilt, transferred as they witnessed their parents' struggles.

The two main characters, Gershon Loran and Arthur Leiden, are both rabbinical students during the Korean conflict and are drafted into the armed forces due to the shortage of Jewish Rabbis in the military. They are both stationed in Korea for their term of duty. Arthur suffers guilt more acutely than Gershon and flies to Japan on every military leave he gets. He stands at the atom bomb site and questions God, begging for an answer about what could be done to atone, in some way, for the tragedy. Arthur dies in a plane crash on one of his Japan excursions, leaving Gershon alone to cope, not only with their weight of guilt, but also with his friend's death.

The end of the book focuses on Gershon back in the United States after his tour of duty. In one of his introspective moments he has a vision. In his vision, Satan comes to him with the accusation that nothing could be done about the catastrophy caused by the atomic bomb. Deep in despair, Gershon sinks to the floor in a paralyzed state. From the depths of his soul, the first line from the Kaddish prayer bubbles up, *Itgadal, v'itkadash, sh'mea rabbah,* "Magnified and sanctified be His Great Name."

As we saw concerning Zerubbabel at the end of God's proclamation, he said "Amen," and all the earth responded, "Amen!" Thus it is so with the Kaddish. Synagogue participants are required to respond to the Kaddish in several places in agreement by saying, "Amen." This is a universal law for all time, that when God is finally revealed in majesty, all creation responds:

By myself I have sworn, my mouth has uttered in all integrity a word that will not be revoked: Before me every knee will bow; by me every tongue will swear.

Isaiah 45:23

In Chaim Potok's book, Gershon seems to be standing by as God puts the words of the Kaddish in his mouth. Then, with Satan standing face to face with him, Gershon arrives at the place in the prayer where he pronounces "Amen." Here we see the unwritten law in operation. Satan is standing there, unwillingly being forced to hear an ancient proclamation of the sovereignty and majesty of God Almighty. There is a long, pregnant silence. In great agony of spirit and mind, Satan must respond with the only answer that is permissable or acceptable: "Amen!"

There are several Scriptures that reveal the existence of this unwritten law of the double affirmation of "Amen."

Ezra praised the LORD, the great God; and all the people lifted their hands and responded, "Amen! Amen!" Then they bowed down and worshiped the LORD with their faces to the ground.

Nehemiah 8:6

Praise be to the LORD, the God of Israel, from everlasting to everlasting. Amen and Amen.

Psalm 41:13

Praise be to his glorious name forever; may the whole earth be filled with his glory. Amen and Amen.

Psalm 72:19

Praise be to the LORD forever! Amen and Amen.

Psalm 89:52

Praise be to the LORD, the God of Israel, from everlasting to everlasting. Let all the people say, "Amen!" Praise the LORD.

Psalm 106:48

From Genesis to Revelation this antiphonal response is evident. Wrapping up time as we know it. John's Revelation of the last days of planet earth also reiterates this law. The subject matter is the return of the Messiah.

Look, he is coming with the clouds, and every eye will see him, even those who pierced him; and all the peoples of the earth will mourn because of him. So shall it be! Amen.

Revelation 1:7

"So shall it be" is the same as saying "Amen." Here again is the double affirmation of an anouncement of the coming of Yeshua, Messiah of Israel. This Scripture even points out that the people will "*mourn* because of him." Nevertheless, all the people of the earth will respond to "So shall it be!" by saying, "Amen."

One day, all created beings in Heaven and earth will come

before the Ancient of Days echoing that heavenly affirmation, "Amen." All titles and accomplishments, both good and evil, will be placed aside as ones such as Nebuchadnezzar, Alexander the Great, Buddha, Confucius, Hitler, Stalin, Mussolini, Mohammed, and yes, even Satan himself and all the fallen angels, will respond to heaven's proclamations with the only answer permitted, "Amen!"

When Daniel saw the courts of Heaven seated, it seemed to underscore the power and authority of the heavenly decree, that the imitation kingdom, forged from arrogant foolishness by the antichrist, will be shattered and then scattered, not leaving even a trace.

Because you have clapped your hands
and stamped your feet,
rejoicing with all the malice
of your heart against
the land of Israel,
therefore I will stretch out my hand
against you
and give you as plunder
to the nations.
I will cut you off from the nations
and exterminate you from the
countries.
I will destroy you
and you will know that I am the LORD.

Ezekiel 25:6, 7
Oracle against Ammon

Alexander's likeness on a Greek coin, in which he sports a lion head as a hat.

On the Banks of the Ulai

Now the Aramaic text of Daniel reverts back to Hebrew. The local Mesopotamian information broadens to encompass the rest of the world. Two years after the vision of the preceding chapter, the future continues to unfold before Daniel in dreams and visions that he still cannot interpret. Scholars also place this chapter before chapter five. Chapter seven took place in the first year of Belshazzar's Empire and chapter eight in the third year of his reign.

In the present vision, Daniel finds himself in Susa, several hundred miles southeast of Babylon, in the province of Elam. Susa was the major city of Elam, located in a fertile plain one hundred and fifty miles north of the Persian Gulf. Susa lies in a place where several rivers head into the Gulf and is graced by an abundance of water and canals that crisscross the area, one of those being the Ulai. From Daniel's description, the palace was near the Ulai Canal. The "voice" speaking to Daniel is recorded as coming from the canal.

It is fairly certain that Daniel was not physically in Susa. The vision most likely centers itself there because it is the seat of the upcoming Medo-Persian government. Daniel's vision is not bound by physical localities. In this, Daniel's story is like the experiences of John, who never physically left the island of Patmos but traversed the heavenlies in the Spirit (Rev. 1:9,10).

The setting of the book of Esther is also in the palace at Shushan (Susa). We certainly get a more detailed description of Susa from the book of Esther. But, even better than that are the finds of archaeologists in the last two centuries. The city sits on four mounds nestled together and is fenced in on one side by the Sha'ur river. The area of the city nearest the river is the acropolis, rising about one hundred feet above the river. The tomb of Daniel sits there to this day. It is amazing that the tomb of a Jewish man is revered as a sacred place by an Islamic populace.

In the third year of King Belshazzar's reign, I, Daniel, had a vision, after the one that had already appeared to me. In my vision I saw myself in the citadel of Susa in the province of Elam; in the vision I was beside the Ulai canal. I looked up,

The Final Kingdom

and there before me was a ram with two horns, standing beside the canal, and the horns were long. One of the horns was longer than the other but grew up later. I watched the ram as he charged toward the west and the north and the south. No animal could stand against him, and none could rescue from his power. He did as he pleased and became great.

Daniel 8:1-4

The Charging Ram

The "ram" that Daniel sees is the combined kingdom of the Medes and the Persians. One horn which appeared larger than the other in the vision meant that Persia was dominant over Media. The areas listed as having been "charged" by the ram omit the east, because east of Persia was desert, which lacked populace. The Fertile Crescent of Mesopotamia, which was discussed in the Introduction, lay to the north, west, and south of the conquering hero nation. The Fertile Crescent was the land area watered abundantly by the Tigris and Euphrates Rivers. These rivers provided irrigation for plants and crops; therefore, they supported large population centers, and over millennia were targets of many conquering nations. The Fertile Crescent extended from the mouth of the Tigris and Euphrates Rivers where they empty into the Persian Gulf, north through what is now Iraq, Syria, and the southeasternmost section of Turkey, where the waters find their source from melting snows on Mount Ararat. Abundant water meant that all armies, merchants, and travelers had to stick close to this crescent. Areas outside the irrigated margin were stark desert wasteland, supporting life only if an oasis existed.

In Mesopotamia, productive fertile crop land was at a premium and was left intact even in times of war. Conquering armies took nobility captive and most of the important city people, but left the peasants and the people who worked the land, so that they, as conquerors, would not "suffer loss." Taxes and tithes on crops were excised on those left behind to financially support the dominant nation. Sometimes there were population exchanges. For instance, the Assyrian's invasion of Israel in 722 B.C. resulted in demographic changes as some of the Jews were taken away to

146

populate Assyria and some of the people from Assyria were brought to Israel to be settled there.

As I was thinking about this, suddenly a goat with a prominent horn between his eyes came from the west, crossing the whole earth without touching the ground. He came toward the two-horned ram I had seen standing beside the canal and charged at him in great rage. I saw him attack the ram furiously, striking the ram and shattering his two horns. The ram was powerless to stand against him; the goat knocked him to the ground and trampled on him, and none could rescue the ram from his power.

vv. 5-7

The rapidly charging "goat" is Greece, and the prominent horn is Alexander the Great, "the first king" of verse 21 later on.

Ixander—the Hero

Ixander (as Arabic and Persian nations call Alexander the Great) is still, to this day, the hero/villain of village storytellers in remote sections of Iraq, Iran, and other places where his influence reached. Children gather in village squares on market day to hear the exciting adventures of Ixander told by traveling bards with gypsy-like wagons decorated as a sideshow. Alexander the Great, portrayed as an aggressive "goat" traveling so fast his feet did not touch the "ground," shatters the power of the ram with two horns—the Medes and the Persians (Dan. 8:21).

The history of Alexander, the Greek conqueror of the world of that day, shows a man with great knowledge of military strategy and wisdom to follow up on conquered areas. He left trained men behind him to govern and groom the conquered nations to become part of a greater empire. He was known to leave places of worship intact and, in fact, even to worship with his conquered peoples from time to time. Therefore, the "rage" with which he attacks the Persians is unique.

This rage probably reflects the hatred emanating from the Greeks toward the Persians for previous battles that had been waged against them from their distant neighbors in the east.

The biblical switch from "panther" to "goat" is interesting. A

147

panther is considered more dignified than a goat. Alexander's previous conquering tactics may have had an air of dignity, but here the rambunctious goat fits the allegory. In Alexander's march of history across the face of the Middle East, when methods other than the sword worked, Alexander used them. When Alexander came to Jerusalem enroute to Babylon, ready to loose his hordes upon the Holy City, he had a dream that persuaded him that a milder method would succeed with his Jewish subjects. According to the historian Josephus, the high priest of Jerusalem at the time had a complementary dream that resulted in a friendly conference between Alexander and himself. The story says that Alexander was shown the scroll of the book of Daniel and that he was so impressed with the prophecy about himself that he negotiated a peaceful occupation with the Jews, granting many of their religious requests. Like the oracle of Delphi, whom Alexander dragged forcibly to the temple to provide him a "good word," Alexander rode high on the clouds of his own glory upon discovering that his path was a predetermined path of destiny and military success recorded hundreds of years before in the scrolls of the Jews.

The unity of the Greek Empire under Alexander is symbolized by the fact that the goat had only one horn. His attack was furious and both horns of the ram were shattered. It does not appear as if he conquered one and then regrouped and conquered the other. Evidently his attack against the Medo-Persian Empire was quick and total—in effect, a shattering of those powers.

The goat became very great, but at the height of his power his large horn was broken off, and in its place four prominent horns grew up toward the four winds of heaven. Out of one of them came another horn, which started small but grew in power to the south and to the east and toward the Beautiful Land. It grew until it reached the host of the heavens, and it threw some of the starry host down to the earth and trampled on them. It set itself up to be as great as the Prince of the host; it took away the daily sacrifice from him, and the place of his sanctuary was brought low. Because of rebellion, the host of the saints and the daily sacrifice were given over to it. It prospered in everything it did, and truth was thrown to the ground.

vv. 8-12

148

The Shattered Empire

At the zenith of his career, the power of Alexander the Great was suddenly broken. He returned to Babylon for the last time in 323 B.C. Worn out by wounds, overindulgence in alcohol, and hardships, Alexander fell ill with a fever. His illness progressed quickly and soon he could neither speak nor move. Within two days Alexander the Great was dead. He was just short of the age of thirty-three. Alexander's empire survived intact for only a few years as his generals were struggling for power. "... *towards the four winds of heaven*" is the Scripture's manner of telling us that the kingdom suffered a division by Alexander's generals (v. 8). It is the horn that started small that should now capture our attention.

The Small Horn

The small horn's attention is turned toward a place called "*the Beautiful Land.*" This is an epithet for Israel. Israel is, in some ways, an unlikely spot to successfully hold the title of "Beautiful Land." Travelers seeking lofty snow-covered peaks and lush green valleys graced with rushing rivers vacation in Europe, not Israel!

Compared with Babylon and Egypt, Jerusalem was provincial. It did not hold a candle to Babylon's massive size and splendor. The glory and splendor of Egypt's dynasties far outshone Israel's humble existence. And yet, in this very fact lies a valuable spiritual lesson. It was not because of any obvious physical characteristic that God chose Jerusalem to place His name eternally. It seems to be an unlikely place to be chosen for such honor. "Unlikely to be chosen" is perhaps most Christians' claim to fame in the Kingdom of God as well. God chose Jerusalem because He wanted to. God also chose us because He chose to do so. The beauty of Jerusalem is God's presence within her. Therefore, we have much in common with the "Beautiful Land" that bears God's name eternally. We, as well, bear God's name eternally. Such a bond of kinship should cause every Christian to identify closely with Jerusalem.

This small horn, with his attention now trained on Jerusalem, seeks a lofty title:

The Final Kingdom

It grew until it reached the host of the heavens, and it threw some of the starry host down to the earth and trampled on them. It set itself up to be as great as the Prince of the host: it took away the daily sacrifice from him, and the place of his sanctuary was brought low.

vv. 10, 11

The "small horn" sought to be the "Prince of the Host." Commentators tell us that this epithet raises Antiochus to the place of a god.

In comparison, the description of the antichrist's deeds stand as a warning to take care against being led astray by outward manifestations of spiritual power in the last days. In the framework of religious parody—"had two horns like a lamb, but he spoke like a dragon"—this final false prophet/priest/messiah replays in real-time Nebuchadnezzar's deeds, with the addition of miraculous visual aids, such as fire being called down from heaven.

Then I saw another beast, coming out of the earth. He had two horns like a lamb, but he spoke like a dragon.

He exercised all the authority of the first beast on his behalf, and made the earth and its inhabitants worship the first beast, whose fatal wound had been healed. And he performed great and miraculous signs, even causing fire to come down from heaven to earth in full view of men.

Because of the signs he was given power to do on behalf of the first beast, he deceived the inhabitants of the earth. He ordered them to set up an image in honor of the beast who was wounded by the sword and yet lived. He was given power to give breath to the image of the first beast, so that it could speak and cause all who refused to worship the image to be killed.

Revelation 13:11-15

With his seat now in the Holy City, Antiochus has tampered with the apple of God's eye. His intent was to destroy the faith of the faithful of that "Beautiful Land."

Because of rebellion, the host of the saints and the daily sacrifice were given over to it. It prospered in everything it did, and truth was thrown to the ground.

Daniel 8:12

150

For a time it seems as if evil has won the battle, with Antiochus pressing the world into his mold. The Jews of Israel suffered greatly under his rule.

Then I heard a holy one speaking, and another holy one said to him, "How long will it take for the vision to be fulfilled—the vision concerning the daily sacrifice, the rebellion that causes desolation, and the surrender of the sanctuary and of the hosts that will be trampled underfoot?" And he said to me, "It will take 2,300 evenings and mornings; and then the sanctuary will be reconsecrated."

vv. 13-14

Morning and Evening Sacrifice

The NIV Study Bible sheds light on this particular Scripture. There were two daily sacrifices for the continual burnt offering (Ex. 29:38-42; Dan. 9:21), representing the atonement required for Israel as a whole. The "2,300 evenings and mornings" probably refer to the number of sacrifices consecutively offered on 1,150 days, the interval between the desecration of the Lord's altar and its reconstruction by Judas Maccabeus 25 Kislev, 165 B.C. The pagan altar set up by Antiochus in Kislev 168, was apparently installed almost two months after the Lord's altar was removed, accounting for the difference between 1,095 days (exactly three years) and the specified 1,150 mentioned in verse 14.

While I, Daniel, was watching the vision and trying to understand it, there before me stood one who looked like a man. And I heard a man's voice from the Ulai calling, "Gabriel, tell this man the meaning of the vision." As he came near the place where I was standing, I was terrified and fell prostrate. "Son of man," he said to me, "understand that the vision concerns the time of the end." While he was speaking to me, I was in a deep sleep, with my face to the ground. Then he touched me and raised me to my feet.

vv. 15-18

How frivolously we speak of a desire to behold heavenly beings. Daniel now encounters an angel and falls prostrate on his face in what he describes as a "deep sleep" (v. 18). He is so completely stupefied, the angel has to raise him—perhaps from the dead—to interpret the vision for him. God is able to keep His servants humble. Daniel, who should by now have an edge on interpretation of dreams and visions, has no clue about what is going on here by the Ulai Canal in Elam.

As Heaven bends down to touch earth, Daniel lies on the ground in a state of altered consciousness. Finally, he is raised by the touch of the angel, who does not even seem to pause in light of Daniel's undoing.

> He said: "I am going to tell you what will happen later in the time of wrath, because the vision concerns the appointed time of the end.
>
> The two-horned ram that you saw represents the kings of Media and Persia. The shaggy goat is the king of Greece, and the large horn between his eyes is the first king. The four horns that replace the one that was broken off represent four kingdoms that will emerge from his nation but will not have the same power.
>
> In the latter part of their reign, when rebels have become completely wicked, a stern-faced king, a master of intrigue, will arise. He will become very strong, but not by his own power. He will cause astounding devastation and will succeed in whatever he does. He will destroy the mighty men and the holy people.
>
> He will cause deceit to prosper, and he will consider himself superior. When they feel secure, he will destroy many and take a stand against the Prince of princes. Yet he will be destroyed, but not by human power."
>
> vv. 19-25

Gabriel's job is detailing for Daniel the Medo-Persian Empire, Greece and Alexander the Great, and the "four horns." Antiochus IV, Epiphanes is the "stern-faced king." This "master of intrigue" was not the rightful heir to the Seleucid throne. He came to this kingdom by deceit. The vision takes in two categories of people: Mighty men and the holy people. He was a powerful warrior and he conquered mighty men, a veiled reference to other armies that came against him. Then the "holy people" are mentioned. He desired in the latter part of his reign to destroy the Jews and

152

Judaism and put a stop to all Jewish practices. His crowning act was building a statue of Jupiter on the altar of sacrifice in the Temple courtyard. There on the altar he commanded the sacrifice of pigs.

> *"The vision of the evenings and mornings that has been given you is true, but seal up the vision, for it concerns the distant future." I, Daniel, was exhausted and lay ill for several days. Then I got up and went about the king's business. I was appalled by the vision; it was beyond understanding.*

vv. 26, 27

No doubt Daniel was extremely distressed to "see" the future of Israel and the gross desecration of the altar of daily sacrifice.

Comfortable with Mystery

The angel Gabriel instructs Daniel to "seal up the vision" because it concerned the distant future. Our future. But the question begs to be asked: *Was there something more to the vision that Daniel never wrote down?* I think we must be content to know that there are unrevealed mysteries saved for a later time. Studying is a godly virtue, but no matter how complete that study is, some things are saved for a time deemed ripe by God. He alone is the Revealer of mysteries. In this day in which we live, God is preparing His people for what is to come. Daniel, sitting ill for a few days, was pondering what he had seen and heard.

Why did Daniel become physically ill? He had already witnessed the seige of Jerusalem, the destruction of the Temple, and his people being carried off captive to a foreign land. But, with his great expectations of the return from their captivity, he is shown a future Jerusalem where the Temple is once again desecrated and his people oppressed. Daniel was shown a vivid picture of the scope of the future of Jerusalem that left him reeling. Twice the city is besieged: once under Antiochus, and again under the antichrist in the end of days.

*This took place to fulfill what was
spoken through the prophet:
"Say to the daughter of Zion, 'See, your king
comes to you, gentle and riding on a donkey,
on a colt, the foal of a donkey.'"*

Matthew 21:4, 5

Yeshua makes known His Messianic mission as he enters Jerusalem on a donkey.

We Have Rebelled

Daniel obviously realized that the time of the prophecy of his people's exile was drawing to a close. A great carefulness seems to have prevailed upon him and remembering the words of Jeremiah, he was moved to intercessory prayer on behalf of his people.

How horrible it would have been to come to the end of the preappointed time of exile and fall short of the mark that God had set for it to accomplish. Daniel's recognition of that fact is evident.

In the first year of Darius son of Xerxes (a Mede by descent), who was made ruler over the Babylonian kingdom—in the first year of his reign, I, Daniel, understood from the Scriptures, according to the word of the LORD given to Jeremiah the prophet, that the desolation of Jerusalem would last seventy years. So I turned to the Lord God and pleaded with him in prayer and petition, in fasting, and in sackcloth and ashes.

I prayed to the LORD my God and confessed:

"O Lord, the great and awesome God, who keeps his covenant of love with all who love him and obey his commands, we have sinned and done wrong. We have been wicked and have rebelled; we have turned away from your commands and laws. We have not listened to your servants the prophets, who spoke in your name to our kings, our princes and our fathers, and to all the people of the land.

"Lord, you are righteous, but this day we are covered with shame—the men of Judah and people of Jerusalem and all Israel, both near and far, in all the countries where you have scattered us because of our unfaithfulness to you. O LORD, we and our kings, our princes and our fathers are covered with shame because we have sinned against you.

The Lord our God is merciful and forgiving, even though we have rebelled against him; we have not obeyed the LORD our God or kept the laws he gave us through his servants the prophets. All Israel has transgressed your law and turned

155

away, refusing to obey you.

"Therefore the curses and sworn judgments written in the Law of Moses, the servant of God, have been poured out on us, because we have sinned against you. You have fulfilled the words spoken against us and against our rulers by bringing upon us great disaster. Under the whole heaven nothing has ever been done like what has been done to Jerusalem.

"Just as it is written in the Law of Moses, all this disaster has come upon us, yet we have not sought the favor of the LORD our God by turning from our sins and giving attention to your truth. The LORD did not hesitate to bring the disaster upon us, for the LORD our God is righteous in everything he does; yet we have not obeyed him.

"Now, O Lord our God, who brought your people out of Egypt with a mighty hand and who made for yourself a name that endures to this day, we have sinned, we have done wrong.

"O Lord, in keeping with all your righteous acts, turn away your anger and your wrath from Jerusalem, your city, your holy hill. Our sins and the iniquities of our fathers have made Jerusalem and your people an object of scorn to all of those around us.

"Now, our God, hear the prayers and petitions of your servant. For your sake, O Lord, look with favor on your desolate sanctuary. Give ear, O God, and hear; open your eyes and see the desolation of the city that bears your Name.

"We do not make requests of you because we are righteous, but because of your great mercy. O LORD, listen! O LORD, forgive! O LORD, hear and act! For your sake, O my God, do not delay, because your city and your people bear your Name."

9:1-19

From these verses several important items come to light. Daniel must have recognized that the Jews time in Babylon had not produced the highest results spiritually. A slow adaptation to a culture is not always healthy since there is the danger of assimilating too much. The tendancy to observe that the Babylonians were successful people seemingly blessed by their gods may have had adverse affects on the exiles.

Several times Daniel prays for God to mercifully restore the city of Jerusalem and the Temple where His name dwelt. No doubt he had been pondering the fact that it was close to the time for God to turn back to His people and return them to His city, Jerusalem. Actually, this prayer of Daniel is a good model to follow as we also desire to interceed for Jerusalem in our present day.

Intercession for Corporate Israel

Up to this point, we have not seen Israel as a corporate entity as in the books of Samuel, Kings, and Chronicles. We have been more focused on Daniel and a few friends and their personal relationships with their God in the midst of crushing adversity.

Now Daniel takes up his people's plight and confesses corporately both on his and their behalf. "We" and "us" now fill his prayer: *"We have sinned, and we have fallen short, and we have not done Your will."*

Daniel exhibits such an example of humility. This book explores the timeless issues of human existence and presents a pinnacle of repentance and obedience. Someone else might have said, *We have followed Your laws, O Lord. We obeyed Jeremiah and Isaiah, and left the city of Jerusalem with our hands bound in surrender to our captors. We gave ourselves up, and did everything You asked us. We have been here almost a generation—how long, O Lord?*

Instead, Daniel is praying a prayer of atonement for corporate rebellion. He knew that Israel, as a whole, would not be obedient until they were back in Israel putting the finishing touches on the Temple in Jerusalem, God's city, and the heart of the Jewish exiles. But, reading the prophetic writings of Ezra and Nehemiah and the exhortation of Haggai to rebuild the Temple of God, we realize that the people encountered stiff opposition.

Nehemiah deals mostly with the construction of the walls around Jerusalem. Ezra, on the other hand, focuses on the rebuilding of the Temple and the stoppages that took place due to the jealousy and complaining of influential friends of Babylon. These individuals dwelt close enough to Jersalem to check on the progress of the rebuilding and to file official complaints to the Babylonian officials.

Daniel's prayer delivers his people, covered in shame, to the throne of God beseeching Him for a covering of mercy. His posture of humility and identification as an intercessor on behalf of his people is supreme wisdom. The God of Israel is a God of mercy and Daniel was certainly appealing to His mercy. *El Shaddai*, the God of the Israelites, possesses an attribute lacking in other known gods of diverse religions. Generally, the attitude about "gods" was: *How can we appease these gods so they do not damage us?* From the wide scope of ancient Mesopotamia and her myriads of gods, to China, and still in our modern times in darkest Africa, appeasement of gods was and is the order of the day.

None of these gods possesses mercy or love for those who worship them. How opposite was Isaiah's message. In the same breath in which he describes the gods of Babylon as "burdensome weights" he conveys God's comforting message to Israel, *"Even to your old age and gray hairs I am he, I am he who will sustain you. I have made you and I will carry you; I will sustain you and I will rescue you"* (Isa. 46:4). God's mercy separates Him from all other gods in all other time periods.

Daniel's prayer of contrition is interrupted by the angel Gabriel:

While I was speaking and praying, confessing my sin and the sin of my people Israel and making my request to the LORD my God for his holy hill—while I was still in prayer, Gabriel, the man I had seen in the earlier vision, came to me in swift flight about the time of the evening sacrifice.

He instructed me and said to me, "Daniel, I have now come to give you insight and understanding. As soon as you began to pray, an answer was given, which I have come to tell you, for you are highly esteemed. Therefore, consider the message and understand the vision. . ."

vv. 20-23

For You are Highly Esteemed

Daniel's prayer was between afternoon and sundown. With the destruction of the Temple in Jerusalem, the Babylonian Jews and priesthood substituted their normal service unto the Lord at the regular animal sacrificial times with prayer and confession. This prayer, in the order of synagogue prayers, is called *Minhah* and involves confession of sin as well as an offering to the Lord, as we see Daniel doing here. The Minhah prayer may be offered anywhere between noon and sunset, but 3:00 o'clock in the afternoon is most common. In the book of Acts, we see the apostles of Yeshua went to the Temple at this same time.

> *One day Peter and John were going up to the temple at the time of prayer—at three in the afternoon.*

> Acts 3:1

Is Daniel a great sinner or a humble man of God? The book of Daniel deals with the weighty issues of humankind—spiritual success and failure, and never being sure exactly where you stand. As Daniel was humbly confessing his and his people's sins, he was brought a message from Heaven. Gabriel brought the comforting news to Daniel, from the mouth of God, that he was "highly esteemed."

How was Daniel expecting God to respond to his period of repenting and confessing? He was certainly aquainted with God's judgment, since he personally lived through the siege of Jerusalem and the ensuing exile. Perhaps Daniel was taken by surprise by the angel's message of encouragement.

Characteristically, even as sincere believers we tend to focus on our own sins, shortcomings, and failures. We have a tendency to look at the things that we *have not* accomplished more than the things that we *have* accomplished. We need God's perspective and encouragement. We need a Gabriel view, at least some of the time.

I have been in the ministry for many years and have spoken with people who have served the Lord thirty or forty years and then come to the end of their service and felt that they may not even *know* the Lord! How could someone possibly serve God that long and dedicate their lives to Him—the best years of their lives—and come to feel that they are a failure to God? There is a reason.

It is human nature, with Satan's helping hand, that we have a tendency to sandwich all our failures together, ignoring the successful days, months, and years. As a result, the shortcomings stack up into one exclamation mark of "failure." During seasons of introspective brooding, we dwell on those shortcomings, sinking down into depression. Rather, it is more refreshing to "number your days."

I do not mean count how many days until you are going to die. Rather, count the good days and thank God for the remaining time to serve Him. Be lifted up and encouraged! Know that God's love and mercy covers our failures, and presses us forward in our desire to serve Him and glorify Him with our lives.

Daniel has been in deep intercession for his people and the city of Jerusalem. It seems that there is another important message that God is bringing to Daniel on this matter.

Gabriel goes on to instruct Daniel:

Seventy 'sevens' are decreed for your people and your holy city to finish transgression, to put an end to sin, to atone for wickedness, to bring in everlasting righteousness, to seal up vision and prophecy and to anoint the most holy.

Know and understand this; From the issuing of the decree to restore and rebuild Jerusalem until the Anointed One, the ruler, comes, there will be seven 'sevens,' and sixty-two 'sevens.' It will be rebuilt with streets and a trench, but in times of trouble. After the sixty-two 'sevens,' the Anointed One will be cut off and will have nothing.

The people of the ruler who will come will destroy the city and the sanctuary. The end will come like a flood: War will continue until the end, and desolations have been decreed. He will confirm a covenant with many for one 'seven.' In the middle of the 'seven' he will put an end to sacrifice and offering. And on a wing of the temple he will set up an abomination that causes desolation, until the end that is decreed is poured out upon him.

vv. 24-27

Without a flurry of trumpets, God simply states facts that are direct answers to Daniel's prayer—the beloved city of Jerusalem and its Temple *would* be rebuilt.

The Babylonian exiles did return to Israel, and Jerusalem and, under the direction of Ezra and Nehemiah, they rebuilt the city and, eventually, the Temple of God.

This "abomination" in the time of Antiochus Epiphanes, was the erecting of a statue of Jupiter on the altar of God outside the Temple and the sacrifice of a pig on that altar, defiling it for further use by the Jews.

Deep in the Citrus Grove

Now we come to the inner reaches of the citrus grove that we mentioned in the introductory chapter. The rare and unusual fruits lie here. Now that we have attempted to understand the time period and the people to whom the book was written, and endeavored to keep the messages in the context of that era as well, we can partake of the deep treasures of Daniel.

I realize much controversy surrounds this section of Daniel. There have been enough presentations of the time line to make one dizzy. I do not approach this in presumption, acknowledging that there are great scholars who spend their lifetimes in study and still do not agree with one another on this issue. I will give you the explanation that seems to make the most sense to someone who is not a scholar, but a popularizer.

There is no doubt that the periods of "sevens" are periods of years. The total time is divided into three sections—seven sevens, sixty-two sevens, and the final single seven. The total number of years is four hundred and ninety to finish the vision. The controversy centers around the 483rd year. This is the year that brings to a conclusion the first two phases of the time line and signals a major milestone in God's final program—the cutting off of the "Anointed One."

There are three possible decrees from which the counting of these years could begin. Number one is the decree of Cyrus. The limiting factor is that Cyrus' decree was to rebuild Jerusalem's Temple. Possibility number two is in the seventh year of King Artaxerxes when he decreed rebuilding further property of the Temple area. Number three, and I think the correct point from which to begin the countdown, is in the twentieth year of Artaxerxes, when he decreed that the city and streets should be rebuilt. Clearly from this section of Scripture the key phrase is, *"It will be rebuilt with streets . . ."* (v. 25b).

This is the decree that determines Israel's renewed national existence, assuring a homeland for the displaced Jewish people right on the mark of seventy years of dispersion. The problem is that this computation takes us racing past the accepted birth of Messiah, the "Anointed One," by some twenty-nine years. This Scripture is not about the birth of the Messiah though, but rather, about His being "cut off."

It is fairly well accepted now that the computation of Jesus' birth could be off, give or take four years. The startling arithmetic then brings us to the exact date of Jesus' triumphal entry into Jerusalem on a donkey, where for the first time He officially presented Himself to His people as their Messiah, in A.D. 29.

Six purposes are determined to be accomplished during the passing of the four hundred and ninety years:

1) To "finish transgression:" *hepesha* (Heb.), which also has the connotation of "crime" and "idolatry."

2) To bring an "end to sin:" *hataot* (Heb.), meaning also to "miss the mark."

3) To make "atonement for wickedness:" *lecaper aven* (Heb.), the root "aven" can also mean "perversion."

4) To bring in "everlasting righteousness:" *tzedek olamim*, (Heb.), which is a good translation by itself.

5) To "seal up vision and prophecy:" *hazon*, and *navie*, (Heb.), "to bring to an end by total fulfillment" the need for vision and prophecy. We will enter into a time of living in the eternal present in God's presence with no need for "seeing" into the future.

6) To anoint a "holiness of holinesses:" *lemschoch kodesh kadashim* (Heb.). This has been construed as several things, from the baptism of Yeshua, to the rededication of the Temple, but must be more closely aligned to the return of the reigning King of kings.

The "stone" that will crush Nebuchadnezzar's statue from the feet up and all will blow away as chaff in the wind will grow into a universal empire.

A notable point on this time line is 168-165 B.C., which were the three years when Antiochus IV Epiphanes was ruling in Jerusalem with the Temple under his control and power. This is noteworthy because it is a picture of the real enemy of God's people that will come in the end of time—the antichrist.

This period, which fell between the Old and the New Testaments, has erroneously been labeled "the silent years." This came to my attention quite by surprise. Many years ago, I was teaching a beginning Hebrew class in a church facility in the Seattle area of Washington State. The church had contacted me the week before my class began and told me which of the church school rooms I had been assigned to use. I was to use a grade 4 and 5 classroom and they had given me the room number. I arrived early, before any of my students, and was preparing the board and getting things in order when I noticed a very well done poster hanging on the wall. It was a birds'-eye-view time line of the Old Testament and New Testament. Between the two testaments was a pleasant face holding up a finger to the mouth in the gesture that means be very quiet. I marveled. At this early age children were being taught that nothing of importance happened during a 400-year biblical period! Nothing could be further from the truth.

Four major historical periods punctuate these four hundred intertestamental years.

The Persian Period: 450-330 B.C.

Somewhere around two hundred years after Nehemiah, the Persians ruled Judah. They caused Israel no serious trouble and allowed them to operate in religious freedom.

The Hellenistic Period: 330-166 B.C.

In 333 B.C. Alexander's rule brought an end to the Persian era. He was convinced that the world needed Greek culture in order to become unified. Flattered by the Jews and their prophecies concerning him, he ruled them favorably. The Septuagint, the Greek translation of the entire Old Testament, came into being in Egypt's glistening city of Alexandria during this era of favor.

The Hasmonean Period: 166-63 B.C.

Under extreme oppression by Selecuid rulers to Hellenize their culture, the Jews rebelled. In ever-increasing degrees, the Syrian/Greek government attempted to squelch Judaism. Under their rule, laws were passed forbidding Shabbat observance, infant circumcision, and the possession of Scripture. The final blow was the desecration of the Temple in Jerusalem.

The Roman Period: 63 B.C.

Pompey conquered Jerusalem and the whole of the land came under subject of Rome through him. Imperially-appointed procurators ruled local governments. Herod the Great was the ruler at the time of the birth of Yeshua.

A fictional novel could not hold more intrigue or imaginative narrative than this period. Historians, who have not fallen under the "spell of silence" and shied away from this block of time, have left us enough information to glean valuable lessons. This period of time actually was the mold out of which the Judaism of Yeshua's time came. The writings of the Essenes were being amassed on the shores of the Dead Sea. The Pharisee and Sadducee parties originated during this time period as well.

The Pharisee party was a grassroots movement to democratize Judaism and wrest it from the control of the Sadducees. Sadducees were sympathizers with the Zadokites, the priestly descendants of Zadok. The Sadducees believed only in the Torah and rejected the authority of the Oral Law. They tended to be in positions of high power and authority in the framework of the priesthood. They firmly believed that only the Torah was valid, therefore the idea of resurrection from the dead ran against their religious grain, since that theology arose from later writings.

The Pharisees, on the other hand, accepted as holy writ not only the Torah but all other writings now canonized, as well as the writings of the prophets. The Pharisee party was popular among the vast majority of the common people. They were attempting to bring to the synagogue and the home certain worship and prayer rituals previously relegated to the Temple and priesthood. The time of political uncertainty had already taken them to Babylon as exiles and could conceivably again upset the operation of formal Judaism centered around a single site for worship.

One of the crowning lessons of that time period comes from the celebration now known as Hanukkah, celebrated by Jewish people the world over.

Hanukkah is a story of survival, bravery, overcoming faith,

and a sovereign God. These lessons are too rich to ascribe to a "silent" past. They cry out, of themselves, to be paid attention to. Perhaps if the historical end of Israel's oppressors had been heeded by the church and taught to the populace instead of a virulent strain of antisemitism, the lives of millions of Jewish people might have been spared during the Holocaust. The story of Hanukkah leaves us an indelible message: in the face of enormous odds, with God we are victorious.

The Menorah

When asked to create a seal for the new State of Israel, David Ben Gurion, the first Prime Minister chose two olive branches surrounding a *menorah*. It stands as the Israeli State seal to this day. On each of the seven cups of the *menorah* (seven-branched candlestick) is one sentence: *"Lo b'chail, u'lo b'koach, ki im b'ruchi,"* (*"Not by might, nor by power, but by My Spirit says the LORD of hosts"*).

This is from Zechariah 4:6 (NKJV), during the time they were rebuilding the Temple after the Babylonian captivity. The word *Hanukkah* in Hebrew simply means "dedication" and specifically refers to the dedication of the Temple of God at Jerusalem.

The menorah stands as an important symbol in so many passages of Scripture. Revelation tells us that each of the seven churches of Asia were represented in the heavenlies by a "golden lampstand" or menorah (Rev. 1:20 KJV). Israel is also represented by the menorah in the book of Zechariah. John 8:12 records that Yeshua is *"the light of the world."* The menorah brings light, just as Israel was meant to be a light to the nations and, indeed, did bring forth the Messiah.

Zechariah provides us another interesting tidbit in relation to this as we read further.

He asked me, "What do you see?" I answered, "I see a solid gold lampstand with a bowl at the top and seven lights on it, with seven channels to the lights. Also there are two olive trees by it, one on the right of the bowl and the other on its left." I asked the angel who talked with me, "What are these, my lord?" Zechariah 4:2-4

165

The Final Kingdom

The Prophet Zechariah asks about the meaning of the vision of the "two olive trees" who are pouring oil from themselves. Of course, the oil is symbolic of the Holy Spirit of God, but it is interesting to note that in Hebrew it does not say that they were pouring just *any* oil from themselves, but rather that they were pouring gold. The word "oil," placed in most Bible translations in this passage of Scripture, is in italics—inferred by the translator. In the context of the rebuilding of the Temple and the power emanating from the Holy Spirit, the Hebrew word picture is without rival. The anointing is as pure and valuable as *gold*. Light proceeds from the Giver of Life and permeates our Scriptures.

In the book of John, Yeshua is recorded as walking in the area of Solomon's Colonnade during the Feast of Dedication, or Hanukkah.

> *Then came the Feast of Dedication at Jerusalem. It was winter, and Jesus was in the temple area walking in Solomon's Colonnade. The Jews gathered around him, saying, "How long will you keep us in suspense? If you are the Messiah, tell us plainly."*

> John 10:22-24

Josephus, the historian of antiquity, left us important documentation. The story of Hanukkah is also found in the apocryphal book of Maccabees, one of the books in the collection of works preserved by the formal church.

There is not a great deal of material written about Hanukkah and the holiday is not mentioned at all in the Old Testament, because the events occured after the writing of the book of Malachi, in the intertestamental time period.

Hellenization of the World

The drama of Hanukkah begins with that ambitious conqueror, Alexander the Great. Through this "leopard"/"horned goat" who charges so swiftly that he does not even touch the ground, the Hellenization of the world began. The ideas of Greek philosophers, glorifying the human body both in sport and in fine art, and the Greek way of perceiving the universe around us permeated the world. These new philosophical ideas changed the existing cultures and sought to influence existing religions in conquered lands.

The Maccabean Revolt

Though our story of the Maccabean revolt against the Syrian-Greeks takes place much later, Alexander's conquest of the world is actually the foundation of those events. At his death, Alexander's empire split into four parts. The four generals of his vast army divided his conquests amongst themselves. Seleucus, one of Alexander's generals, took what later became modern Syria in 311 B.C. It was under the iron fist of this sector of the divided empire that Israel came into a time of great trouble.

Several generations from Seleucus, a maniacal ruler came to power known as Antiochus Epiphanes. His Greek name actually means "god in the flesh." Antiochus ruled from Syria, but set up a military garrison in Jerusalem. This garrison was to oversee the Hellenization of the population of Israel in 168-165 B.C.

Antiochus had Jerusalem's high priest, Onais, murdered. He demanded that the circumcision of all Jewish baby boys cease. He had a statue of Jupiter erected on the Temple Mount and the sacrifice of swine on the altar was instituted.

The Syrian-Greek military garrison met their demise upon entering a small village outside Jerusalem called Modi'in. The soldiers built an altar and demanded a "show of allegiance" by having the local elders sacrifice a pig there, in direct contradiction to Levitical laws. An old priest named Mattathias became so enraged when he saw what was taking place that he killed the Jew who was complying with the orders. He and his sons fled to the nearby mountains to regroup and prepare to wage guerrilla warfare against the oppressive authorities of Syria.

Mattathias, being elderly, passed his leadership on to his son, known as Judah "the Maccabee" (meaning "hammer"), just prior to his death. Judah, his brothers, and their followers, the Hasmoneans, defeated every attempt by Antiochus to end the Jewish uprising. Their strategy and bravery could not be matched by the other side. In the face of astounding odds, Judah led his followers to Jerusalem where he drove the Syrian force from the Temple and out of the city.

Judah faced the grief of having to fight against his own Jewish brothers who had joined the side of the Hellenizers. Some forsook their Jewishness for monetary gain, others for prestige. Some Israeli males even went so far as to surgically reverse their circumcisions in order to participate in nude Greek sporting events. They thereby erased any sign of their Jewish heritage and the covenant in the flesh with the God of Israel.

On the twenty-fifth day of the Hebrew month Kislev, exactly the same day that three years earlier the Temple had been defiled by unholy sacrifices, the Hasmoneans liberated the city of Jerusalem and began in earnest to undo what their Syrian oppressors had done. The Jews rushed to rededicate the desecrated Temple.

Temple Consecration

Arriving at the Temple site, they began removing the stones of the defiled altar and toppling the statue of Jupiter. In the Holy Place, inside the Temple, stood the huge menorah. The rejoicing Jewish conquerors found earthenware oil cruses holding only enough consecrated oil to light the menorah for one day. The joy of the conquest of liberation was diminished due to the Levitical laws requiring that the Temple menorah must burn "continually." It normally took eight days to process enough consecrated olive oil to replenish the menorah. How could they possibly begin the process and let the light go out again? Nevertheless, they lit the Temple menorah and began the process of procuring more oil.

God's affirmation of their deeds of valor and zeal was evident when the oil, which should have lasted for only one day, miraculously lasted the entire eight days until new oil was processed and consecrated. For this reason this eight-day winter holiday is also known as the "Festival of Lights."

Traditions

The traditions of the Feast of Hanukkah that have evolved over the years are the lighting of an eight-branched menorah (candle holder) called a *hanukkiah*. One candle is lit each night by using a candle known as the *shamash,* or "servant" in English. Thus, the hanukkiah candle holder has a total of nine candles including the shamash. The candles are lit in a right-to left-hand order. Each night a new candle is added until the eighth day when all candles are ablaze with light. Hanukkah candles come in boxes of forty-four, since lighting an additional candle each night of the eight nights, including the shamash, adds up to forty-four.

The frying of potato pancakes in oil is also a modern tradition, to commemorate the oil used to light the Temple menorah during those eight days so long ago.

Games are played with a four-sided top called a *dreidel.* Each side of the dreidel has a Hebrew letter on it, standing for the slogan, *Nes Gadol Hiyah Po,* "A Great Miracle Happened Here." (Outside Israel, the Hebrew letters of the dreidel differ slightly, *Nes Gadol Hiyah Sham,* "A Great Miracle Happened *There.*")

Hanukkah Storytelling

During Hanukkah, the book of Maccabees is read, wherein lies the story of the bravery of those people zealous for God's ways. Women also played a very important role in this great drama as well. These accounts are retold concerning Israel's women of valor connected with this holiday.

One story, from the Apocrypha, is about Judith who, upon seeing the desperate plight of her people, left Jerusalem and arrived at the Syrian encampment. Her beauty pleased the Syrian general and thinking to have her for himself he consented to her preparing him a meal. Judith knew serving salted cheese would make the general thirsty, whereby she could overindulge him with drink. He complied, drinking wine until he passed out. Judith seized the opportunity and cut off his head. When the Syrians learned of Judith's deed and saw the Jews with their leader's head held aloft on a pole while advancing to attack, they fled.

Another story of a woman of valor relates that the Syrian governor passed a law that every Jewish bride would be brought to his own bed chamber first on the night of her wedding. The daughter of the high priest, upon hearing this, made plans for her own wedding ceremony. After her vows she stood amidst the people disrobing, almost like the prophet Jeremiah at a much earlier time.

This, of course, enraged the crowd. Her brothers shouted that they would kill her, to which she replied, "Over my being disrobed you are angry, but about what the Syrian governor will do to me tonight you remain silent?" Being roused to righteous anger, her brothers stormed the palace and killed the Syrian governor and the Jewish revolt began.

These stories also show us the extent of the cruel treatment the Israelites were experiencing at the hands of the ruling empires.

What Does This Mean For Us?

This story is a tale repeated time and time again by the Jewish people. It is a story of overcoming, in the face of overwhelming adversity, with a mighty God. From the book of Genesis to the Maccabees the Jews have overcome Egyptians, the desert and its dangers, felled the walls of Jericho with rams' horns, quelled the giants of the promised land, and led three Babylonian kings to the throne of God Almighty.

From the Maccabees to present day there have been a string of miracles in Israel—too long to list. And, to answer Isaiah's rhetorical question, "Can a nation be born in a day?"—yes, indeed it can! In fact, it did happen, in the face of such overwhelming odds as to be absurd! Israel continues to stand as an amazing miracle of God's faithfulness.

Our lesson from these Hanukkah stories is that we can overcome with God. The spirit of Antiochus will rise again in the person of the antichrist in the end of time. But, despite the fact that when he appears on the scene again, he will fulfill all that was prophesied about him, God's people will overcome. Satan's empire will once again be shattered. This time, God's people will watch because it will be done miraculously and without human hands, according to Daniel.

While you were watching, a rock was cut out, but not by human hands. It struck the statue on its feet of iron and clay and smashed them.

Then the iron, the clay, the bronze, the silver and the gold were broken to pieces at the same time and became like chaff on a threshing floor in the summer.

The wind swept them away without leaving a trace. But the rock that struck the statue became a huge mountain and filled the whole earth.

Daniel 2:34, 35

From this we can see that *all* oppression indeed will come to an end, so we can take courage. The message of the story of Hanukkah is that God is ever present in the annals of men and, even greater, that His sovereign plan will be carried out, without fail. That plan is the overthrow of all oppressive leaders, earthly governments, and empires.

Daniel's vision describes the "rock" striking the statue and all elements of the statue becoming like chaff on a summer threshing floor. At first glance, New Testament descriptions of the coming of the Lord reveal a secondary element of Daniel's vision.

And then the lawless one will be revealed, whom the Lord Jesus will overthrow with the breath of his mouth and destroy by the splendour of his coming.

2 Thessalonians 2:8

Upon closer consideration it becomes evident that the "wind" that sweeps away the gold, and silver, and bronze, leaving nothing behind, is the very breath of the Yeshua, the Messiah Himself.

Then I saw another
mighty angel coming down
from heaven.
He was robed in a cloud,
with a rainbow above his head;
his face was like the sun,
and his legs were like fiery pillars.

He was holding a little scroll,
which lay open in his hand.
He planted his right foot on the sea
and his left foot on the land,
and he gave a loud shout
like the roar of a lion.

Revelation 10:1-3

# The Long Road Home

A great war now take center stage in Daniel's visions. His desperation to hear from Heaven through a season of denying himself in a modified fast paid off in an amazing visitation. Heavenly visitations previous to this chapter have left Daniel physically ill and exhausted. In a storm of heavenly messages, Daniel is the lightning rod of prophecy.

According to the books of Ezra and Nehemiah, the edict of Cyrus puts into motion the beginning of the return of the exiles from Babylon. They were going home to their own land. God inspired them to brave the treacherous obstacles that they would face, and to gird themselves up to rebuild Jerusalem, the Holy City, and their Temple.

If this is the third year of Cyrus, king of Persia, then two years have already passed since the Jewish people were given permission to return to Jerusalem and rebuild their Temple.

It is generally overlooked, but this long road home has taken over two thousand years. There was a continuum of Jewish presence in Babylon and the neighboring nation, now known as Iraq, for millennia. As I said in the preface, the final exodus of the Iraqi Jewish population took place between the years of 1947 and 1952.

But, concerning those who went in this initial phase, there are varied explanations as to why Daniel does not return to Israel with his people. The most likely thing to take into consideration was his age by this time, as well as the difficult months of travel to Jerusalem from Babylon. An uncertain but plausible reason is that Daniel may have been forced to become a eunuch. The Scriptures tell us he was under the authority of the "chief of the eunuchs" in chapter one (1:3, NKJV). If this was so, Levitical prohibition forbade entrance to the Temple area by men maimed in this manner. It is certain, though, that Daniel was concerned for the wellbeing of his people and may have chosen to stay with those who did not return home to Israel.

Unlike the book of Esther and her fast of deliverance for her condemned people, Daniel's three week fast seems to have been aimed specifically at understanding the series of heavenly messages he had been given (10:2, 3).

When Heaven Stoops Down

Successive visions from other biblical episodes echo this particular visitation of Daniel's. Saul, on the road to Damascus, was the only one to see the Lord standing above him, yet his compatriots trembled in fear and fell to the ground (Acts 26:14). Likewise, Daniel's companions, unable to see the vision with their eyes, must have heard something or sensed in their spirits indicating that something monumental was taking place.

> *I, Daniel, was the only one who saw the vision; the men with me did not see it, but such terror overwhelmed them that they fled and hid themselves. So I was left alone, gazing at this great vision; I had no strength left, my face turned deathly pale and I was helpless. Then I heard him speaking, and as I listened to him, I fell into a deep sleep, my face to the ground.*

> 10:7-9

The visitor, standing on the banks of the Tigris River, "dressed in linen" and girded with the "finest gold," possessed other characteristics with which we as humans cannot identify. The Scriptures desire us to identify with Daniel, absorb his lessons and rejoice in his triumphs, but of these apparitions we are to simply stand in awe, if indeed we can stand at all. Daniel was face to face with a being whose body was like a diamond, with a face as bright as a bolt of lightning.

I imagine the best of movie makers' magic of special effects could not hold a candle to this slice of reality placed before Daniel. Abandoned by his friends who ran away terrified, Daniel stood gazing at the vision unfolding before him. Finally overwhelmed, he fell to the ground unconscious.

Although the description of his vision might at first lead you to think that this is an epiphany, there are indicators that it is a heavenly being—but not of the most powerful order. He reports that the prince of Persia "resisted" him twenty-one days and that Michael, one of the chief princes, came to his aid.

> *But the prince of the Persian kingdom resisted me twenty-one days. Then Michael, one of the chief princes, came to help me, beause I was detained there with the king of Persia.*

> v. 13

174

How humbling but encouraging it must have been to have the heavenly messenger tell Daniel that he was "highly esteemed." We may discuss prayer attitudes and become dull to the power of Heaven, thinking it is acceptable to take a less-than-awestruck stance when petitioning the Lord. When the powers of Heaven reveal how temporal earthly existence is and that it is a thin veil, all the breath goes out of the beholder.

Enemies in High Places

The "prince" of Persia is most likely a demonic authority figure which hovers over that region. From all we see in our day and age, I would venture to say it is *still* over the land of Persia. The Persian people have been held in dark, oppressive, spiritual bondage for centuries.

As westerners, we have a tendency to project upon the rest of the world our own characteristics. I learned a very important lesson in the 1970's when I was at Bible school in Southern California. I heard fire trucks in our neighborhood and went out to see a garage burning nearby.

I noticed the man next to me in the crowd looked Middle Eastern. I introduced myself to him and we began talking. He was a college student at the University. We became very good friends over the next ten months or so. Even though I was very interested in the Middle East at the time, I was naïve about political situations there. He was from Iran.

One evening at his house, where I had been invited for tea, three of his friends dropped by. They gathered themselves around the table where we were sitting and I must have seemed to be invisible as they verbally launched into plans to overthrow the Shah of Iran. With my simple American mentality I was thinking, *These guys are such braggarts. High-level wishful thinking!* It was not much more than a month after that, that the news media reported the overthrow of the Shah of Iran, with the Ayatollah Khomeini returning to Iran from his long period of exile in France. In that short period of time, I received an eye-opening understanding of Middle East politics. It was then that I realized that the rest of the world truly does not operate like the West. This is particularly true of Islamic countries.

Jan Goodwin, former senior editor of *Good Housekeeping Magazine*, compiled real-life stories in her book called *The Price of*

The Final Kingdom

Honor. After retiring from her position with *Good Housekeeping Magazine*, she spent many years living in various Islamic countries of the Middle East. Her book is an exposé of the lifestyle of the Islamic nations and the plight of their women. The heavy cloud of spiritual oppression still hovers over the area spoken of in Daniel. The "prince of Persia" still seems to be at work, just in a new guise.

Michael: Prince Over Israel

"Then Michael, one of the chief princes, came to help me, because I was detained there with the king of Persia" (v. 13). Michael is later described in Daniel 12:1 as the *"great prince who protects your people."* He serves as the angelic overseer of the nation of Israel, evidently, wherever they might be. In the following verse, the interpreter of the vision refers to Michael as "your prince" when speaking to Daniel. This is another glimpse into the heart of God. A nation in the midst of the consequences of disobedience has a heavenly archangel appointed for their protection, even in exile.

> *Now I have come to explain to you what will happen to your people in the future, for the vision concerns a time yet to come." While he was saying this to me, I bowed with my face toward the ground and was speechless. Then one who looked like a man touched my lips, and I opened my mouth and began to speak. I said to the one standing before me,*
>
> *"I am overcome with anguish because of the vision, my lord, and I am helpless. How can I, your servant, talk with you, my lord? My strength is gone and I can hardly breathe." Again the one who looked like a man touched me and gave me strength.*
>
> *"Do not be afraid, O man highly esteemed," he said. "Peace! Be strong now; be strong." When he spoke to me, I was strengthened and said, "Speak, my lord, since you have given me strength." So he said, "Do you know why I have come to you? Soon I will return to fight against the prince of Persia, and when I go, the prince of Greece will come; but first I will tell you what is written in the Book of Truth." (No one supports me against them except Michael, your prince . . .)"*
>
> vv. 14-21

At times I have beseeched the Lord for a heavenly vision to refresh in me the fear and reverence of God Almighty. I realize our position in Messiah and am grateful and bold when need be, but I think many times we lose sight of the awesome and fearful power of Heaven. The flesh-consuming glory of its inhabitants makes me want to restore my vision again and again and maintain respect of the Kingdom to which we belong.

And yet more humbling than that, the book of Romans tells us that the entire creation "groans and travails in pain" waiting for God to unveil who we, his sons, really are.

> *The creation waits in eager expectation for the sons of God to be revealed. For the creation was subjected to frustration, not by its own choice, but by the will of the one who subjected it, in hope that the creation itself will be liberated from its bondage to decay and brought into the glorious freedom of the children of God.*
> *We know that the whole creation has been groaning as in the pains of childbirth right up to the present time. Not only so, but we ourselves, who have the firstfruits of the Spirit, groan inwardly as we wait eagerly for our adoption as sons, the redemption of our bodies.*
>
> Romans 8:19-23

So, this angelic visitor, glorious being that he is, has come to aid Daniel in understanding the vision for the sake of those who will be affected by it.

Now, although he says he is going back to fight against the "prince of Persia," but then mentions the "prince of Greece." In verse 21 he says, *"But first I will tell you what is written in the Book of Truth."* This may be the annals of the kings and empires of the world. As we stand before God in judgment we will stand before Him in varied capacities. Those who were peasants will stand before him as peasants, those who were world leaders and kings will stand before Him as world leaders and kings. Not having been a world leader, I will not have to answer to God for a nation that I led, but a king, president, or prime minister will. He who leads a nation of people has a much greater responsibility before God on Judgment Day.

This "Book of Truth," may still be in process of being written for the day it will be laid out before the Judge of all the earth.

The beast I saw resembled a leopard, but had
feet like those of a bear
and a mouth like that of a lion.
The dragon gave the beast
his power and his throne and great authority.

Men worshiped the dragon
because he had given authority to the beast,
and they also worshiped the beast
and asked,
"Who is like the beast?
Who can make war against him?"

Revelation 13:2-4

The great bear raised up and devoured three ribs in Daniel's vision.

An Ancient Melodrama

The untimely death of Alexander the Great is the platform for the story line of Daniel chapter eleven. The upheaval surrounding his passing holds much intrigue. Alexander's passion for adventure had been wearing on his men for some time. There were times on his long tiring journeys when mutiny was barely averted. His death itself is shrouded in mystery. Some sources say that he fell ill, while others suggest he was poisoned. Whatever the truth of his death was, his kingdom began to disintegrate even before he took his last dying breath. The advice of one of Alexander's generals, Perdiccas, was to await the birth of Alexander's baby by his wife Roxane. If the baby were a son, then the dilemma would be averted and he could be enthroned.

The simple plan had adversaries. Ptolemy, another of Alexander's generals, refused to be ruled over by the son of an Asian mother. Roxane was not Greek. General Meleager did not like General Perdiccas, who seemed intent on holding the reigns of the kingdom during the three days of Alexander's illness and shortly after his death. Meleager stormed out of the presence of the king upon hearing the royal plans and joined a band of disgruntled soldiers who were plotting rebellion.

Upon Alexander's death in June of 323 B.C., Perdiccas placed Alexander's royal ring upon the vacant throne in a symbolic act of placing the kingdom in "suspended animation." Perdiccas arranged that the three hundred men who had rebelled with Meleager be stampeded to death by the army's elephants. Meleager was later murdered in a temple complex.

Finally, a plan was drawn up to avert war within the ranks of Alexander's military structure which would spread to all those within the circles of influence of those particular military men. Civil war was avoided by appointing Phillip, Alexander's mentally-retarded brother, to the throne as Phillip III. Though mentally impaired, he had enough wits to keep war from breaking out until a solution could be found.

It was finally decided that Phillip III would hold supreme power, with several satraps in various provinces ruling over their own corners of Alexander's world. The polarization that began with these decisions is not detailed here, but it was extensive. This

The Final Kingdom

chapter of Daniel skims the troubled waters of history and gives the highlights of the time with the focus, of course, centered around God's people, Israel.

"No one supports me against them except Michael, your prince," And, *"In the first year of Darius the Mede, I took my stand to support and protect him."* By these verses (11:21 and 12:1) we know we have entered the kingdom of Darius.

A Parade of Kings

A sensational bas relief carving of King Darius, the Mede was uncovered in Babylon by archaeologists. He is a majestic-looking fellow in a domical hat. A finely-curled head of hair and matching beard grace his masculine features. His kingly garment flows to his ankles as he sits on a throne of beautifully carved wood—which looks almost as if it were machine-turned on a lathe. The king is wielding a long rod in his right hand which extends to the floor, signifying his kingly authority, and perhaps its length symbolizing his hopes for the duration of his kingdom. In his left hand he bears the kingly cup, a vessel of the fruit of the vine and directly indicative of the prosperity of his reign. Biblical descriptions of prosperity always pictured a man sitting under his own vine and fig tree (Micah 4:4).

The next verse is a warning about the era we are now about to embark upon:

Now then, I tell you the truth. Three more kings will appear in Persia, and then a fourth, who will be far richer than all the others. And when he has gained power by his wealth, he will stir up everyone against the kingdom of Greece.

Daniel 11:2

The four "kings" referred to here are:

- Cambyses, 530-522 B.C.
- Gautama, also known as Pseudo-Smerdis, 522 B.C. (his reign was short lived)
- Darius I, from 522-486 B.C.
- Xerxes, from 486-465 B.C.

Xerxes, the fourth king, attempted to conquer Greece in 480 B.C. In this section of chapter eleven, the kings listed are documented historical figures who reigned in history.

Making sense of this chapter involves some historical backtracking to discover who is who.

Then a mighty king will appear, who will rule with great power and do as he pleases.

After he has appeared, his empire will be broken up and parcelled out towards the four winds of heaven. It will not go to his descendants, nor will it have the power he exercised, because his empire will be uprooted and given to others.

vv. 3, 4

The "mighty king" is, as we have mentioned, another view of Alexander the Great. It is amazing that chapter eleven affords Alexander less than one sentence. The chapter is not about Alexander's empire but about the *disintegration* of his kingdom! It is living proof that "Where there is no vision, the people perish" (Prov. 29:18). Alexander, the provider of "vision" for his empire, was gone. The Scriptures are clear that the kingdom would not be handed down to his descendants and that his amazing world-conquering prowess would no longer be the vital force in the kingdom. The phrase "broken up and parceled out toward the four winds of heaven" (v. 4) suggests that the succeeding verses are going to relate the story of a shattered kingdom.

Alexander's other sons, Hercules and Alexander II, were either too young to rule or did not have the world-conquering drive of their father. Historical sources tell us little about them. Instead, the history books are filled with the stories of the abandonment of Alexander's political philosophy by his military leaders and of the world he tried to unite under one banner which they shattered, leaving his realm in unraveling fragments.

The king of the South will become strong, but one of his commanders will become even stronger than he and will rule his own kingdom with great power.

After some years, they will become allies. The daughter of the king of the South will go to the king of the North to make an alliance, but she will not retain her power, and he and his power will not last. In those days she will be handed over, together with her royal escort and her father and the one who supported her.

vv. 5, 6

The kingdoms succeeding the death of Alexander are Macedon and Greece, Thrace and Asia Minor, Israel and Egypt under the Ptolemys, and Syria under the Seleucid Empire. The biblical narrative centers itself around the struggles that raged between

The Final Kingdom

the southern kingdom of Egypt and the northern kingdom of Syria and the central point where all roads met in the Middle East— Israel. It is important to note in the following drama that the title Antiochus is mentioned several times prior to arriving at the reign of "the Antiochus" who foreshadowed the coming of the antichrist. Several rulers bore the title name "Antiochus." The saga of the kings and their queens and children from Alexander's kingdom are as follows:

Ptolemy I Lagi Soter was the king of the south, a Macedonian (323-285 B.C.) who ruled Egypt, the southernmost quadrant of Alexander's kingdom.

Seleucus I Nicator was his commander who is mentioned in the same verse. He spread his wings in rebellion and ruled from Babylonia (311-280 B.C.). He spread out his kingdom to the east and to the west. They were rivals, but according to verse six, they later became allies.

Ptolemy II Philadelphus followed. He ruled the South, or Egypt (285-246 B.C.), and his daughter Berenice was given to **Antiochus I Soter**, who ruled the North (280-261 B.C.) in order to wed the two rival kingdoms in a shaky union.

Laodice was Antiochus' jealous ex-wife hidden in the wings. The plot thickens because Laodice conspired to have Berenice and Antiochus put to death. Her father Ptolemy died almost simultaneously.

Ptolemy III Euergetes I who was next in the line of succession ruled Egypt (285-246 B.C.) while **Antiochus II Theos** ruled the Seleucids.

> *One from her family line will arise to take her place. He will attack the forces of the king of the North and enter his fortress; he will fight against them and be victorious.*
>
> *He will also seize their gods, their metal images and their valuable articles of silver and gold and carry them off to Egypt. For some years he will leave the king of the North alone.*
>
> *Then the king of the North will invade the realm of the king of the South but will retreat to his own country.*
>
> *His sons will prepare for war and assemble a great army, which will sweep on like an irresistible flood and carry the battle as far as his fortress.*
>
> *Then the king of the South will march out in a rage and fight against the king of the North, who will raise a large army, but*

it will be defeated.
When the army is carried off, the king of the South will be filled with pride and will slaughter many thousands, yet he will not remain triumphant.
For the king of the North will muster another army, larger than the first; and after several years, he will advance with a huge army fully equipped.

vv. 7-13

"One from her family line" speaks of this same **Ptolemy III**, Berenice's brother, who had Laodice killed.

Seleucus II Callinicus, mentioned in the same verse, was the "king of the north" (246-226 B.C.) who ruled over Syria from Antioch. Ptolemy invaded Seleucus' kingdom and carried away his images of Syrian deities, as well as recovering Egyptian gods that had been carried away by Cambyses, the previous Persian ruler. His two sons **Antiochus III the Great** (223-187 B.C.) and **Seleucus III Ceraunus** (226-223 B.C.) followed in his footsteps, assembling a great army and attacking Ptolemy's fortress in Raphia in southern Israel.

Ptolemy IV Philopater, the "king of the South" (Egypt) (221-203 B.C.), charged out in a rage against the "king of the North" (Israel, at Raphia again) and **Antiochus III the Great** then lost Raphia. "Filled with pride," **Ptolemy IV** slew 10,000 of Antiochus III's army, according to the historian Polybius.

Ptolemy V Epiphanes, the succeeding king, was joined in the next battle by Jewish people in Israel, probably sick of being a sacrificial pawn in the great chess match between the North and South. According to Daniel 11:14, *"In those times many will rise against the king of the South. The violent men among your own people will rebel in fulfillment of the vision, but without success."* In spite of the Jewish men who joined his forces, he lost the battle.

We now revisit a famous area from the conquests of Alexander the Great in the very next verse:

Then the king of the North will come and build up siege ramps and will capture a fortified city. The forces of the South will be powerless to resist; even their best troops will not have the strength to stand.

v. 15

The Final Kingdom

This refers to the city of Sidon, now located in Lebanon, north of present-day Israel. Tyre and Sidon are sister cities on the Mediterranean sea coast.

Alexander the Great conquered Tyre in a great show of strength in spite of Tyre's strong resistance to his forces. The logistics that brought forth the fulfilling of the prophecy against Tyre were the physical fact that the seat of administration of Tyre sat on a small island just off the coast. The island was close enough for Alexander and his army to harness teams of horses to logs chained together and drag the buildings of the city into the sea as if done by an enormous bulldozer. Thus, he constructed a causeway to the small island to conquer the city.

> Son of man, because Tyre has said of Jerusalem, 'Aha! The gate to the nations is broken, and its doors have swung open to me; now that she lies in ruins I will prosper,' therefore this is what the Sovereign LORD says: I am against you, O Tyre, and I will bring many nations against you, like the sea casting up its waves.
> They will destroy the walls of Tyre and pull down her towers; I will scrape away her rubble and make her a bare rock.
> Out in the sea she will become a place to spread fishing nets, for I have spoken, declares the Sovereign LORD. She will become plunder for the nations, and her settlements on the mainland will be ravaged by the sword. Then they will know that I am the LORD.
>
> Ezekiel 26:2-6

Continuing on in chapter eleven of Daniel, we still are viewing **Antiochus III the Great** not yet Epiphanes. *"The invader will do as he pleases; no one will be able to stand against him. He will establish himself in the Beautiful Land and will have the power to destroy it"* (v. 16). The year is 197 B.C. and Antiochus is in control of the kingdom of Israel, the "Beautiful Land" mentioned in this Scripture.

> He will determine to come with the might of his entire kingdom and will make an alliance with the king of the South. And he will give him a daughter in marriage in order to overthrow the kingdom, but his plans will not succeed or help him.
>
> v. 17

Antiochus III the Great's daughter is **Cleopatra**. She was given in marriage to **Ptolemy V Epiphanes**.

Antiochus is still on the move militarily:

Then he will turn his attention to the coastlands and will take many of them, but a commander will put an end to his insolence and will turn his insolence back upon him. After this, he will turn back toward the fortresses of his own country but will stumble and fall, to be seen no more. His successor will send out a tax collector to maintain the royal splendor. In a few years, however, he will be destroyed, yet not in anger or in battle.

vv. 18-20

The "coastlands" are most likely Asia Minor and mainland Greece. The commander is **Lucius Cornelius Scipio Asiaticus**, who defeated Antiochus at Magnesia in Asia Minor in 190 B.C.

Antiochus lost his life a few years later in the province of Elymais while plundering a temple.

Seleucus IV Philopater was his own son who succeeded him. He reigned from 175-167 B.C. Heliodoros was Seleucus' finance minister and was responsible for gathering taxes from his colonial empire so that his kingdom would remain fiscally strong. This verse tells us that he would be "destroyed, yet not in anger or in battle." Heliodoros engineered an in-house conspiracy against him.

Someone arrives on the scene, from the wings, whom the next verse describes as a "contemptible person."

He will be succeeded by a contemptible person who has not been given the honor of royalty. He will invade the kingdom when its people feel secure, and he will seize it through intrigue.

v. 21

This word "contemptible" used to describe Seleucus' younger brother, **Antiochus Epiphanes**, was probably coined due to the manner in which he came to power. The word "intrigue" in Hebrew, *ca-lak-la-kaw* means slipperiness or flattery. Demetrius I, the son of Seleucus, was rightful heir to the throne, but while he was too young to hold power, Antiochus Epiphanes seized the throne. This Antiochus is the ruler who foreshadows the coming antichrist.

A Modern Poet on Antiochus

Edgar Allen Poe wrote a piece of prose regarding the history of Antiochus Epiphanes. The setting is the city of Antioch of Syria, where the seat of authority of the Seleucid Empire was situated. In the poem, Poe paints a portrait of Antiochus' maniacal character for us. The name of the prose poem is a riddle in and of itself. The unity of four beasts is mentioned, but only three at most can be deduced from the second half of the title—*Homo sapien*, meaning "man," and "cameleopard," a combination of two animals. The combination name "cameleopard" means "giraffe" in Latin. If you look at a giraffe without spots, indeed he looks somewhat like a camel, and with the spots of a leopard added, you have a giraffe. This was the origin of the name given the African animal. But coming to a conclusion about the fourth beast seems to transcend the obvious and enter the realm of the symbolic. The fourth must be the character of Antiochus himself, which is neither camel nor leopard and in the end of his horrible reign, not even human, but is the embodiment of the coming antichrist.

FOUR BEASTS IN ONE—THE HOMO-CAMELEOPARD
by Edgar Allan Poe (1850)
Chacun a ses vertus.
CREBILLON'S Xerxes.

ANTIOCHUS EPIPHANES is very generally looked upon as the Gog of the prophet Ezekiel. This honor is, however, more properly attributable to Cambyses, the son of Cyrus. And, indeed, the character of the Syrian monarch does by no means stand in need of any adventitious embellishment. His accession to the throne, or rather his usurpation of the sovereignty, a hundred and seventy-one years before the coming of Christ; his attempt to plunder the temple of Diana at Ephesus; his implacable hostility to the Jews; his pollution of the Holy of Holies; and his miserable death at Taba, after a tumultuous reign of eleven years, are circumstances of a prominent kind, and therefore more generally noticed by the historians of his time than the impious, dastardly, cruel, silly, and whimsical achievements which make up the sum total of his private life and reputation.

Let us suppose, gentle reader, that it is now the year of the world three thousand eight hundred and thirty, and let us, for a few minutes, imagine ourselves at that most grotesque habitation of man, the remarkable city of Antioch. To be sure, there were, in Syria and other countries, sixteen cities of that appellation, besides the one to which I more particularly allude. But ours is that which went by the name of Antiochia Epidaphne, from its vicinity to the little village of Daphne, where stood a temple to that divinity. It was built (although about this matter there is some dispute) by Seleucus Nicanor, the first king of the country after Alexander the Great, in memory of his father Antiochus, and became immediately the residence of the Syrian monarchy. In the flourishing times of the Roman Empire, it was the ordinary station of the prefect of the eastern provinces; and many of the emperors of the queen city (among whom may be mentioned, especially, Verus and Valens) spent here the greater part of their time. But I perceive we have arrived at the city itself. Let us ascend this battlement, and throw our eyes upon the town and neighboring country.

What broad and rapid river is that which forces its way, with innumerable falls, through the mountainous wilderness, and finally through the wilderness of buildings? That is the Orontes, and it is the only water in sight, with the exception of the Mediterranean, which stretches, like a broad mirror, about twelve miles off to the southward. Everyone has seen the Mediterranean; but let me tell you, there are few who have had a peep at Antioch. By few, I mean, few who, like you and me, have had, at the same time, the advantages of a modern education. Therefore, cease to regard that sea, and give your whole attention to the mass of houses that lie beneath us. You will remember that it is now the year of the world three thousand eight hundred and thirty. Were it later—for example, were it the year of our Lord eighteen hundred and forty-five, we should be deprived of this extraordinary spectacle. In the nineteenth century Antioch is—that is to say, Antioch will be—in a lamentable state of decay. It will have been, by that time, totally destroyed, at three different periods, by three successive earthquakes. Indeed, to say the truth, what little of its former self may then remain, will be found in so desolate and ruinous a state that the patriarch shall have removed his residence to Damascus. This is well. I see you profit by my advice, and are making the most of

your time in inspecting the premises—in—
satisfying your eyes
With the memorials and the things of fame,
That most renown this city.—
I beg pardon; I had forgotten that Shakespeare will not flourish for seventeen hundred and fifty years to come. But does not the appearance of Epidaphne justify me in calling it grotesque?
It is well fortified; and in this respect is as much indebted to nature as to art.
Very true.
There are a prodigious number of stately palaces.
There are.
And the numerous temples, sumptuous and magnificent, may bear comparison with the most lauded of antiquity.
All this I must acknowledge. Still there is an infinity of mud huts, and abominable hovels. We cannot help perceiving abundance of filth in every kennel, and, were it not for the overpowering fumes of idolatrous incense, I have no doubt we should find a most intolerable stench. Did you ever behold streets so insufferably narrow, or houses so miraculously tall? What gloom their shadows cast upon the ground! It is well the swinging lamps in those endless colonnades are kept burning throughout the day; we should otherwise have the darkness of Egypt in the time of her desolation.
It is certainly a strange place! What is the meaning of yonder singular building? See! it towers above all others, and lies to the eastward of what I take to be the royal palace.
That is the new Temple of the Sun, who is adored in Syria under the title of Elah Gabalah. Hereafter a very notorious Roman Emperor will institute this worship in Rome, and thence derive a cognomen, Heliogabalus. I dare say you would like to take a peep at the divinity of the temple. You need not look up at the heavens; his Sunship is not there—at least not the Sunship adored by the Syrians. That deity will be found in the interior of yonder building. He is worshiped under the figure of a large stone pillar terminating at the summit in a cone or pyramid, whereby is denoted Fire.
Hark—behold!—who can those ridiculous beings be,

half naked, with their faces painted, shouting and gesticulating to the rabble?

Some few are mountebanks. Others more particularly belong to the race of philosophers. The greatest portion, however—those especially who belabor the populace with clubs—are the principal courtiers of the palace, executing as in duty bound, some laudable comicality of the kings.

But what have we here? Heavens! the town is swarming with wild beasts! How terrible a spectacle!—how dangerous a peculiarity!

Terrible, if you please; but not in the least degree dangerous. Each animal if you will take the pains to observe, is following, very quietly, in the wake of its master. Some few, to be sure, are led with a rope about the neck, but these are chiefly the lesser or timid species. The lion, the tiger, and the leopard are entirely without restraint. They have been trained without difficulty to their present profession, and attend upon their respective owners in the capacity of valets-de-chambre. It is true, there are occasions when Nature asserts her violated dominions;—but then the devouring of a man-at-arms, or the throttling of a consecrated bull, is a circumstance of too little moment to be more than hinted at in Epidaphne.

But what extraordinary tumult do I hear? Surely this is a loud noise even for Antioch! It argues some commotion of unusual interest.

Yes—undoubtedly. The king has ordered some novel spectacle—some gladiatorial exhibition at the hippodrome—or perhaps the massacre of the Scythian prisoners—or the conflagration of his new palace—or the tearing down of a handsome temple—or, indeed, a bonfire of a few Jews. The uproar increases. Shouts of laughter ascend the skies. The air becomes dissonant with wind instruments, and horrible with clamor of a million throats. Let us descend, for the love of fun, and see what is going on! This way—be careful! Here we are in the principal street, which is called the street of Timarchus. The sea of people is coming this way, and we shall find a difficulty in stemming the tide. They are pouring through the alley of Heraclides, which leads directly from the palace;—therefore, the king is most probably among the rioters.

The Final Kingdom

"Yes,";—I hear the shouts of the herald proclaiming his approach in the pompous phraseology of the East. We shall have a glimpse of his person as he passes by the temple of Ashimah. Let us ensconce ourselves in the vestibule of the sanctuary; he will be here anon. In the meantime let us survey this image. What is it? Oh! it is the god Ashimah in proper person. You perceive, however, that he is neither a lamb, nor a goat, nor a satyr, neither has he much resemblance to the Pan of the Arcadians. Yet all these appearances have been given—I beg pardon—will be given—by the learned of future ages, to the Ashimah of the Syrians. Put on your spectacles, and tell me what it is. What is it?

Bless me! it is an ape!

True—a baboon; but by no means the less a deity. His name is a derivation of the Greek Simia—what great fools are antiquarians! But see!—see!—yonder scampers a ragged little urchin. Where is he going? What is he bawling about? What does he say? Oh! he says the king is coming in triumph; that he is dressed in state; that he has just finished putting to death, with his own hand, a thousand chained Israelitish prisoners! For this exploit the ragamuffin is lauding him to the skies. Hark! here comes a troop of a similar description. They have made a Latin hymn upon the valor of the king, and are singing it as they go:

> Mille, mille, mille,
> Mille, mille, mille,
> Decollavimus, unus homo!
> Mille, mille, mille, mille, decollavimus!
> Mille, mille, mille,
> Vivat qui mille mille occidit!
> Tantum vini habet nemo
> Quantum sanguinis effudit!

Which may be thus paraphrased:

> A thousand, a thousand, a thousand,
> A thousand, a thousand, a thousand,
> We, with one warrior, have slain!
> A thousand, a thousand, a thousand, a thousand.
> Sing a thousand over again!
> Soho!—let us sing
> Long life to our king,
> Who knocked over a thousand so fine!

Soho!—let us roar,
He has given us more
Red gallons of gore
Than all Syria can furnish of wine!

Flavius Vospicus says, that the hymn here introduced was sung by the rabble upon the occasion of Aurelian, in the Sarmatic war, having slain, with his own hand, nine hundred and fifty of the enemy.

Do you hear that flourish of trumpets?

Yes: the king is coming! See! the people are aghast with admiration, and lift up their eyes to the heavens in reverence. He comes;—he is coming;—there he is!

Who?—where?—the king?—do not behold him—cannot say that I perceive him.

Then you must be blind.

Very possible. Still I see nothing but a tumultuous mob of idiots and madmen, who are busy in prostrating themselves before a gigantic cameleopard, and endeavoring to obtain a kiss of the animal's hoofs. See! the beast has very justly kicked one of the rabble over—and another—and another—and another. Indeed, I cannot help admiring the animal for the excellent use he is making of his feet.

Rabble, indeed!—why these are the noble and free citizens of Epidaphne! Beasts, did you say?—take care that you are not overheard. Do you not perceive that the animal has the visage of a man? Why, my dear sir, that cameleopard is no other than Antiochus Epiphanes, Antiochus the Illustrious, King of Syria, and the most potent of all the autocrats of the East! It is true that he is entitled, at times, Antiochus Epimanes—Antiochus the madman—but that is because all people have not the capacity to appreciate his merits. It is also certain that he is at present ensconced in the hide of a beast, and is doing his best to play the part of a cameleopard; but this is done for the better sustaining his dignity as king. Besides, the monarch is of gigantic stature, and the dress is therefore neither unbecoming nor over large. We may, however, presume he would not have adopted it but for some occasion of especial state. Such, you will allow, is the massacre of a thousand Jews. With how superior a dignity the monarch perambulates on all fours! His tail, you perceive, is held aloft by his two principal concubines,

191

Elline and Argelais; and his whole appearance would be infinitely prepossessing, were it not for the protuberance of his eyes, which will certainly start out of his head, and the queer color of his face, which has become nondescript from the quantity of wine he has swallowed. Let us follow him to the hippodrome, whither he is proceeding, and listen to the song of triumph which he is commencing:

> Who is king but Epiphanes?
> Say—do you know?
> Who is king but Epiphanes?
> Bravo!—bravo!
> There is none but Epiphanes,
> No—there is none:
> So tear down the temples,
> And put out the sun!

Well and strenuously sung! The populace are hailing him "Prince of Poets," as well as "Glory of the East," "Delight of the Universe," and "Most Remarkable of Cameleopards". They have encored his effusion, and do you hear?—he is singing it over again. When he arrives at the hippodrome, he will be crowned with the poetic wreath, in anticipation of his victory at the approaching Olympics.

But, good Jupiter! what is the matter in the crowd behind us?

Behind us, did you say?—oh! ah!—I perceive. My friend, it is well that you spoke in time. Let us get into a place of safety as soon as possible. Here!—let us conceal ourselves in the arch of this aqueduct, and I will inform you presently of the origin of the commotion. It has turned out as I have been anticipating. The singular appearance of the cameleopard and the head of a man, has, it seems, given offence to the notions of propriety entertained, in general, by the wild animals domesticated in the city. A mutiny has been the result; and, as is usual upon such occasions, all human efforts will be of no avail in quelling the mob. Several of the Syrians have already been devoured; but the general voice of the four-footed patriots seems to be for eating up the cameleopard. "The Prince of Poets," therefore, is upon his hinder legs, running for his life. His courtiers have left him in the lurch, and his concubines have followed so excellent an example. "Delight of the Universe," thou art in a sad predicament!

"Glory of the East," thou art in danger of mastication! Therefore never regard so piteously thy tail; it will undoubtedly be draggled in the mud, and for this there is no help. Look not behind thee, then, at its unavoidable degradation; but take courage, ply thy legs with vigor, and scud for the hippodrome! Remember that thou art Antiochus Epiphanes. Antiochus the Illustrious!—also "Prince of Poets," "Glory of the East," "Delight of the Universe," and "Most Remarkable of Cameleopards!" Heavens! what a power of speed thou art displaying! What a capacity for leg-bail thou art developing! Run, Prince!— Bravo, Epiphanes! Well done, Cameleopard!—Glorious Antiochus!—He runs!—he leaps!—he flies! Like an arrow from a catapult he approaches the hippodrome! He leaps!—he shrieks!—he is there! This is well; for hadst thou, "Glory of the East," been half a second longer in reaching the gates of the Amphitheatre, there is not a bear's cub in Epidaphne that would not have had a nibble at thy carcase. Let us be off—let us take our departure!— for we shall find our delicate modern ears unable to endure the vast uproar which is about to commence in celebration of the king's escape! Listen! it has already commenced. See!—the whole town is topsy-turvy.

Surely this is the most populous city of the East! What a wilderness of people! what a jumble of all ranks and ages! what a multiplicity of sects and nations! what a variety of costumes! what a Babel of languages! what a screaming of beasts! what a tinkling of instruments! what a parcel of philosophers!

Come let us be off.

Stay a moment! I see a vast hubbub in the hippodrome; what is the meaning of it, I beseech you?

That?—oh, nothing! The noble and free citizens of Epidaphne being, as they declare, well satisfied of the faith, valor, wisdom, and divinity of their king, and having, moreover, been eye-witnesses of his late superhuman agility, do think it no more than their duty to invest his brows (in addition to the poetic crown) with the wreath of victory in the footrace—a wreath which it is evident he must obtain at the celebration of the next Olympiad, and which, therefore, they now give him in advance.

❖ END OF POEM ❖

An Ancient Usurper

The prose poem is tongue-in-cheek, but just as Poe's last line suggests, Antiochus was a man who took things that did not belong to him—the Seleucid Empire from his own nephew; the Olympic crown before the race had been run; the city of the Great King, Jerusalem; but finally, the honor and glory belonging to God Almighty Himself in His Temple.

If the Scriptures would aid us in recognizing the antichrist when he comes on the scene, we can fully expect to behold a man who gains honors not earned and consumes riches not belonging to him on every level.

Then an overwhelming army will be swept away before him; both it and a prince of the covenant will be destroyed. After coming to an agreement with him, he will act deceitfully, and with only a few people he will rise to power.

11: 22, 23

Onais the high priest is most likely the "prince of the covenant" spoken of, who served in Jerusalem and was murdered in 170 B.C.

When the richest provinces feel secure, he will invade them and will achieve what neither his fathers nor his forefathers did. He will distribute plunder, loot and wealth among his followers. He will plot the overthrow of fortresses—but only for a time.

v. 24

The "rich provinces" are most likely further areas that were yet unconquered in both Israel and Egypt.

With a large army he will stir up his strength and courage against the king of the South. The king of the South will wage war with a large and very powerful army, but he will not be able to stand because of the plots devised against him. Those who eat from the king's provisions will try to destroy him; his army will be swept away, and many will fall in battle. The two kings, with their hearts bent on evil, will sit at the same table and lie to each other, but to no avail, because an end will still come at the appointed time.

v. 25

Antiochus attacked the king of the South, **Ptolemy VI**, and evidently an inside conspiracy and a covenant of lies was struck

194

between those two, but yet without coming to any helpfulness to him.

The king of the North will return to his own country with great wealth, but his heart will be set against the holy covenant. He will take action against it and then return to his own country.

v. 28

Antiochus' sins then reached the heavens as he stretched out his arm and defiled the people of the Covenant in Jerusalem. He set up a garrison in God's chosen city, massacred Jewish people, but then left for the North. He still had not situated himself permanently in Jerusalem.

At the appointed time he will invade the South again, but this time the outcome will be different from what it was before. Ships of the western coastlands will oppose him, and he will lose heart. Then he will turn back and vent his fury against the holy covenant. He will return and show favor to those who forsake the holy covenant.

vv. 29-30

The "ships" of the "western coastlands" spoken of here are the ships of the Roman army now coming on the scene. Defeated by them and unable to vent his fury against them, he sublimated his rage and turned back in a fury against the Jewish populace of Jerusalem.

His armed forces will rise up to desecrate the Temple fortress and will abolish the daily sacrifice. Then they will set up the abomination that causes desolation. With flattery he will corrupt those who have violated the covenant, but the people who know their God will firmly resist him. Those who are wise will instruct many, though for a time they will fall by the sword or be burned or captured or plundered. When they fall, they will receive a little help, and many who are not sincere will join them. Some of the wise will stumble, so that they may be refined, purified and made spotless until the time of the end, for it will still come at the appointed time.

vv. 31-35

This last verse is filled with hidden promise. The picture is much like the list of heroes in Hebrews chapter eleven who chose to endure in the face of great adversity, even death—persevering in faith because they "saw him who is invisible" (Heb. 11:29). Actually, this verse is probably one of the most important verses in the entire book of Daniel. "But, the people who know their God

195

will firmly resist him." Daniel's underlying message throughout is that God's power is strongest in the darkest circumstances; His light shines when it seems there is no chance of light anywhere. What follows here in Daniel also underscores this concept.

Now those mountains of prophecy that have seemed just a purple backdrop on the horizon develop detail as we draw closer. Shadows separate themselves and foothills are distinguishable from higher mountain peaks. The scenery actually has dimension to it. The activity spoken of has moved beyond the kingly possibilities of Antiochus Epiphanes and is detailing the coming antichrist.

> *The king will do as he pleases. He will exalt and magnify himself above every god and will say unheard-of things against the God of gods. He will be successful until the time of wrath is completed, for what has been determined must take place. He will show no regard for the gods of his fathers or for the one desired by women, nor will he regard any god, but will exalt himself above them all. Instead of them, he will honor a god of fortresses, a god unknown to his fathers, he will honor with gold and silver, with precious stones and costly gifts. He will attack the mightiest fortresses with the help of a foreign god, and will greatly honor those who acknowledge him. He will make them rulers over many people and will distribute the land at a price.*

vv. 36-39

Against the God of Gods

Up to this point, the kings of Babylon have reserved some measure of respect for the "God of gods." Even in their wickedness there was a line that was drawn in the sand which was not crossed over. Now the king who has exalted and magnified himself will speak "unheard-of things against the God" above all earthly gods. There is no reverence for God any longer. Things are said against Him that have never been heard before. Antiochus Epiphanes did not fulfill this. We are seeing a "being" who will boast himself against the God of Heaven. All fear of God is gone.

Jesus himself warns:

> *So when you see standing in the holy place 'the abomination that causes desolation', spoken of through the prophet Daniel—let the reader understand—then let those who are in Judea flee to the mountains. Let no one on the roof of his house go down to take anything out of the house. Let no one in the field go back*

to get his cloak. How dreadful it will be in those days for pregnant women and nursing mothers! Pray that your flight will not take place in winter or on the Sabbath. For then there will be great distress, unequaled from the beginning of the world until now—and never to be equaled again.

Matthew 24:15-21

Paul joins Jesus' admonition:

Don't let anyone deceive you in any way, for [that day will not come] until the rebellion occurs and the man of lawlessness is revealed, the man doomed to destruction.
He will oppose and will exalt himself over everything that is called God or is worshiped, so that he sets himself up in God's temple, proclaiming himself to be God.

2 Thessalonians 2:3, 4

This "man" being portrayed for us discards all vestiges of religion but one: He embraces and honors a god of fortresses. *"Instead of them, he will honor a god of fortresses; a god unknown to his fathers he will honor with gold and silver, with precious stones and costly gifts"* (Dan. 11:38). Raw, cruel power will accompany his reign.

The price of his worship is costly. The Hebrew word tells us he is pledging his honor to *maoz'im*, which is in the plural form (its root is *maoz*) and is interpreted as "strongholds." The primary character in Scripture depicted as a "man of war" and of "strongholds" was Nimrod.

Cush was the father of Nimrod, who grew to be a mighty warrior on the earth. He was a mighty hunter before the LORD; that is why it is said, "Like Nimrod, a mighty hunter before the LORD." The first centers of his kingdom were Babylon, Erech, Akkad and Calneh, in Shinar.

From that land he went to Assyria, where he built Nineveh, Rehoboth Ir, Calah and Resen, which is between Nineveh and Calah; that is the great city.

Genesis 10:8-12

Nimrod's reputation came to be linked with the building of the tower of Babel, the city of Babylon, and the other cities of reknown listed above including Nineveh. Historians say that he subverted the patriachal system of government and was the first to establish a regal government where he ruled as king. He supposedly founded the kingdom of Babylon in 2245 B.C. and reigned one hundred and twenty-one years. Nimrod was deified after his death and placed in

The Final Kingdom

the constellation of Orion—the "Great Bear" by his worshipers.

The propensity of Antiochus to take what is not his surfaces—exposing him as the "man of perdition."

He will attack the mightiest fortresses with the help of a foreign god and will greatly honor those who acknowledge him. He will make them rulers over many people and will distribute the land at a price."

Daniel 11:39

A colonial rule will reemerge from his authority and he will set up governors over the lands that he will conquer.

Government systems in the last centuries have alarmed many. Communism was tagged as the great antichrist. In spirit that is true, but in fact, it is not. Communism lost its mysterious ability to instill fear in the kingdoms of the world in our lifetimes. Its seventy years of rule came to an abrupt end. In the meantime, Islam has busied itself over the last several hundred years spreading out over the face of the earth. I do not believe either of these to be the final enemy.

Seeds of deterioration in Islam surfaced in the war between Iraq and Iran in the 1980s. As a matter of fact, tactics of the "coming man of perdition" were used by Saddam Hussein to forge his nation into a battering ram of hate toward their own Moslem brothers across their eastern border. He began to tout himself as being in the direct line of Nebuchadnezzar, king of Babylon. Great murals of himself and Nebuchadnezzar sprang up in the major cities of Iraq. Massaging his nation's awareness of their past glorious history as Babylon, he then reminded them that it was the Persians who brought their glories to an end—and although they have changed their names, they still exist just over the border in Iran. Therefore, a war of Moslem brother against Moslem brother raged for eight years and millions of young boys were sacrificed by a madman promising "paradise" if martyred in the "just" cause of *jihad* ("holy war") against their enemies.

But we have not yet seen the rulership that will emerge from the marriage of the "man of perdition" with the "god of fortresses."

At the time of the end the king of the South will engage him in battle, and the king of the North will storm out against him with chariots and cavalry and a great fleet of ships. He will also invade many countries and sweep through them like a flood. He will also invade the Beautiful Land. Many countries will fall, but Edom, Moab and the leaders of Ammon will be delivered from his hand. He will extend his power over many countries; Egypt will not escape. He will gain control of the treasures of gold and silver and all the riches of Egypt, with the Libyans and Nubians in submission. But reports from the east and the north will alarm him, and he will set out in a great rage to destroy and annihilate many. He will pitch his royal tents between the seas at the beautiful holy mountain. Yet he will come to his end, and no one will help him.

vv. 40-45

The problems presented to invading armies in reaching Edom, Moab, and Ammon may have preserved those kingdoms. The main trade route between the north and south at that time was the coastal road which was known in Roman times as the *Via Maris*, "The Way of the Sea." This road lay the length of Israel, connecting Assyria and Egypt, close to the Mediterranean Sea. This answer may be too simplistic and neglect a spiritual application. The physical aspects and difficulty are the obvious reason for the first century B.C. deliverance. On a clear day, from the mountain on which Jerusalem sits one can see the tallest buildings of the Jordanian city of Amman, which sits on another mountain separated by the Jordan Valley rift. The journey for an army would have been fraught with danger on descent from Jerusalem. The road is dry, dusty, and riddled with canyons in which small segments of an opposing army could hide with great advantage over a large number of men. The same would have been true of the successive ascent to the mountains of Moab, Ammon, and Edom.

But, present day peace agreements between Jordan and Israel may have something to do with the fullness of the prophecy and the fact that they are spared from destruction and wrath. Egypt is also mentioned as finding favor in the sight of God, once more, and they too signed a peace treaty with Israel in the 1980s.

Jerusalem, that city named by God the "Beautiful Land," becomes the downfall of the antichrist. Bad news from the east and north enrages him: Syria, Iran, and Iraq. Finally, in verse 45, "He will pitch his royal tents between the seas at the beautiful holy *mountain*"—of course, that is Jerusalem—"and yet he will come to his end, and no one will help him." Touching the "apple of God's eye"—the Jews and their land—may have been appealing in the beginning, but in the end, it will crush him and all his evil intentions.

*But if you return to me
and obey my commands,
then even if your exiled people are
at the farthest horizon,*

*I will gather them from there
and bring them
to the place I have chosen
as a dwelling for my Name.*

Nehemiah 1:9

The Wrap-up of Time

In this "end of all things" chapter, Michael "the great prince" is still on the scene. His job description flies in the face of modern-day attempts to dismiss Israel as God's chosen people. He has been appointed the guardian of the Jewish nation, and according to our final chapter, is still busy with that calling in the end of time.

> *At that time Michael, the great prince who protects your people, will arise. There will be a time of distress such as has not happened from the beginning of nations until then. But at that time your people—everyone whose name is found written in the book—will be delivered.*

> Daniel 12:1

Sometimes, it is the small details, such as Michael's continuing role, that tell the bigger story.

The Other Israel

The modern attempt to eradicate Israel from the pages of the Bible is finding fresh fuel these days. While pastoring in Washington state, one of my congregants who was attending seminary in the area came to me very distressed. He told me the seminary was about to show a video that he was extremely troubled by. I asked him to try to get me a copy to preview so I could decide what action to take. The video was entitled "The Other Israel." I viewed the video in horror. It opens in a charismatic church in Oregon during their worship service. After about thirty seconds of the church service, the narrator steps in front of the camera and describes a "danger" to these folks that we have been watching.

"The Jews of the modern nation of Israel are not really Jews," he warns. In the thirty minute video, he pulls together a most amazing array of distorted information and absurd theories about the Jewish people that have been disproven time and time again, painting a black picture of the entire Jewish society worldwide.

I could not remember seeing such attacks against the Jewish people since Joseph Goebbels, Hitler's public relations mastermind in Germany during the Third Reich. Mr. Goebbels perfected a cinematic ploy called "photomontage." Photomontage is so often used in advertising today that it seems to be second nature. It is hard to imagine that there was a time when photomontage was *not* used as a persuasive tool. This tool has been overused and we are now advertising savvy. We know that if we see a bright red sports car advertised, the pretty girl in the swimsuit sitting on the hood does not go with it. Through cinematic media, Goebbels married bubonic-plague-infested rats to the ultra-Orthodox Jewish population of Germany's ghettos, in the minds of the German people. He accomplished this via cinema shots of narrow, attic crawl spaces—with rats darting in and out of little openings—closely followed by shots of the narrow streets of the Jewish ghetto—and bearded Jewish men darting in and out of shop and apartment doors.

In Goebbel's time, two separate ideas brought together by a mastermind of media held untold power. By his documentaries, Goebbels prepared the German mind to accept the Holocaust. His films have been banned by all nations of the world with the exception of some Arabic nations, still embroiled in hate campaigns against Israel today.

One of the most vile sectors of "The Other Israel" is the narrator entering a synagogue in the Los Angeles area and taking a volume of the Talmud off the shelf. Turning to a passage whose context is carefully hidden, the video allows it to seem to say that sex with a three-year-old is permissible. Actually, this section of the Talmud deals not with sex at all but with the betrothal of a priest to the daughter of another priest since they could not marry outside the line of the *Cohenim* (priestly line). It was understood that the marriage would not be consummated until the daughter was of marriageable age, but given the "The Other Israel" antisemitic treatment, what is white was cleverly made to appear black.

Our senior pastor and I, with some very able congregants, went into action. We telephoned the institution with a query as to why they would ever show such a video in a seminary. They seemed shocked and distressed that outsiders knew of the showing. They claimed it was purely for "educational purposes," although their plan of presentation involved no explanation of the unjustifiable slander against the Jewish people.

Over the next few weeks, and with the threat of informing the local newspaper of the seminary's intents, they allowed us to be present at the showing to explain, step by step, the error of the film maker.

The sad part of the story is that over ten years later, a man identifying himself as Keith Richard, a representative of an organization called the Militia of Montana, was interviewed on a radio broadcast on the Cape Talk radio station in South Africa on September 26, 1999. He described Israel as "that litterbox in the Middle East," and said verbatim: "If you're practicing Judaism, I know exactly what that filthy thing says. It says we should have sex with three-year-old children and it will be all right."

To see the same thoughts expressed in almost identical phraseology crop up in South Africa means that antisemites are busy spreading their propaganda far and wide.

Thank God, Michael, the guardian of the Jewish people, is still on the job. The evil one still has a program to undo Israel, and thereby ultimately attempt to prevent the return of the Messiah. Our earlier visitation of Antiochus Epiphanes painted a picture for us of the attempt to erase Jerusalem and her purpose in the calendar of God. History books are punctuated with records of those who attempted to annihilate the Jews, accompanied in many instances by records of their final ends.

Life from the Dead

Multitudes who sleep in the dust of the earth will awake: some to everlasting life, others to shame and everlasting contempt. Those who are wise will shine like the brightness of the heavens, and those who lead many to righteousness, like the stars for ever and ever.

Daniel 12:2,3

This is one of the only very clear references to the resurrection of the dead in the First Covenant. With that in mind, it is obvious that directing others to God yields great rewards.

But you, Daniel, close up and seal the words of the scroll until the time of the end. Many will go here and there to increase knowledge.

v. 4

Knowledge is increasing greatly. Simply counting the advances in technology in the last two centuries brings us in agreement with the Scriptures. Electricity, telephone, television, air travel, computers, the Internet network that links us worldwide, and the list goes on. We have shrunk the globe to a virtual marble. We communicate with people daily now via e-mail. On the Worldwide Web, one can go anywhere and find almost anything.

The Final Kingdom

> *Then I, Daniel looked, and there before me stood two others, one on this bank of the river and one on the opposite bank. One of them said to the man clothed in linen, who was above the waters of the river, "How long will it be before these astonishing things are fulfilled?"*
>
> *The man clothed in linen, who was above the waters of the river, lifted his right hand and his left hand toward heaven, and I heard him swear by him who lives forever, saying, "It will be for a time, times and half a time. When the power of the holy people has been finally broken, all these things will be completed."*
>
> *I heard, but I did not understand. So I asked, "My lord, what will the outcome of all this be?" And he replied, "Go your way, Daniel, because the words are closed up and sealed until the time of the end. Many will be purified, made spotless and refined, but the wicked will continue to be wicked. None of the wicked will understand, but those who are wise will understand."*
>
> vv. 5-10

This prophetic line of thought is in a closed loop and the message is brought to its conclusion by John on Patmos in a similar angelic visitation when he is instructed to "not seal up" the prophetic words:

> *Then he told me, "Do not seal up the words of the prophecy of this book, because the time is near. Let him who does wrong continue to do wrong; let him who is vile continue to be vile; let him who does right continue to do right; and let him who is holy continue to be holy."*
>
> Revelation 22:10, 11

Fulfillment, Then and Now

The time periods do not work out to have been fulfilled in total by Antiochus Epiphanes. He reigned for three years, not for three and a half years. We see that though he was a foreshadowing of the final antichrist, the full prophecy does not apply to him.

> *From the time that the daily sacrifice is abolished and the abomination that causes desolation is set up, there will 1,290 days. Blessed is the one who waits for and reaches the end of the 1,335 days, As for you, go your way till the end. You will rest, and then at the end of the days you will rise to receive your allotted inheritance.* Daniel 12:11-13

Again, as in the desecration of the Temple in Antiochus' day, we must expect the antichrist to do the same in the city of the Jews. Exactly what that desecration will be is speculative.

The book ends in mystery. The forty-five days tacked on to the end of the terrible time period seem to have stumped even great commentators. It is interesting, though, that Jewish sources suggest that the forty-five days would be a time when the Messiah would be hidden again after having been revealed. This is found in *Midrash (Raba) Ruth*. There is no real clear explanation of what the Jewish commentators mean by that time period either. Exactly what will happen is wrapped up in the angel's words a few verses back:

> *Go your way, Daniel, because the words are closed up and sealed until the time of the end.*

v. 9

Nevertheless, we did not stop at the gate of the citrus grove because we were afraid we could not understand all. We entered expectantly to find out what has been revealed. The journey through the garden of Daniel has been a revelation of the final Kingdom. And not just the promise that there is a final Kingdom on its way, but details of how it will happen. Encircled by the history, culture, and manners of the Fertile Crescent, Daniel serves us a feast of applicable lessons to digest and appropriate.

The frontispiece of C.S. Lewis' book *That Hideous Strength* has a fragment from a poem from Sir David Lyndsay's "Ane Dialog" and describes the Tower of Babel.

The shadow of that hyddeous strength
Sax myle and more it is of length

(The shadow of that hideous strength
Six miles and more it is of length)

The wonder of the citrus grove is that we can sense, as strongly as the sense of smell, the coming of the final Kingdom which will end, once and for all, "that hideous strength," whose "shadow" has stretched itself over the face of the earth.

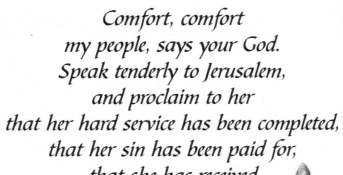

*Comfort, comfort
my people, says your God.
Speak tenderly to Jerusalem,
and proclaim to her
that her hard service has been completed,
that her sin has been paid for,
that she has received
from the LORD's hand
double for all her sins.*

Isaiah 40:1, 2

The Beginning of the End

The modern Hebrew word *moreshet* means to "impart to the next generation the traditions of the past." The word has a fuller meaning than simply "heritage." It encompasses igniting the spirit of another with the flame of their culture. In reality, it is the passing of the torch wherein lies a legacy of knowledge, inheritance, language, corporate legends, possessions, a unified identity and, of course, personal stories of the extensive existence of the Hebrew people.

This book has been an attempt to ignite the hearts of Christians with what God has done in the past, with what He is doing right now, and with what is to come. Sometimes, books on prophecy are static. God's endtime program is in process at this moment and we can all participate with Him in it.

This transferring of the torch in modern Israel is complex. So many Jewish cultures intertwine here. Jewish people returning home to Israel, bringing cultures from well over one hundred countries, come together in a state only three hundred miles long and fifty-four miles wide.

One does not have to be Jewish to be involved in *moreshet*. The call of God, which began with the Jewish people, comes full circle back in Israel. This great drama, whose stage from the beginning was the Middle East, spread throughout all the world and now returns for the wrap-up of the ages. This boomerang effect—dispersion and return—is most clearly portrayed in the stories of the exodus from Egypt and the return from Babylon. The treasures gathered along the way are for us all.

Returning to Rebuild Jerusalem

It would have been unthinkable for the Jews to return from the Babylonian exile and not keep Jerusalem foremost in their rebuilding plans. Ezra and Nehemiah urged the people to engage in active, "zealous" rebuilding—even amidst terrible opposition, ridicule and insults from their neighbors.

So it is in our day. As the former captives of Zion return to their homeland, Jerusalem remains the heart of the people—the eternal capital. It must be also be noted that throughout the history of the

The Final Kingdom

Israelites, Jerusalem has always remained central and in fact represents the full and complete return of the Jews to their Promised Land! The ancient Jewish prayer of Passover is "Next year in Jerusalem!" annually proclaimed and desired by every celebrating Jewish person worldwide. Even today, as I write this final chapter, governmental leaders are meeting to discuss the future "final" status of Jerusalem. In God's view, what is the future status of Jerusalem? What role will it play in the last days?

At that time they will call Jerusalem the Throne of the LORD, and all nations will gather in Jerusalem to honor the name of the LORD. No longer will they follow the stubbornness of their evil hearts. In those days the house of Judah will join the house of Israel, and together they will come from a northern land to the land I gave your forefathers as an inheritance.

Jeremiah 3:17-18

In the book of Revelation, the Lord makes clear to John through his vision the future status of Jerusalem from an eternal vantage point. Jerusalem is represented as the desire of us all and as the Holy City of God's presence in the New Heaven.

I saw the Holy City, the new Jerusalem, coming down out of heaven from God, prepared as a bride beautifully dressed for her husband.

And he carried me away in the Spirit to a mountain great and high, and showed me the Holy City, Jerusalem, coming down out of heaven from God. It shone with the glory of God, and its brilliance was like that of a very precious jewel, like a jasper, clear as crystal.

Revelation 21:2,10,11

The contrast in the book of Nehemiah is evident when the returning exiles, including a representation of Levite Temple musicians and singers, are gathered to take up their daily ministry activities once again in Jerusalem:

Uzzi was one of Asaph's descendants, who were the singers responsible for the service of the house of God. The singers were under the king's orders, which regulated their daily activity.

At the dedication of the wall of Jerusalem, the Levites were sought out from where they lived and were brought to Jerusalem to celebrate joyfully the dedication with songs of thanksgiving and with the music of cymbals, harps and lyres.

And on that day they offered great sacrifices, rejoicing because God had given them great joy. The women and children also rejoiced. The sound of rejoicing in Jerusalem could be heard far away.

Nehemiah 11:22, 23; 12:27; 12:43

The time for mourning was over. The joyfulness of their celebrations resulted in the noisiest "worship service" this side of Heaven!

The prophets of Israel foretold of the singing in the streets of Jerusalem that would once again occur upon their return to the Land. The fact is, *aliyah*, "going up" (the Hebrew word used for one immigrating to Israel), is cause for rejoicing and singing in the heart of the one returning to the Land given by God to the Jewish people.

When the LORD brought back the captives to Zion, we were like men who dreamed.

Our mouths were filled with laughter, our tongues with songs of joy. Then it was said among the nations, "the LORD has done great things for them.

The LORD has done great things for us, and we are filled with joy.

Psalm 126:1-3

We have an admonition to *"Pray for the peace of Jerusalem; may they prosper who love you"* (Ps. 122:6, NKJV). This echoes the promise of God given to Abraham, Isaac, and Jacob, for those nations (Gentiles) who "bless" their descendants—the Jewish people. There is a prosperity and blessing for those who seek the good of Jerusalem and the Jewish people.

The Face of the Past All Around Us

My wife and I and our three children have lived in the city of Jerusalem for thirteen years. Here, remnants of ancient cultures can be found everywhere. That reality came as a shock to me during a city bus ride after poring through books and archaeological records during my research on Mesopotamian culture. *Bas* relief panels discovered by archaeologists in both the Assyrian city of Nineveh and Babylon show great detail in the facial features of the inhabitants of those cities. The finds are extensively popularized in many different publications. After so many viewings, those facial features and physical characteristics become somehow imprinted on the subconscious.

During that morning ride to work on the bus, I realized that sitting directly across from me was a young man with the distinct features of King Darius. I did a double take. The only difference was that he was dressed in a leather jacket, T-shirt, jeans, and a new pair of Nikes on his feet. For a moment my mind could not reconcile that face and those clothes. A long flowing robe and the staff of a king went with that face. Full lips, a royal semitic nose, and heavy-lidded eyes stared back at me, just like in the Babylonian murals. He must have wondered why I was staring at him.

I then looked around the bus and recognized other faces that would have been at home on a Mesopotamian mural—some from distinct areas of the land between the rivers and others suggesting surrounding nations of the ancients. It seemed as if the cultures still existed but were now cloaked in modern, western garments representing the melting pot of modern Israeli life.

I am not against progress. I had just never looked at the society that I had been living in in quite that manner before. Since that day I have looked more carefully at the faces around me. I have also realized that the story of the exiles is ongoing.

The dispersion of the Jewish people happened in several phases. Babylon was the first scattering of God's elect. Rome, and the destruction of Jerusalem in A.D. 70, was the second. The first few chapters of the book of Acts record for us the demographics of Jewish population centers in Asia, Africa, and Europe.

Now there were staying in Jerusalem God-fearing Jews from every nation under heaven. When they heard this sound, a crowd came together in bewilderment, because each one heard them speaking in his own language.
Utterly amazed, they asked: Are not all these men who are speaking Galileans? Then how is it that each of us hears them in his own native language? Parthians, Medes and Elamites; residents of Mesopotamia, Judea and Cappadocia, Pontus and Asia,
Phrygia and Pamphylia, Egypt and the parts of Libya near Cyrene; visitors from Rome (both Jews and converts to Judaism); Cretans and Arabs—we hear them declaring the wonders of God in our own tongues!

Acts 2:5-11

Return from Baghdad

One of the books I used for research, *To Baghdad and Back*, was written by Mordechai Ben-Porat. Throughout his life, Iraqi-born Mordechai Ben-Porat served Israel, as an emissary to Iraq and Iran and as a member of the Israeli Parliament (known as the Knesset). He is the founder of the Babylonian Jewry Heritage Center, which he established on the original site of the transit camp in the coastal city of Or Yehudah, south of Tel Aviv, where the final scenes of the return of the Jewish people from Babylon took place in 1948.

Over 130,000 Jews emigrated to Israel from Iraq, thanks largely to the efforts of emissaries from Israel and activists of the "Halutz Movement" (Pioneer Movement) in Iraq. This astounding accomplishment, known as "Operation Ezra and Nehemiah," gave a final and glorious curtain call to the ancient Babylonian exile.

Excited about the research I was doing of the ancient Orient, I longed to actually meet some of those who had returned from Baghdad in the movement of the late '40s and early '50s. Several events took place close to the completion of this book that facilitated this opportunity.

The Mountains and the People

I recently lectured a group about Jesus' first-century Passover meal with His disciples at Jim Fleming's Scripture Garden here in Jerusalem. After the meal, Barak Rimon, the Israeli tour guide, and I were talking and I discovered that his father had escaped from Iraq in 1949. Seeing my interest, Barak extended an invitation to visit his family in Haifa.

Several weeks later, I drove north to meet the family. Being early for the interview, I decided I had time to take the scenic route and drive through the famous Mount Carmel National Park to get to their house in the foothills on the other side of the mountain.

I turned off the highway coming from Tel Aviv to Haifa at the Mount Carmel sign. The national park sign welcomed me and the road narrowed and began to climb immediately. In many years of living in Israel, I had never been to the top of Mount Carmel! As I have experienced in so many other sites in Israel, the characters and events that made those places famous played themselves out in my mind. As my car wound up the mountain through the pine

The Final Kingdom

forest I "saw" Elijah and the prophets of Baal on the mountain in my imagination. I wondered where the exact site was. It was such an expansive forest that my car was winding its way through. The events of Elijah's story could have taken place anywhere.

Then, just the fact that I was on a high mountain in Israel, was enough to bring voices out of the past. Ezekiel's words echoed in my mind:

Son of man, prophesy to the mountains of Israel and say,
O mountains of Israel, hear the word of the LORD. This is what
the Sovereign LORD says: The enemy said of you, "Aha! The
ancient heights have become our possession."' Therefore
prophesy and say, 'This is what the Sovereign LORD says:

Because they ravaged and hounded you from every side so
that you became the possession of the rest of the nations and
the object of people's malicious talk and slander, therefore, O
mountains of Israel, hear the word of the Sovereign LORD:

This is what the Sovereign LORD says to the mountains and
hills, to the ravines and valleys, to the desolate ruins and the
deserted towns that have been plundered and ridiculed by
the rest of the nations around you—this is what the Sovereign
LORD says: In my burning zeal I have spoken against the rest
of the nations, and against all Edom, for with glee and with
malice in their hearts they made my land their own
possession so that they might plunder its pastureland.

Therefore prophesy concerning the land of Israel and say to
the mountains and hills, to the ravines and valleys: 'This is
what the Sovereign LORD says: I speak in my jealous wrath
because you have suffered the scorn of the nations. Therefore
this is what the Sovereign Lord says: I swear with uplifted
hand that the nations around you will also suffer scorn. But
you, O mountains of Israel, will produce branches and fruit
for my people Israel, for they will soon come home . . .'"

Ezekiel 36:1-8

I knew that at least eighty percent of the mountainous regions in Israel existed in the contested "West Bank." Political negotiations to give up those areas seemed unthinkable in light of the prophetic admonition. But, the phrase "for they will soon come home," was my reason for being on Mount Carmel.

I continued to experience the "drive-thru-panorama-of-history" on the way to Barak's father's house to hear his homecoming story first-hand.

212

A Valued Contact

Barak's heart had been knit to ours, as an organization, when our Bridges for Peace tour group was using him as their tour guide through the land of Israel. They discovered that he was missing a memorial day service for his best friend who had been killed in the war in Lebanon. A scheduling mistake had placed the beginning of the tour and the memorial on the same day. John Howson, our Canadian National Director of Bridges for Peace, who was hosting the tour that day, suggested that Barak would not miss the memorial if they all went together as a group to the service. The tour could proceed as scheduled and they would all attend the memorial at the same time. Barak agreed and the tour group was elated. The young man's family were so grateful for the comfort and support they felt from Barak and the tour group that they wept. Since that time, Barak has been close to our organization and regularly leads our Canadian groups.

An Ancient People Come Home

Arriving at the home of the Rimon family, I was warmly greeted by Barak and Zvi, his father. Barak was to interpret for me in difficult areas where my Hebrew was not good enough to get all the colorful details.

While Barak fixed cold drinks and sliced cool melons on that very hot day, I quickly learned that his father, Zvi Rimon, was born in 1934 in a village called Twarige, many miles south of Baghdad. In Iraq, Zvi's Iraqi name was Saba, and the family name was Rachamim. Both names were changed upon arriving in Israel. Zvi had four brothers and one sister. The Iraqi village was fifteen thousand people total, with thirty Jewish families residing there.

The Rachamim family moved from Twarige to Hela in 1944. Zvi's father, Salman, worked as an irrigation specialist. In Hela there were sixty-five Jewish families and three synagogues in which to worship. Zvi proudly told me that this village was the home of the prophet Ezekiel, according to tradition.

Barak now joined us from the kitchen and the story became more animated, as he was obviously hearing portions of his father's story apparently for the first time.

In Twarige there was no Halutz Movement, the Hebrew name for the "Zionist Youth Movement," but there was in their new home of Hela. Zvi's brother, Rachamim, became a member upon their move to the new city. (Barak saw that I was confused and clarified that Rachamim's first name was indeed also their family name—Rachamim Rachamim.) The movement had begun in 1942 and was young in Iraq. Some ninety percent of the population voiced intentions to one day immigrate to Israel. Several things kept them from that goal. At this particular time, Israel was under the Mandate government of the British, and immigration numbers were being strictly controlled. At the same time, the Iraqi government was unwilling to let their Jewish population leave the country, as many of them held important government jobs.

Over a period of about five years, from 1944 to 1949, the desire to immigrate became an all-consuming preoccupation of many of the Jews in Iraq. Positive Zionist propaganda from the Halutz Movement and the curtailing of many jobs and educational possibilities for the Jewish community gave the idea of leaving Iraq new importance. There was little meaning to life without that goal in front of them. Those deeply involved in the Halutz Movement met often and learned the Hebrew language of the modern State of Israel. The Jews of Iraq used the Sephardi Hebrew script known as Rashi, named after the highly esteemed Ashkenazi Rabbi, Rashi. The letters of the modern Hebrew alphabet are only somewhat similar, therefore, these hopeful Iraqis had to learn the modern Hebrew script.

Zvi voiced his belief that it was miraculous that his father actually let him leave Iraq. He was the "baby" of the family and protected from danger by all the other members. At the time he was only fifteen years old. But, Go! was the message from all members of the family when the time for them to escape finally arrived. The last straw was when the Jews were banned from attending Iraqi schools in 1948. The stage was set, the time had come, and now the adventure began.

The monthly salary of Zvi's father was only twelve dinar. The cost that the smugglers demanded to take Zvi to Israel was five hundred dinar. By scraping, saving, and selling everything that they could, the family raised the money to send Zvi and his brother Itzhak to Israel. They knew their only hope of a future was in the land of their forefathers. What they did not know at the time, is that Zvi and Itzhak would not be allowed to travel together.

214

Time to Go!

In October of 1949, the Rachamim family got word that Zvi was to prepare to leave. Word came on a Sunday, and on Monday, Zvi's mother began preparing foods that would last on the long trip. No one knew exactly how long the trip would take, neither did they know what route they were to travel. Each step was given one at a time and that is when the boys found out that they would not even be traveling together.

On Wednesday, a lady dressed in the Islamic *abaya*, a full-body covering, called at the house for Zvi. Covered from head to foot, she took him to a house where they were joined by another young lady, also dressed in Islamic dress. There they ate dinner and slept. In the morning at 5:00 a.m., the party rose and headed for the train station. The route to the train station passed the Rachamim house but Zvi could not even say goodbye to the family now that he was on his way. From their village they headed to Baghdad, with only the instructions that "someone" would meet the group at the train station. There was no word of who they should look for or how they would recognize them. Amazingly, in the Baghdad train station, someone caught Zvi's eye, winked, and with a nod of the head, motioned in which direction he should move.

The group was taken away from the train station to the city, placed into a taxi, and taken to the home of a Jewish family. Here they were fed lunch and waited until 4:30 p.m. At that time they were told it was time to move again. They were joined by several other travelers and taken back to the train station. The train station was extremely crowded and the travelers were instructed to wait until the last minute before loading their baggage on the train so it would be close to the exit doors.

Shaking Any Informants

Once baggage was carefully loaded on the train, and the positioning of it checked, the undercover passengers were allowed to board the train. They were instructed not to take seats far from the door. The group was instructed to keep their eyes on the ladies who were their guides at this very important juncture. The train they were on was headed south, back past their village, to the Iraqi city of Basra, almost to the Persian Gulf. One could not take the train straight from Hela to Basra but rather a connection had to be made in Baghdad.

The Final Kingdom

Once the train had pulled out of the station, the lady dressed in the abaya softly but firmly gave an order for everyone to immediately join her in the space between the train cars. All complied to find her instructing them now to throw their luggage from the moving train and jump off after it! The strategy for getting on last was becoming clear.

Rattled and confused they found themselves scattered over a several block area along the train track. Gathering their luggage together, they hailed taxis and traveled through Baghdad to Masbah, a resort suburb of Baghdad on the banks of the Tigris River, to the home of a very wealthy Jewish merchant. The quick train change ordeal was to confuse anyone who might have been following them and to throw them off track. Here, at this luxurious villa, they remained for two weeks, never going out of the house and being careful not to be seen on the premises.

It was becoming evident that the Halutz Movement had members at every level of Iraqi society. The wealthy Iraqi citizens were doing all they could to help their people realize their Zionist dream of immigrating to Israel.

Finally, on *Erev Shabbat*, the Friday evening beginning the Jewish Sabbath, the group was told that in the morning they would be leaving again. More people had joined the group during this two week time period, and all the Jewish women were dressed in the abaya. Zvi was dressed as a Baghdad businessman in a nice suit, but to disguise himself better he was made to wear many layers of undergarments to add some bulk to his young body. Everyone was so excited to be leaving that they could not eat breakfast that morning.

What could barely be called a bus came to pick them up. It was more in the fashion of a British lorry, with a cover overhead. All the travellers sat in the back. Zvi met a nail in the roof with his head each time the bus hit a bump. He quickly learned to dodge and miss the sharp stabbing pain.

Singing for Joy and Anxious Moments

As soon as they knew they were out of range of crowds and well on the road, they were so happy they sang. They sang loudly in Hebrew and in Arabic. They were going to the Promised Land. Later that night, their hopes sank for the first time. The truck ground to a halt and the driver, after tinkering around for some time, announced that a very important part was broken beyond repair. They tried not to despair and sat waiting, wondering what to do. A car appeared on the horizon and the driver flagged him down. Negotiations took place and the driver of the car sped off back the way he had come.

The bus driver had hired him to drive back to Baghdad to pick up the spare part and told him he would only be paid if he arrived back that *very* night. At about 4:00 a.m., the man returned and in a short time, the group was on the road again.

With the truck now fixed they headed to Amara, a southern city, well over halfway to Basra, situated on the Tigris River. Because it was a fairly large city, the hired guides felt it important to stay on the outskirts and not chance being caught there. Many years later, Amara became the battleground between Iraq and Iran in their eight-year territorial war during the 1980s. The driver made his way around the city and out into a wilderness that is known as the Jezera. This region is a flat desert stretching for many miles. Once out of the populated area these Iraqi Jews were breathing easier, when just up ahead they spotted a policeman coming their way. The driver announced that if the officer tried to stop the lorry he would have to run him down with the truck and leave him for dead. They simply could not take the chance of being caught.

As the truck approached, the policeman was making the sign with his hand for *baksheesh,* the Arabic word for a "bribe." The quick-thinking bus driver wadded several bills up and threw them at him as they passed at high speed! The truck then traveled unhindered for hours.

The terrain changed little by little, and the desert soon gave way to low-growing vegetation and some reeds, but no trees. The reason for the shrubs and vegetation became apparent. They had arrived at the southern swamps. Reeds now rose high above their heads and water stretched out before them as far as the eye could see. This was the Shat-al-Arab, an area where the Tigris and Euphrates Rivers meet and spread themselves in a wide delta of marshland. The size of the swamp is as wide as the state of Israel in some places.

The Shat-al-Arab

Reeds and water meet in the Shat-al-Arab and form a tangled

mass of waterways, some large and wide, others medium sized, while still others are barely passable even with a small boat. The swamp is so large and complex that it takes an experienced navigator to keep from getting hopelessly lost.

In the village close to the shore of the swamp is buried a revered Moslem prophet named Robah. Since it would be improper for women to address a sheik, the guides instructed Zvi, "Ask the men to see the village sheik and tell him we have all traveled far to visit the tomb of the prophet on a pilgrimage."

The sheik arrived with great pomp and circumstance. Two body guards accompanied him with swords and guns and a small procession.

When the sheik addressed the visitors, no one but Zvi could understand him. The southern Iraqis rarely have communication with the outside world, and tend to be provincial in manner, education, and dialect. In Zvi's younger years, while learning his father's irrigation trade, he had learned to deal with merchants from some of these southern villages. As a result, he was able to learn to speak their unique dialect of Arabic. At this point in the dangerous journey, Zvi recognized that God had prepared him from that early time for just this moment.

Zvi overheard the conversation of the two body guards who had accompanied the sheik. Thinking they could not be understood by these northern travelers, they discussed how they thought these people were being "smuggled" out of the country. Zvi quickly responded to their accusations, in their own dialect, that the entourage had come to visit the tomb of the prophet. The answer seemed to satisfy the body guards, and they retreated to allow the sheik to conduct business. The driver then used Zvi to translate in arranging for boats and oarsmen to accompany the group into the swamp and deposit them at the other side. A large sum of money was paid to the sheik and four boats with navigators were brought. The boats were not motorized, but rather simple row boats.

With much fear and trepidation, the group arranged themselves in the boats and the party left the shore behind them. Night fell, and they rowed on for what seemed like an eternity. Fear settled around them like fog. Only the sound of the oars and an occasional plop of a fish or some small water animal could be heard. Suddenly, the oarsman in the front boat seemed to loose his mind. He began screaming and making the most disgusting sounds imaginable. The Jewish passengers thought he had gone crazy. No one could quiet him long enough to try to make sense of what was happening to him. Being filled with fear themselves they naturally projected their own emotional state upon him and were sure he was suffering from stress. Then, as quickly as it came on him, it left.

Wild Boar and Knives

Now, once again in the quiet, he explained that a very large wild water boar inhabited this particular area of the swamp. Some of these animals can reach several meters in length. They have been known to turn a boat over and tear the humans in pieces. He had spotted one in the reeds and had to make horrible noises to scare him off for the protection of his passengers.

The temperature in the swamp was now quickly dropping. The air was becoming increasingly colder and the water temperature was numbing. The rowing continued on for eight hours when, finally, the oarsman spotted two men coming toward them in another boat from the other direction.

These men turned out to be the contacts from their next point of destination, the other side of the swamp, who were now to take over leading the people out to the safety of the opposite shore. The oarsman from the sheik's side of the swamp instructed the other boatsmen to go get his boats and transfer the people to them. The boatsmen had a different idea and demanded the money first. This seemed like a bad idea to the sheik's oarsman and he refused. An argument ensued and continued on for half an hour. Finally, the boatsmen pulled their boat up alongside the other boat and attacked both the oarsman and the Jewish passengers with knives. The boats overturned and the people were swimming in the freezing water. All the boats sunk and the stronger swimmers were trying to find any shallow place to get people to safety. After some minutes someone shouted that there was dry ground not far away. They all headed that direction. Zvi said the water was so cold that he could not feel his feet.

Finally, they got the people to a dry island and sat down to wait—for what, they did not know. In the cold and wet, and from the horrible fear, one of the men lost his mind. For the remainder of the journey, he was a liability to the group, who now had to care for him as if he were a child. When the light of morning came, some of the bags were found floating on the river and were recovered.

The Final Kingdom

Soon three men arrived from Kaoon, a place where the river gets very wide. Arrangements were made for new boats and the group was able to travel to a place called Dabeyeh. All the buildings in this village are constructed like very large quonset huts, as the only building material available is river reeds. These reeds are bound together by the hundreds to create tall makeshift logs. These extremely tall logs are erected, standing upright like palm trees along a narrow foundation slab of dried mud. Then they are made to lean over until they touch one another where they are lashed together by reed rope. This skeletal structure is then covered quite artistically with thick reed matting to create an attractive building.

In Dabeyeh, the group was taken to one of these reed buildings that served as the city police station. The man in charge demanded *baksheesh*. There was nothing they could do but comply. He left the group of forty-five people in a small room in the building and disappeared. Soon, another policeman came and began questioning them aggressively. When he did not like an answer, he beat them. Zvi moved between the women and the police officer to protect them and was beaten severely. That night, he came down with a fever from the severity of the beating.

More *baksheesh* got them out of the police station and on their way to the next city, Pseytin. The authorities in Pseytin felt sorry for the man who had lost his mind, so they brought some food. The members of the group were allowed to sleep at Pseytin and a bus picked them up the next morning and headed for Sarhand, a larger city. In Sarhand, a police captain came to them and disclosed that he himself was Jewish and treated them quite nicely. By this time, they realized that their route was taking them into Iran, most likely to Tehran, which was still further away than they had already traveled. The route lead over the Zagros mountains, high and covered with snow. In the night another young man lost his senses and rose up screaming, "They are going to kill us!"

Tehran

They next morning they headed over the border into Iran, to Ahwaz, a city in the foothills of the Zagros mountains. At the police station they were questioned, but had been briefed by the guides not to disclose their careers, if they were at all technical or skillful, as the government authorities would keep them there to use their skills. Finally some members of the Persian Halutz

Movement came to encourage them in their journey and see how the travelers were doing. They took them to the synagogue in Ahwaz, which was full of Halutz smugglers, for the Shabbat morning service. One young orthodox man, who had not eaten for a week, was beside himself when he realized the food there was not *Kosher* and he could not eat it! One of the others convinced him that the biblical injunction to "save life" overruled the *Kosher* law at that moment and promised that any sin he would incur by eating non-kosher food, would be on his own head. With this, the boy ate.

The next morning the group was preparing to leave for Tehran when a high ranking police officer pulled Zvi aside and stated, "You are not going." Zvi's heart pounded as if it would burst. He could not understand why he was being detained. "You must see the Doctor," the officer responded gruffly. Zvi was taken to another building and stripped. He was searched thoroughly to see if he was smuggling something into Iran. Coming from a rural area of Iraq, he had never been treated in such a manner and was humiliated by the extent of the examination. Fairly sure he would be left behind, he wept in despair. Some time later, it was discovered that he had been mistaken for someone else and was allowed to rejoin his group, who were just leaving for Tehran on another bus.

The bus slowly climbed the Zagros mountains for four days, in steadily falling snow. About the third day, chains had to be put on the bus and then finally on the fourth day, the snow was so deep the bus could move no further. The driver said that he thought there were some abandoned buildings not far from the road and suggested that the people find them, set up camp, and make fires to keep from freezing to death. The following day, amazingly, the snow stopped and they were able to continue on. Day after day passed driving toward Tehran. Five-hundred kilometers traveling on a rickety bus was taking its toll on the members of the group.

Just when they were sure that they could take it no longer, they arrived at the Tehran transit camp. It was situated in the cemetery outside the city. There were already hundreds in the immigrant camp and the new arrivals were led to a quonset hut about two hundred meters long. Just in the simple act of sitting down they realized that there were lice everywhere. The place was so depressing Zvi took action. He knew he had an uncle in Tehran who was very wealthy, if he could just get out long enough to find him. He went to someone in charge to request permission to go to find his uncle. He found a Jewish man who worked at the transit camp that everyone called "Haji" and made his request known to him.

Haji immediately slapped him in the face and told him to get back to his hut and leave him alone. Questioning others about Haji, he found that this Jewish man was taking advantage of everyone he could in the camp and had made himself out to be someone of reputation to the authorities. He was stealing from the refugees and cutting their food rations to his own benefit.

Heavy-hearted, Zvi sat down to make a fire and warm himself when he heard someone calling his name from outside the quonset hut. Miracle of God! It was his uncle who had heard he might be there! Zvi's uncle had left Iraq thirty years before and Zvi had never met him. Yehezkiel Kookoo was his name and he was a very wealthy and influential man in Tehran. After a joyful reunion, Zvi was taken to Yehezkiel's lavish home. The structure was palatial. One room was kept just as a 24-hour reception room where guests could be entertained. Tables were kept loaded with food of every kind. There, Zvi related the story of their journey. Yehezkiel began to weep, saying that they were paying so much money to get the Jews out of Iraq and were led to believe that they were being brought out in the best manner possible.

Zvi was later introduced to members of the Persian Halutz Movement, who were busy forging false identity papers for the immigrants. They had to create fake families to pose as tourists leaving Iran, completing the final leg of their journey. Zvi was placed in one of those "families" and flown from Tehran to Tel Aviv on an American airline.

Home at Last

January 1950, Zvi finally arrived "home" in Israel. Another Babylonian exile had returned to his homeland. He sobbed at the airport, happy about being home, and feeling the release of the incredible stress of the three-month journey. There was a mental identification with those early returning Babylonian Jews, simply because it had taken them the same amount of time to make the same journey. But Zvi's ordeal was not yet over. At the airport he was met by British absorbtion personnel who took him to another transit camp in Haifa. He was put immediately into a delousing chamber and then taken to a tent where he would be registered and placed somewhere in Israel, in due course.

Zvi had had enough. Out of the transit camp he ran and took off for Jerusalem, skirting the British army on every side. His mind almost could not comprehend that he was home in Israel and yet he was still running to keep from being caught. Finally, arriving in Jerusalem, he went to the huge central open market, *Mah'neh Yehuda*, where he had been told to ask for one of his uncles, and everyone there would know him. Asking the first booth vendor he came to, he was greeted with the response, "Ha! You are nothing but an Arab!!! Get out of here!" Then he realized he had been speaking to the man in Arabic, his mother tongue.

Zvi did find his family in Jerusalem and later joined Gan Shmu'el, a kibbutz near the port of Caesarea between Tel Aviv and Haifa. He lived there for two years which helped him adapt to life in Israel and learn the language well.

The Gabi Family

A similar contact came through my Israeli coworker, Eli Ken, one of our Bridges for Peace Distribution managers in Jerusalem. He was able to make contact with a family who also managed to get out of Iraq during the same time period.

Aryeh Gabi, son of Ephraim Gabi, hosted me in his home to tell me the story of his father's family's escape.

Unlike the provincial village of Zvi's birth, Ephraim, Aryeh's father, was born in Baghdad in 1909, where he lived most of his life. Aryeh's grandfather, Ovadiah Abdullah Gabi, was a fabric merchant in Baghdad. Ovadiah's wife's father was the *Chacham Bashi*, or Chief Rabbi of the Jewish community of Baghdad. He was also the Jewish representative to the Iraqi government.

The situation for the Jewish population of Iraq until 1946 was fairly good. After 1946, stirrings in the Iraqi populace to break away from the British colonial government and proclaim independence birthed an ever-growing animosity toward the Jewish population in the larger cities. Ongoing efforts of men like Mordechai Ben-Porat to smuggle his people out of Iraq added to the ill-feelings of the Iraqis toward the Jews.

The six-year time span between 1946 and 1952 was dramatic. Jews were emprisoned as spies; the Jewish underground movement began to smuggle their people out of Iraq via several different routes, both east and west; costly bribes were paid;

223

exhausting journeys were endured overland by foot; some were flown out under the false pretenses of emigrating to Europe, then secretly rerouted to Israel. Nevertheless, there are 130,000 stories like these. This was the amazing number of Jewish people who made the journey to Israel from Iraq during this time.

During our interview, Aryeh's eyes brightened with a question:

"Do you know the secret code that was used by the Iraqi Jews to communicate their escape plans to one another," he asked? I could sense his drawing out the pause while I pondered what it could possibly be.

"Morse Code," I guessed?

"No, not morse code," he answered still smiling at the secret.

I was formulating a few other plausible possibilities when he said:

"They used the high formal Arabic language, in which the Koran was written. The ordinary Iraqi could not understand it! Only the very well educated and those who could afford formal training could master the difficult and complex classical Arabic," he added.

Such irony! We all laughed at such a mental picture.

Aryeh's Uncle Achram was arrested as a Zionist spy and sentenced to death. Time passed as he languished in prison. Iraqi prisons were not as we might think of a prison. Filthy conditions and the possibilities of torture were too real. The family went into overtime activities to try to get him out of prison. Finally, a high bribe was paid and Uncle Achram was released.

Prior to the announcement of a Jewish state in 1948, family members who were succeeding in getting out of the country were thrown headlong into a cultural chasm in Palestine. Holdover laws from the Turkish Ottoman Empire were still in effect. Aryeh's father was able to get out on a tourist visa. The authorities had no idea that he never planned to return to Iraq. He was sent by the family as an emissary to purchase property so that when each family member succeeded in getting out of Iraq, they would have a place to live in Israel.

Family members from Iraq smuggled him money to purchase small homes for them. Little did he know that the very small places he purchased would also house the family members of the previous owners, until they had found their own suitable housing arrangements. Islamic Ottoman laws forbade a new buyer to evict the sellers until they had aquired suitable housing. In the slow-moving Middle East that could take many months or even years. Therefore, a two-room home might have as many as fifteen people living in it from two different families, and one protected by law from being evicted!

Coming Home from Babylon

By 1950, the Iraqi government was so anxious to expel their Jewish population that they conspired how they might destroy the emerging infant State of Israel and ease their own plight as well. The conspiracy was to quickly release all the Jewish inhabitants of Iraq and send them into Israel in such numbers that they would bring the economy of the fledgling nation crashing down. Thus, the final phase of the Babylonian dispersion was ending. God had different ideas about the new state of Israel. The purpose was clear: He would return the remnant of these He had dispersed centuries before—now scattered—to His land.

From a land of dreams, Babel—Gate of God came His people. From the land known for visions and heavenly visitations we learn a valuable lesson: God is not in a hurry. Two thousand five hundred and fifty years of history pass and a move of God is complete.

Kingdoms rise and fall. No nation is forever, however permanent we might think it to be. No nation, that is, but Israel.

With Israel's various periods of exile in mind, it would appear (as some would have us believe) that God rejected His people, the Jews, and took the Church as His chosen people instead. This erroneous theology took many insidious turns over the centuries. In the last century, we only have to see the pogroms and finally the Holocaust to understand where antisemitic sentiments lead. Today, the Lord is causing the Church to take its proper position toward the Jewish people, and Israel.

What position then, does God require us, specifically Gentile Christians, to take toward His people?

This "outsider" stance might be clarified by the story of Balaam. You might call him the pagan "rent-a-prophet." Balak hired him to curse the Israelites coming out of the wilderness, as recorded in the book of Numbers chapters 23-24. It is a long and very interesting story, but the short of it is that, regardless of Balaam's motives, he arrived on the scene to do Balak's bidding. Balaam was not a Jewish prophet, he was from Pethor. He was doing the bidding of a Moabite king against God's chosen people.

Several points must be made here. God does not send non-Jewish prophets to His people. Balaam's prophecy was serendipitous, in that Balaam went perhaps with monetary gain in his mind and may have been surprised at what came out of his mouth at the moment of utterance.

It is surprising to us because we see Israel from a heavenly perspective rather than a "facts on the ground" viewpoint. We know what Israel had been through in the wilderness of Sinai and yet Balaam's first oracle pronounces:

> *He hath not beheld iniquity in Jacob, neither hath he seen perverseness in Israel: the LORD his God [is] with him, and the shout of a king [is] among them.*

> Numbers 23:21 (KJV)

This begs questioning! No iniquity? No perverseness? The books of Exodus and Numbers are filled with the woes of Moses and the wanderers in the wilderness. The accounts of the sin and idolatry are numerous. The content of Baalam's utterances tells me that the spiritual stature of Israel is between them and their God. He is calling us to come alongside the Jewish nation and interceed on their behalf, beseeching Him for His mercy. In short, this means that "outside" pronouncements of judgment and cursing, as Balak sought, are not tolerated by God. He alone is their final judge.

Balaam's pronouncements continue to be surprising until Numbers 24:17-19, when they rise right off the pages of the Bible and prophetically shout out the announcement of the coming of the Messiah. Balaam desired to curse Israel, but God, rather, commands a blessing through the lips of Balaam. This is another view of Daniel's vision of the "Rock" that will crush the feet of the statue.

> *I see him, but not now; I behold him, but not near. A star will come out of Jacob; a scepter will rise out of Israel. He will crush the foreheads of Moab, the skulls of all the sons of Sheth.*

> Numbers 24:17

We are presently in the midst of this drama. The stage has not changed, although the scenery has been replaced. At the turn of the millenium, another scene took place in Iran. The heads of several Jewish families were arrested as spies on trumped up charges. At the printing of this book, some of those Jews have been handed lengthy prison sentences. The message is clear: the only place for a Jewish person to be safe is home in the land of Israel.

Acts chapter two is enlightening in regard to the demographic location of Jewish populace in the first century. The Assyrian captivity, and the Babylonian exile, had taken many communities of the Jews to the far ends of the earth.

Pontus (modern Turkey), the Parthian Empire (modern Iran), Asia, and Rome were the northern-most communities. One of the three pilgrimage festivals in which all Jewish families had to come up to Jerusalem was the setting for the scene in Acts at *Shavuot* (Pentecost). Representatives from every nation were there.

The Roman seige and destruction of Jerusalem in A.D. 70, was the last scatteration of the Jews of Israel. These times of exile for God's people has, in fact, scattered them over the face of the earth. Here in *The Final Kingdom*, we have concentrated on the Babylonian captivity and the return from such—but, the return is much more broad sweeping than that. The return home for the Jewish people is worldwide in our day.

To Russia with Love

In the last decade, my wife and I, through the ministry of Bridges for Peace in Jerusalem, have been greatly involved in this process of the return of the Jewish people. During this period of time, we have witnessed over one million Jewish immigrants coming to Israel, mainly from the former Soviet Union. We see this as fulfillment of the prophecy of Jeremiah:

> *"So then, the days are coming, declares the LORD, when the people will no longer say, 'As surely as the LORD lives, who brought the Israelites up out of Egypt,' but they will say, As surely as the LORD lives, who brought the descendants of Israel up out of the land of the north and out of all the countries where he had banished them.' Then they will live in their own land."*

> Jeremiah 23:7, 8

According to this Scripture, the latter-day exodus rivals the one from Egypt!

The Final Kingdom

Through cooperation with the Ebenezer Emergency Fund/Operation Exodus, under the direction of Gustav and Elsa Scheller, and representing Bridges for Peace, we were privileged to be part of the team of Christian volunteers on the second sailing of ships that regularly sail from the Israeli port of Haifa to the Black Sea port of Odessa. Our mandate was to pick up several hundred Russian Jewish people who had, by that time, successfully applied for immigration to Israel, and bring them home! The voyage encompassed a number of exciting—and at times disturbing—experiences and observations.

Our voyage was mid-winter—December 26, 1991—and we quickly learned why Paul thought it not good to travel the Mediterranean Sea in the winter! As it turned out, the Mediterranean region was experiencing the worst storm in several decades, only it did not begin its fury until we had left the breakwater out of the port of Haifa. I never knew a large sailing vessel could move in so many different directions all at the same time. From Haifa to the Greek Islands (three days), we had to hold onto the sides of our bed to keep from being thrown to the floor. Nearly everyone on board—ship crew included—got horribly seasick. Few escaped the sickness that resulted in the extreme motions of the ship, and the sounds of it were evident in most cabins.

Because the route of the ship would pass through the Bosphorus Straits, the narrow channel connecting the Mediterranean Sea and the Black Sea that slices Istanbul in half, there was a potential danger of terrorist acts against our ship. The government of Israel posted on board our ship a team of about fifteen Israeli security men on high alert—who were prepared for any eventuality we might encounter. Traveling from Israel through the waterway of an Islamic city to pick up Jewish passengers from Russia, made us targets for Islamic extremists. The team of Christian believers were on a serious prayer watch at that particular time. There were tense moments as we passed directly under the bridges of Istanbul around midnight. With praise to God, we glided through without incident and all breathed a sigh of relief as we made the last leg of our journey on to Odessa.

Normally, the food of a Greek luxury liner is something to write home about! However, on our journey, we would not experience such tasty delights. This ship was turned into an Israeli Absorption Center, staffed with a team of about fifteen government officials, who would process the Russian immigrants as they

228

boarded the ship, expediting their arrival and destination assignments when we finally arrived back in Haifa. The cuisine crew did not understand that a Kosher menu is wonderfully varied and delicious. As a result, the menu for the meals was simple, and in a word, bland. For ten days we ate fish and rice with a few canned vegetables, and little variation. For people who were experiencing serious seasickness, this daily fare of fish only made matters worse! After several days of these scanty, tasteless meals, the undercover Israeli security men—bulging with well-toned muscles—were making their complaints known. Comically, at one particular evening meal, one of the security guards called over a kitchen crew member. We overheard his conversation in very broken English:

"Do you have any other food other than this," the Israeli asked? He received an apologetic negative reply from the Greek crew member. This hulking security guard, with a slow, determined, sweeping, circular motion with his hand over his plate said, "I do not like *any* of this food." His complaints went unheeded. The next day, we had fish for dinner.

Docking in Odessa five days after we had begun our journey, the Ukrainian Government officials were going through the arduous and painstaking procedures of processing the immigrants, inspecting them with excruciating detail. Because of the long delay, we would not be able to receive them on board until the following morning. That evening was spent in prayer for the whole operation that was about to take place, as well as the five-day journey back to Israel. Along the way, we had encountered numerous situations that presented themselves as opposition to what we were doing. All we could do was to present our requests to the Lord, knowing full well the mandate He had given us to carry His people home on this vessel.

There were poignant moments for the team during our times of prayer and worship as we waited on the Lord each day. I remember several Scriptures in particular that my wife and I came across as we read our Bibles—particularly what the prophets had foretold of the very thing we were doing.

The LORD will have compassion on Jacob; once again he will choose Israel and will settle them in their own land. Aliens will join them and unite with the house of Jacob. Nations will take them and bring them to their own place.

Isaiah 14:1-2a

The Final Kingdom

We could relate to being the aliens, or foreigners from other nations. However, even more specifically, as we sat on a "ship of Tarshish" chartered for this journey, we read:

> *Surely the islands look to me; in the lead are the ships of Tarshish, bringing your sons from afar, with their silver and gold, to the honor of the LORD your God, the Holy One of Israel, for he has endowed you with splendor.*

> Isaiah 60:9

Early the next morning, the Ukrainian Government officials began to allow a trickle of immigrants to come aboard. They had spent the night holed up in the room where they were processed and were anxious to board the ship that would take them far from the horrible persecution and treatment they had just been through, and on to their new home! Our team was ready to carry their suitcases up the long gangplank, welcome them on board, and show them to their private cabins.

Two Ukrainian Police officials had demanded that they be posted atop the gangplank on board the ship. We were horrified to observe them harassing the passengers—as if for one more time— before they left for Israel. Harshly, they would demand the passports of the families as they came on board. We stood back watching and waiting to receive them, praying all the while. The fear in the eyes of our passengers was obvious. *Is this all a cruel hoax? Did we come this far—traversing across the whole of Russia to Odessa, spending all we had—just to be turned away? Will they keep my passport and send me back to Russia?*

When finally the passports were slowly returned to them, and with an obvious despising smirk, the family members would be immediately greeted by us with a warm and welcoming, "Shalom!" Tears of relief, and often falling into our arms as we gathered up their belongings, made us thankful we had come. This was quite emotional for all of us.

About mid-morning, the Russian officials had arranged a quick bus tour of the city of Odessa. This we welcomed, as we were only in Odessa for 24 hours. We were hoping to be dropped off downtown after the "official" tour, and asked permission to be able to, but were refused. About an hour into the tour, the bus had mechanical failure and broke down! Now we *had* to get off the bus, and so were allowed to wander downtown at our leisure, agreeing to meet the new bus at an assigned point. This thrilled us! Finally as Westerners, we could see for ourselves a Soviet city that we had only heard about. However, we were in for a big shock. Hoping to find a little gift shop, or a supermarket to buy real food, we were amazed to see the stores emptied of merchandise of any kind. We considered ourselves blessed to even find some fresh bread! It saddened us to see this. Over the years since this trip, the economic situation for Soviet Russia has only worsened. We experienced firsthand a nation that had severely persecuted its Jewish communities, and the end result of that persecution.

Our new bus picked us up in town and we returned to the dock. This time, we were to go through the large customs room where the processing of the immigrants was still in progress. We were once again horrified at what we saw. Here were Soviet government officials combing through every single item that was packed. They even went so far as to look through every single page of a book or magazine. These Russian Jews were not allowed to bring more than a very small amount of gold, nor anything precious or of great value out of the country. The rest was confiscated, usually by force. The residue of cruelty from the former Soviet regime hung in the air like a mist. We made our way slowly through the customs room taking in the agonizing procedure that each man, woman and child was experiencing before they came on board of our ship. It gave us a fresh burden for them.

On board once again, I noticed a gentleman hanging onto the railing gazing out towards the sea. Engaging him in conversation, he began to tell me the story of his journey thus far.

"Twelve years ago I decided to immigrate to Israel—on a ship! [At that time, there were no ships going to Israel.] I was a member of the secret underground Jewish organization in my city and began in earnest to master the Hebrew language as part of my preparation for the time when I would finally be released to go to Israel. I wanted to be able to speak Modern Hebrew as soon as I landed. For the past several years, I have been teaching Hebrew in my community. Now here I am, finally realizing my goal after twelve years," he beamed!

Ya'acov was bringing with him his pregnant wife and their thirteen-year old daughter. Expressing his gratitude to us, the Christians who had made the way possible for him, was a moment I will never forget. My years of ministry among the Jewish people could not compare to this one poignant moment. The Lord had heard the desire of my heart to somehow aid His people, relieving their times of trouble and return them to their rightful homeland.

Not too long after this, I heard a woman screaming. Peering over the top of the railing, I could see family members surrounding this woman and attempting to quiet her hysteria at the bottom of the gangplank. At one point, her husband slapped her face. As she finally quieted and made her way up to the top of the ship, standing before the two Russian authorities she burst out screaming again, in obvious fear. Mercifully, their passports were returned to them quickly and they were now in *our* care. The reason for her hysteria soon became apparent as the family told their story.

Upon arriving in the customs processing room, the officials demanded that this woman give over all her jewelry. She was more than willing to part with anything—with the exception of an heirloom that her mother had given her on her deathbed, her wedding ring. This was not an expensive ring per se, but it had enormous sentimental value to her. She must take this to Israel with her. It was nearly impossible for her to even remove the ring from her finger. At this, the officials assured her they would forcibly remove the finger, if necessary. They demanded that she get the ring off. This last act of unfounded cruelty, coupled with the long arduous and painful journey to this point, caused her to break into hysterics. She simply could not take any more of this treatment. The officials had their way. The ring was forcibly removed injuring her finger.

At the same there was another drama unfolding in the customs room. Another woman and her young daughter were experiencing similar demands by these Russian officials. The ten-year old girl had a small gold Star of David necklace ripped from her neck, and had the marks on her neck to prove it. These incidents gave us even greater compassion for our passengers.

In light of all this, I questioned God about the "thawing" of Russia—that change that had finally allowed the Jewish people who wanted to immigrate to Israel be allowed to do so. What I was seeing here on the boat really was the "old Russia" that I was more familiar with. There were many years of my joining demonstrations for the freedom of Jewish "refusniks"—those who wanted to immigrate to Israel but were imprisoned instead. I needed some kind of indication that Russia was really changing its attitude toward its Jewish population. Witnessing all the harassment, I feared the Jewish exodus might stop.

I had gone down below deck to the loading door to help bring aboard the luggage of our passengers, taking my camera with me just in case. During a break in the work, I stepped outside, onto Russian soil, and caught the attention of a young Russian guard. I raised my camera to snap a photo of him and was halted with a gruff voice and gesticulation which clearly meant that I was not welcome to take his photograph. I complied and let my camera drop to its place around my neck. I was getting used to disappointment here in this cold, snowy outpost of the Soviet Empire.

I returned to loading luggage and organizing the ship's hold. About ten minutes later, I passed the huge open doorway again and heard someone whistling and calling out, obviously trying to get my attention. The young Russian officer had positioned himself out of the sight of his superiors and had taken a position motioning me that it was now permissable to take his photograph. I felt God had let me know that on the surface Russia was still gruff, but down deep, where it counted, there were changes that were going to benefit the Jewish people and their desire to come home to Israel. In reality, over the next nine years we saw over a million realeased from the grip of communist Russia.

Throughout the day, members of the team were busy carrying luggage aboard and generally assisting the passengers in any way that would make the process easier for them. There were a number of disabled elderly people, mothers with babies, and pregnant women, who were carried or assisted onboard, echoing the words of Jeremiah:

> *See, I will bring them from the land of the north and gather them from the ends of the earth. Among them will be the blind and the lame, expectant mothers and women in labor; a great throng will return. They will come with weeping; they will pray as I bring them back. I will lead them beside streams of water on a level path where they will not stumble, because I am Israel's father, and Ephraim is my firstborn son.*

Jeremiah 31:8, 9

On the maiden voyage of Operation Exodus, the week preceding ours, and during the cruel customs inspections, Jewish mothers had been stripped of all their baby items. They had no baby formula, bottles, diapers or other essentials needed to properly care for their small infants and children as they made the

The Final Kingdom

five-day journey to Haifa. This came to the attention of Clarence Wagner, Jr., Director of Bridges for Peace, who immediately prepared the necessary supplies for the subsequent journeys. A special room was prepared on board the ship where we could give these items out to the traveling mothers once aboard the ship.

The following day all passengers were aboard and with much relief we began our journey back to Israel. We were going home. The horrible winter storm that had accompanied us on the way to Odessa completely lifted, so that the trip back resembled a pleasure cruise in the Greek islands! Where we had had snow and heavy rains, we now had sun; where we had had wind and rough, rolling seas, now not even a ripple on the water. Sunning and strolling on the deck gave opportunity for us to hear firsthand accounts of the horrific testimonies of our passengers. The woman who came on board hysterically weeping and wailing, told her story to any who would listen. As she recounted her difficulties over the months of preparation for this trip, she would fall on her husband's shoulder crying. There was a residue of heaviness upon many of them, and many carried feelings of uncertainty as to what lay ahead for them in their new land. They were leaving the land of their birth, their families, and all that was familiar. We could understand these feelings of uncertainty as they shared with us. Nevertheless, we sensed the blessing of God on such an unforgettable trip.

One morning, as the team was just finishing prayer and worship time together, we noticed that several Israeli government officials had slipped into our room unnoticed, and were quietly listening to the music. Afterwards they approached my wife, commenting on her voice and suggested that she consider doing a concert for the passengers on the evening before we were scheduled to pull into the port of Haifa.

Prayerfully, and realizing that this concert could be a wonderful opportunity to encourage our passengers, Carol received a word from the Lord. As she was praying, the Lord gave a wonderful promise that His presence would be with His people and that He would remove their sorrows and replace it with joy. She had the picture of the hysterical woman that had came on board weeping and "wailing." The Lord confirmed this to her with following Scripture:

> *You turned my wailing into dancing; you removed my sackcloth and clothed me with joy, that my heart may sing to*

you and not be silent. O LORD my God, I will give you thanks forever.

Psalm 30:11,12

On the night of the concert, the room where we gathered was packed to overflowing. Nearly everyone it seemed had turned out: the Russian immigrants, the volunteer team of Christians, the Israeli government officials, the Israeli security guards, and even a number of ship crew members. Here we all were gathered into this ballroom, now converted into a concert hall!

The sadness and pain of the immigrants was still so evident on their faces and posture. Heads bowed low, shoulders stooped, quietly talking among themselves as they moved about and settled into the room. A mournful sadness hung over them like a cloud. My wife is a worship leader and she later related to me that she could sense these things in her spirit as she stepped up to begin.

The songs she selected were familiar Israeli songs—all of them from the Hebrew Scriptures or the Hebrew liturgy—well known and loved by Jewish people around the world. As soon as she began to play her guitar and sing, the lowered heads lifted up. Shortly, people began to clap and their faces turned into smiles. Hesitantly and quietly at first, they began to sing with her, becoming more confident and gaining in strength. The words of these Hebrew songs spoke of trusting in the God of Israel and many were prayers from the Psalms—heart-cries in the midst of adversity.

Suddenly, it was as if joy exploded in the room. At this point, two Israeli government officials who had placed themselves alongside of Carol as she sang, jumped up on their feet and began to dance a familiar Israeli dance. A couple of our volunteers and I joined the circle, whirling around together in celebration. A moment later, and bursting into the circle, was the lady who came on the ship weeping and "wailing!" She was quickly followed by the other woman whose daughter had had her necklace torn from her neck. Here was a picture of what God intended to do in the hearts of His people: return them to His Land in great joy! It was exactly what the Lord had promised to Carol: turning their wailing into dancing!

By now, the faces of all those in the room reflected joy, excitement, and anticipation. It seemed as if God had come and replaced their sadness.

Ending the concert, Carol sang the song, *Shalom Havarim*

("Goodbye Friends") as each person filed past her, tears rolling down their faces and gesturing good-bye, as they blew kisses of gratitude for an evening of encouragement. All of us on the ship that night were inspired by the God of Israel, and our faith to trust Him was increased.

Something tangible and obvious had happened in that room. Surrounding my wife afterwards, the Israeli security team quizzed her for quite sometime, inquiring, "What happened in that room? What did you *do* that caused such a change in those people?" God's presence was there. He loves His people and He is the One who comforts them, drawing them to Himself.

The Lion of Babylon

Signs of the times exist in such unlikely places. These indicators of where we are on God's time line, as we race toward the end of the age, are exhilarating.

On Nablus Road, not more than a mile from my office in Jerusalem, sits a six-foot by three-foot by four-foot quarried stone specifically prepared for the cornerstone of the Third Temple. It was cut by an Orthodox Jewish group here in Jerusalem, known as the "Faithful of the Temple." Obviously, it is not quite time to see that building stone installed, but God *is* building Jerusalem. Living stones are coming by the hundreds of thousands and the demographics of Israel change monthly. We are in the last days and need more than ever to be "busy about the King's business."

All we have learned here in the pages of the book of Daniel are now ours to keep and to appropriate. Calm assurance in the midst of turmoil, quiet strength, and perseverance when all seems to be against us, are qualities of the king of beasts—the lion—which characterize Daniel.

Slowly walking through the pages of the Old Testament, Daniel takes in all that is around him, assesses the situation in the confidence of his Heavenly Father, and reigns—bringing kings to their knees. He is the reflection of the Lion of Judah, that Heavenly King of creation, the Lion of Babylon.

Photographs

Last of the Babylonian Exiles

Zvi Rimon (left)
and his son
Barak Rimon (right)

To Russia With Love

Left: Ron, Carol and a friend explore Odessa.
Below: The concert in the ballroom.
Bottom left: Dancing breaks out during Carol's concert.
Bottom right: Russian lady whose ring was forcibly removed from her finger with her husband and dog.

Ron aboard the ship. The hills of the European half of Istanbul can be seen in the background covered in a light dusting of snow.

And Then Back Again

Right: Ron assisted an elderly Jewish man on board the ship, who was too weak to board by himself.
Below: Jerusalem Bridges for Peace food bank.
Below left: Russsian soldier who forbade his photo to be taken, then changed his mind!
Below right: All those wonderful people we traveled with.

Bibliography

Ben-Porat, Mordechai. *To Baghdad and Back, The Miraculous 2,000 year Homecoming of the Iraqi Jews.* Gefen Publishing House Ltd., Jerusalem, New York, 1998.

Budge, E. A. Wallis. *Babylonian Life and History.* Dorset Press, 1992.

Cantrell, Ron. *The Feasts of the Lord, Rehearsals for the End.* Jerusalem, Israel, second edition 1999, copyright 1998.

De Koven, Rabbi Ralph. *A Prayer Book with Explanatory Notes.* KTAV Publishing House Inc., 1965.

The Encyclopedia Judaica. Keter Publishing House, Ltd., Jerusalem, Israel, 1978.

Ferm, Vergilius; (ed.), *Encyclopedia of Religion.* New Students Outline Series, Littlefield, Adams & Co., Patterson, New Jersey, 1959.

Finegan, Jack. *Myth and Mystery: An Introduction to the Pagan Religions of the Biblical World.* Baker Book House Company, Michigan, 1989.

Fleming, Jim. *Jesus in the Biblical Feasts.* Biblical Resources, Jerusalem, Israel.

Hamel, Ken. *Online Bible.* Online Bible Software, POB 168, Oakhurst, NJ 07755, USA, Copyright 1995.

Herodotus. *Histories.* Wordsworth Classics of World Literature, Wordsworth Editions Ltd., Cumberland House, 1996.

Herzog, Isaac. *The Royal Blue and Biblical Purple.* Keter Publishing House, Jerusalem Ltd., 1987.

The Holy Bible. King James Version, Oxford University Press, New York, USA, 1967.

Josephus. *Complete Works of Josephus.* Kregel Publications, Grand Rapids, Michigan, 1960.

Jordan, Michael. *Encyclopedia of Gods.* Kyle Cathie Ltd., Great Britain, 1992.

Kramer, Samuel. *Cradle of Civilization.* Time Incorporated, New York, 1970.

Lewis, C.S. *That Hideous Strength.* Collier Books, Macmillan Publishing Company, New York, 1965.

National Geographic Society. *Greece and Rome, Builders of Our World.* National Geographic Society, 1968.

Pearl, Chaim, ed. *The Encyclopedia of Jewish Life and Thought.* Jerusalem, Carta, 1966

Poe, Edgar Allen. *The Homo-Cameleopard.* Selected poem.

Potok, Chaim. *The Book of Lights.* Fawcett Crest Books, 1982.

Sandberg, Gosta. *The Red Dyes, Chochineal, Madder, and Murex Purple.* Lark Books, 1994.

Seiss, Joseph. *Voices from Babylon.* Muhlenberg Press, Philadelphia, Pennsylvania, 1879.

Shakespeare, William. *The Sonnets.* Barrie & Jenkins, Ltd., London, Great Britian, 1988.

Siegal, Richard; Strassfeld, Michael; Strassfeld, Sharon. *The First Jewish Catalog.* The Jewish Publication Society of America, 1973.

Soden, Wolfram von. *The Ancient Orient: An Introduction to the Study of the Ancient Near East.* William B. Eerdmans Publishing Co, Grand Rapids, Michigan, 1994.

Steinsaltz, Adin. *The Essential Talmud.* Bantam Books, 1976.

Steinsaltz, Adin. *The Talmud: The Steinsaltz Edition.* Random House, New York, 1989.

Strassfeld, Michael. *The Jewish Holidays: A Guide and Commentary.* Harper & Row, New York, 1985.

Telsner, David. *The Kaddish: Its History and Significance.* Tal Orot Institute, Jerusalem, Israel, 1995.

The Apocrypha. Oxford University Press, London/New York/Toronto, 1879.

The New Open Bible. New King James Version, Thomas Nelson Publishers, Nashville, TN, USA, 1967. Copyright 1983,1985,1990.

Twain, Mark. *The Innocents Abroad.* The American Publishing Company, Hartford, CT, USA, 1869.

Yamauchi, Edwin M. *Persia and the Bible.* Baker Books, Grand Rapids, Michigan, 1996.